IMAGES
of America

SKIING IN OLYMPIC NATIONAL PARK

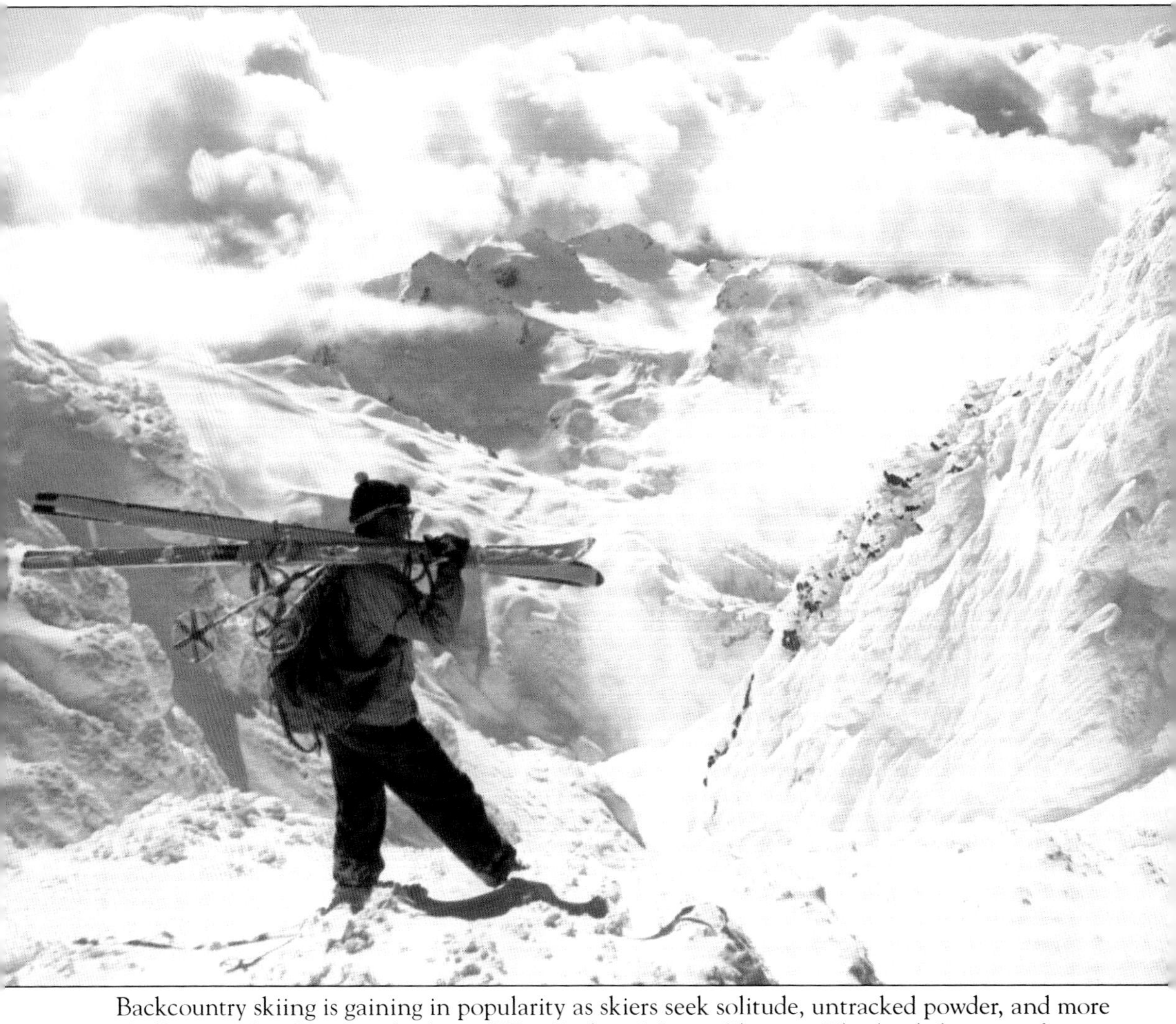

Backcountry skiing is gaining in popularity as skiers seek solitude, untracked powder, and more challenges. This skier is at the foot of West Peak on Mount Olympus. This book, however, focuses on the history of the two alpine ski areas in Olympic National Park: Deer Park and Hurricane Ridge. (Courtesy of ONP.)

ON THE COVER: In this 1938 photograph, a solitary skier enjoys the view looking down a ski slope at Deer Park on Blue Mountain and out toward the Olympic Mountains, with the Needles being the prominent peaks in the distance. In the clouds below lies Three Forks, the confluence of Grand and Cameron Creeks as they come together and then join the Graywolf River. (Photograph by USFS, courtesy of ONP.)

IMAGES
of America

SKIING IN OLYMPIC NATIONAL PARK

Roger Merrill Oakes
Foreword by Jack Hughes

ARCADIA
PUBLISHING

ISBN 978-1-4671-3248-0

Published by Arcadia Publishing
Charleston, South Carolina

Printed in the United States of America

Library of Congress Control Number: 2014938649

For all general information, please contact Arcadia Publishing:
Telephone 843-853-2070
Fax 843-853-0044
E-mail sales@arcadiapublishing.com
For customer service and orders:
Toll-Free 1-888-313-2665

Visit us on the Internet at www.arcadiapublishing.com

To all volunteers of the Hurricane Ridge Winter Sports Club and supporters of its Education Foundation, and to my lifelong friend and hiking partner Tucker Thompson, whose hiking days are over

CONTENTS

Foreword by Jack Hughes 6

Acknowledgments 7

Introduction 8

1. The Olympics: Olympic National Park 11

2. Roads and Lodges: Deer Park and Hurricane Ridge 23

3. Deer Park: 1936–1957 51

4. Hurricane Ridge: 1957–Present 95

Bibliography 127

Foreword

It was 1965 when I arrived at Olympic National Park, bringing my wooden skies from Yellowstone. As a new park ranger, I was assigned to Hurricane Ridge, where there was a ski-tow operation. During the 1930s, there was a Civilian Conservation Corps (CCC) camp run by the US Forest Service at mile-high Deer Park. The Forest Service allowed the skiers to use the CCC buildings as a ski lodge during the winter. The road was plowed for weekends, and there was a series of rope tows and a ski jump.

With the outbreak of World War II, skiing was on hold at Deer Park. The lookouts at Deer Park and Hurricane Hill were manned and supplied by skiing rangers to watch for enemy aircraft. After the war, the National Park Service began planning a new road to Hurricane Ridge. Once the road was completed in 1957, the ski area was moved to Hurricane Ridge.

There were problems with this move. The weather was more severe, and the new road required more heavy-duty snowplows, which the park did not have. Olympic had to depend on cast-off equipment from other parks. A grand opening was planned for New Year's Day, but a series of severe blizzards moved in, and the road crew was not able to keep up. One plow was stuck in a drift and could not move up or down. Other plows could not reach the operator, Dave "Maggie" McGraw. He had to spend the night in the plow, covered with snow. The site and the ski run above it are now informally named after him ("Maggie's"). The grand opening was cancelled.

During the 1960s, there was a revived interest in cross-country skiing, and I was a leader in encouraging this activity at Hurricane Ridge. I recall "pine-tar parties," where we prepped our wooden skis and enjoyed glogg (wine with spices and blueberries) provided by our Scandinavian friends.

I first met Roger Oakes when I led a search for two overdue hikers in 1965. They were medical students who grew up in Port Angeles. Later, I learned that Roger spent a year in Vietnam with the Army Medical Corps. We were reacquainted when he returned to practice in Port Angeles and became involved with the ski-lift operation. We share a love of skiing and hiking in the Olympic Mountains.

–Jack Hughes

Jack Hughes is a retired park ranger and has been described by his colleagues as "a ranger's ranger," well known for his search-and-rescue skills as well as being a skiing ranger.

ACKNOWLEDGMENTS

The idea for this book has been in my head for many years, but it was Jacilee Wray at Olympic National Park who encouraged me to work with Arcadia Publishing. I thank her and my acquisitions editors—Rebecca Coffey, Amy Kline, and Matthew Todd—for their direction.

My biggest challenge has been securing images and working on their adequate resolution. The National Park Service provided many images, and I thank curator Gay Hunter for her assistance with that. I want to give a special thanks to Karen McCormick for her willingness to help with images and my challenged computer skills. Also, thanks go to Jim Ude and Daniel Hudgings in that regard.

Many others provided images, including Bernice Byrne, Don Johnson, Kaye C. Winters, Malcolm White, Carolyn Brown Mackey, Jock Broadbent, Robert and Alexis Sorensen, Steve Baxter, Joan Morrish, Daniel Hudgings, Jerry Fagerlund, Avon Miller, Craig Hofer, Jim Cahill and his family, Bill Tiderman, Rex Gerberding, Jake Seniuk, Keith Thompson, Jim Wengler, and Dave Logan. Also, thanks go to Jeanne Humphreys at Pixel Perfect for her expertise with images.

Thanks are also extended to all who gave of their knowledge, some through recorded oral histories and others through informal interviews, including Leo White, Jim Cahill, Bob Allman, Avon Miller, Ted Simpson, Craig Hofer, Vance and Rosalee Bingham, Georgia Spencer, Jack Hughes, Glenn Wiggins, Gloria Spencer, Harley Hollatz, Ted Byers, Harold Byers, Dan Peacock, Tom Tinkham, Bill Reidel, David Bower, Shirley Stolz Clark, and Gordon Grall.

Finally, I thank all those who gave encouragement, remembrances, and perspectives of their times skiing in the Olympics. A special thanks goes to my wife, Maura, for her patience and encouragement. Also, thanks go to Kathy Monds at the Clallam County Historical Society, Larry Lang, Mike Macdonald, Myles Phipps, Peggy Owens, Dave Bovy, Rod Farlee, Dorothy Munkeby, Maureen Conniff, Rosalee Secord, Bea Ralston, Claud Johnson, Alice Alexander, Roy Jones, and Sidney Cays.

Some of the images in this volume appear courtesy of the United States Forest Service (USFS) and Olympic National Park (ONP).

INTRODUCTION

In the 1930s, recreational skiing was just becoming popular in America. Ski lifts were being constructed, first with simple rope tows. Then, in 1936, Northern Pacific Railroad engineers designed America's first chairlift at Sun Valley, Idaho. In the Olympic Mountains of Washington State, circumstances were such that a premier ski area was developed. In a time of economic depression and a New Deal response that created a ready labor force along with a Forest Service that wanted projects and development, a ski area was in the making at a place called Deer Park.

Other circumstances afforded the opportunity for better access to another ski area in the Olympics at Hurricane Ridge 20 years later. This time, it was a National Park Service movement to improve park facilities, which led to the creation of a modern highway and new lodge in the alpine reaches of Olympic National Park and a new ski area. Deer Park was abandoned as a ski resort and the lifts moved over to Hurricane Ridge. This is a pictorial story about skiing at these two areas.

When it was created in 1916, the National Park Service was given a complex mission "to conserve the scenery and natural and historic objects and the wildlife therein," yet "provide for the enjoyment of the same in such manner and by such means as will leave them unimpaired for the enjoyment of future generations." In its early years, it clearly emphasized enjoyment, development, and recreation, often to the detriment of the natural environment. As the country has gradually recognized the importance of wilderness preservation, this emphasis has changed. As a result, Olympic National Park is a fairly well-preserved ecosystem of mountains, forests, and ocean coastline, road building has stopped, and most of the park is designated wilderness.

Today, the Deer Park ski area is just a memory, while Hurricane Ridge remains a small recreational ski area where children learn to ski and visitors enjoy a variety of winter recreational activities. This access is increasingly enjoyed by sightseers, cross-country skiers, snowboarders, snowshoers, and backcountry skiers, most of whom appreciate the opportunity and value the protected wilderness of Olympic National Park.

The Olympic Mountain Range on the Olympic Peninsula of Washington State was formed millions of years ago by powerful tectonic forces with undersea lava flows (basalt) and the effects of ice and water. Its rivers run radially into the Pacific Ocean, the Strait of Juan de Fuca, Puget Sound, and south to the Chehalis River, forming what has been called an "Island of Rivers."

These mountains are rugged and steep, surrounded by dense old-growth forests, and incised by deep valleys. They are largely composed of sedimentary rock, with a crescent of basalt stretching from the northwest corner, forming an arc eastward and then to the southwest corner of the range. The range is not volcanic and contains no granite, except for occasional glacial erratics deposited by previous ice sheets.

Recent archaeological evidence shows that Native Americans explored the Olympic high country centuries ago. The first European explorers cruised by in the 16th century. In 1787, British fur trader Charles W. Barkley named the Strait of Juan de Fuca after the fabled Greek explorer who possibly visited the strait in 1592. Spanish explorer Juan Perez, said to be the first European explorer to see the Olympic Mountains, named them Cerro de La Santa Rosalia. In 1788, Capt. John Meares renamed the tallest peak Mount Olympus after the Greek mountain of a similar name.

Another Spanish explorer, Manual Quimper, explored the strait in 1790 and established a small fort at Neah Bay, securing Spanish claim to the area on August 1, 1790. Exploration into the interior of the Olympics did not start in earnest for another century.

From the early days of exploration of the Olympic Mountains, people recognized that these wilderness lands and the wildlife within deserved preservation. While Olympic National Park was not created until 1938, preservation efforts date back to the time of these explorations and were most significantly supported by the two Roosevelts, Theodore and Franklin Delano. Teddy Roosevelt encouraged Pres. Grover Cleveland, a somewhat reluctant conservationist, to proclaim the Olympic Forest Reserve in 1897 using the Forest Reserve Act of 1891.

In 1909, Pres. Theodore Roosevelt used the Antiquities Act of 1906 to establish Mount Olympus National Monument. Roosevelt was said to have had an abiding fascination with the Olympics and would have visited the area if not for lack of a railroad and time constraints. That visit was left to his fifth cousin FDR, who made the trip in 1937 when he advocated for a large Olympic National Park, which he signed into law on June 29, 1938.

Largely because of its vast temperate rain forests with acres of potential timber harvest, Olympic National Park has had a long and contentious history. Once it became apparent that a park would be established, there was an immediate call for an expanded road system. Some thought the first thing the Park Service should do was reconstruct the road to Deer Park and connect with a road to Obstruction Point. Another proposal was to build a high-country road connecting Olympic and Sol Duc Hot Springs.

Under the jurisdiction of the US Forest Service, the 1930s was an active period of road, trail, and shelter building. The Forest Service took full advantage of FDR's New Deal, which created the Civilian Conservation Corps and the Works Progress Administration. The CCC established several camps on the Olympic Peninsula and was instrumental in most of the development in the Olympics during that period.

Given Blue Mountain's location in the front range of the Olympics close to the Dungeness Valley and Port Angeles, it was an obvious choice for a road to the high country. And Deer Park, which sits on a small bench on the south side of the mountain, afforded an obvious destination. Its southern exposure, panoramic views, and low precipitation made it an ideal place to visit and camp.

Deer Park is a uniquely beautiful spot in the Olympics and has a rich geological, archaeological, and cultural history. Geologically, its gently rolling bench is formed by a wall of basalt that traps the softer sandstone and shale beds whose erosion forms the bench. The colored rocks near the summit are a result of shale and limestone lying near the lava flows, whose iron and manganese create the varied colors. Many fossilized small animals have been found here, helping scientists date the geologic age of Blue Mountain.

Blue Mountain looks out over one of North America's most interesting archaeological discoveries. In 1977, Emanuel "Manny" Manis was digging a pond on his property in Happy Valley when he uncovered a mastodon tusk. He had the foresight to contact archaeologists working an excavation on the Washington coast. Carl Gustafson of Washington State University would end up spending his summers excavating the sight until 1985. He made an interesting discovery: One of the mastodon's ribs was penetrated by a spiked piece of bone. He suspected it might have come from a human, which would mean man lived here longer ago than previously thought; however, Gustafson's tools were limited to carbon dating and x-ray, and his theory was not widely accepted.

In 2011, new techniques—including CT scanning, DNA sequencing, carbon dating, and protein analysis—showed that the penetrating shaft was a bone that had been sharpened to a tip, and the age was narrowed to about 13,800 years ago, which means humans were here with mastodons before Clovis man (previously thought to be the first humans here, about 13,000 years ago). Gustafson was vindicated, and Manis's Happy Valley site was listed in the National Register of Historic Places.

Culturally, Deer Park became a premier ski area for skiers from across the region in an era of skiing enthusiasm across the country. With a new Forest Service road to the top of Blue Mountain at 6,000 feet completed in 1934, a government commitment to establish a ski area, a CCC barracks to serve as a ski lodge, and strong community interest, it was only a matter of time before Deer Park became one of the premier ski areas in the Northwest.

While Northern Pacific Railroad engineers were designing the country's first chairlift at Sun Valley, Idaho, Port Angeles businessman Leo White was busy borrowing a friend's hill-climb motorcycle engine to drive a short rope tow at Deer Park. He returned the engine each summer to its owner, who continued using his motorcycle during the summer. Two years later, Leo upgraded to a Ford V-8 engine.

In 1937, a Port Angeles ski club was formed, and the Olympic Winter Sports Association, which became the Olympic Ski Club in 1938, was formed to sponsor races. Developments soon followed, with an addition to the CCC cookhouse in the summer of 1937 and the creation of a new mile-long ski run. The US Forest Service hired three landscape and recreational engineers to study future improvements.

In March 1938, Olympic Ski Club had its first championship meet at Deer Park, a Pacific Northwest Ski Association event. At this time, Deer Park was the premier ski area in the state. The event drew 800 competitors and spectators. One can only imagine a crowd of this size driving the one-lane dirt road, exposed to precipitous drops into the Morse Creek Valley. The Seattle Mountaineers were well represented at the meet. They were enticed by a Black Ball Line ad describing "a new, unsurpassed ski field" and "good road to ski lodge." The line ran a ferry from Edmonds, Washington, to Port Ludlow for $3 round-trip, car and driver. Accommodations were at the local Masonic Temple, with sleeping bags and blankets on the floor.

And there was this admonition in the *Port Angeles Evening News*: "Local people wishing to greet the visitors may call on them at the Masonic Temple Saturday night, BUT they are asked not to stay too late. The Mountaineers must get up early Sunday for a strenuous day." The Mountaineers would be on the road by 7:00 a.m., leaving Port Angeles in a caravan of cars convoyed by the state patrol. They received preference in the parking lines at Deer Park (their cars would be turned around by the "bouncing method") so they could make the 6:00 p.m. ferry at Port Townsend. The Deer Park lodge was reserved for officials and contestants. Lodging was 75¢, breakfast 50¢, lunch 60¢, and dinner 75¢, or $2.60 for the works. Lodging was dormitory style, and visitors brought their own bedding. On race day, it was announced that Olympic Ski Club was the second-largest organization in the Pacific Northwest Ski Association, with a membership of 230 or more.

World War II brought a halt to Deer Park skiing, except for a ranger or two stationed at the lookout atop Blue Mountain to observe for enemy planes. Skiing resumed in the winter of 1946–1947 and continued until 1957, when the new road to neighboring Hurricane Ridge was completed. With its paved two-lane road and better snowfall, Hurricane Ridge was chosen as a better ski venue.

The 1950s saw a resurgence of road and facility construction in national parks. In 1956, the National Park Service launched an ambitious program called Mission 66, so named because it was to conclude in 1966, the 50th anniversary of the Park Service.

For skiers, the move to Hurricane Ridge meant a much-improved road and better snow and slopes, but the loss of overnight lodging and lots of nostalgia. Not lost was the equipment for the tows, including a 1929 Hercules motor that served until 1998 and two engines still in service today.

Brothers Tom and Larry Winters were running the tows at Deer Park and continued to do so at Hurricane Ridge until 1965, when they sold to Avon Miller and Ted Simpson, who made significant improvements. In 1969, the corporation Olympic Ski Lifts, Inc. was formed, and shares were sold to fund the installation of a surface lift made by Poma of America.

In 1986, Olympic Ski Lifts was dissolved, and nonprofit corporation Hurricane Ridge Winter Sports Club was formed. This club has run the area to the present day.

While the rest of America has seen a vast expansion of ski areas and advances in chairlifts and facilities, Hurricane Ridge has continued its small operation of rope tows and a surface lift. Hundreds of young skiers have learned to ski on its slopes. Many think that small, affordable ski areas like this will make a comeback.

That downhill skiing has survived here all these years is a testimony to the dedicated volunteers of the local skiing community.

One

The Olympics
Olympic National Park

There is a lot to be thankful for in Olympic National Park. With its mountains, glaciers, rivers, rain forests, wilderness ocean beaches, and many recreational opportunities, it has something for everyone.

Thanks to moving tectonic plates, recurrent ice sheets, and the current temperate climate with considerable rainfall, there are rugged mountain ranges, cascading rivers, and large ice-scoured, densely forested valleys. The Ice Age isolated the Olympic Mountains, resulting in several endemic animals and plants. In large part, preservation centered on saving the Olympic elk (often called Roosevelt elk), once thought to be a distinct species but now recognized as a subspecies.

Thanks to the ruggedness and isolation of the interior, there was no significant exploration by humans, other than archaeological evidence of visiting Native Americans, until relatively recent times. Thanks to circumstances and the interest of many conservationists, many roads and other intrusions into the park were never completed, and a large part of the park remains a wilderness minimally touched by human activities.

Thanks to FDR's New Deal and the interest of people like US senator Henry Jackson, there is road access into the periphery of the park in places like Deer Park and Hurricane Ridge, affording winter recreation to many people. At the same time, efforts to open places like Soleduck Park, Marmot Pass, Flapjacks Lake, and the Little River Valley to roads and skiing interests did not come to fruition, thus preserving some of the most beautiful areas of the park in their pristine state.

Thanks to dedicated local recreation enthusiasts, many opportunities (and memories) have been created in the park. Olympic Hot Springs was developed in 1909 and Sol Duc Hot Springs in 1912. The Klahhane Hiking Club was formed in 1915, and skiing at Deer Park on Blue Mountain started in 1935, with the first rope tow installed in the winter of 1936–1937.

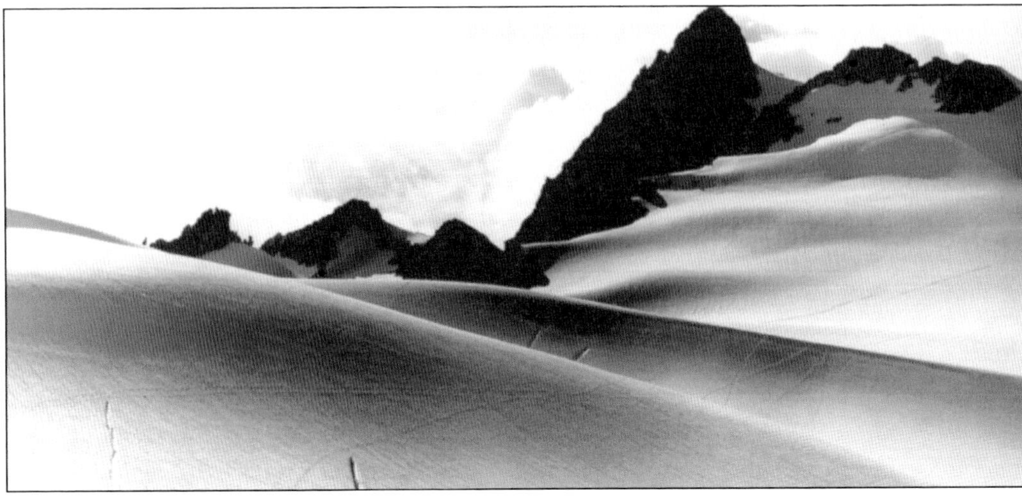

Mount Olympus, the tallest peak in the Olympics, is heavily glaciated. It receives over 200 inches of precipitation each year, mostly in the form of snowfall. However, its glaciers are shrinking. Between 1930 and 1953, Blue Glacier melted back 815 feet. There are over 300 glaciers in Olympic National Park, but in the last 100 years, they have lost 55 percent of their area. These photographs show the broad expanse of ice fields on the upper slopes and the dramatic ice fall below the snow dome. (Above, photograph by Keith Thompson; below, photograph by the author; both, courtesy of the author.)

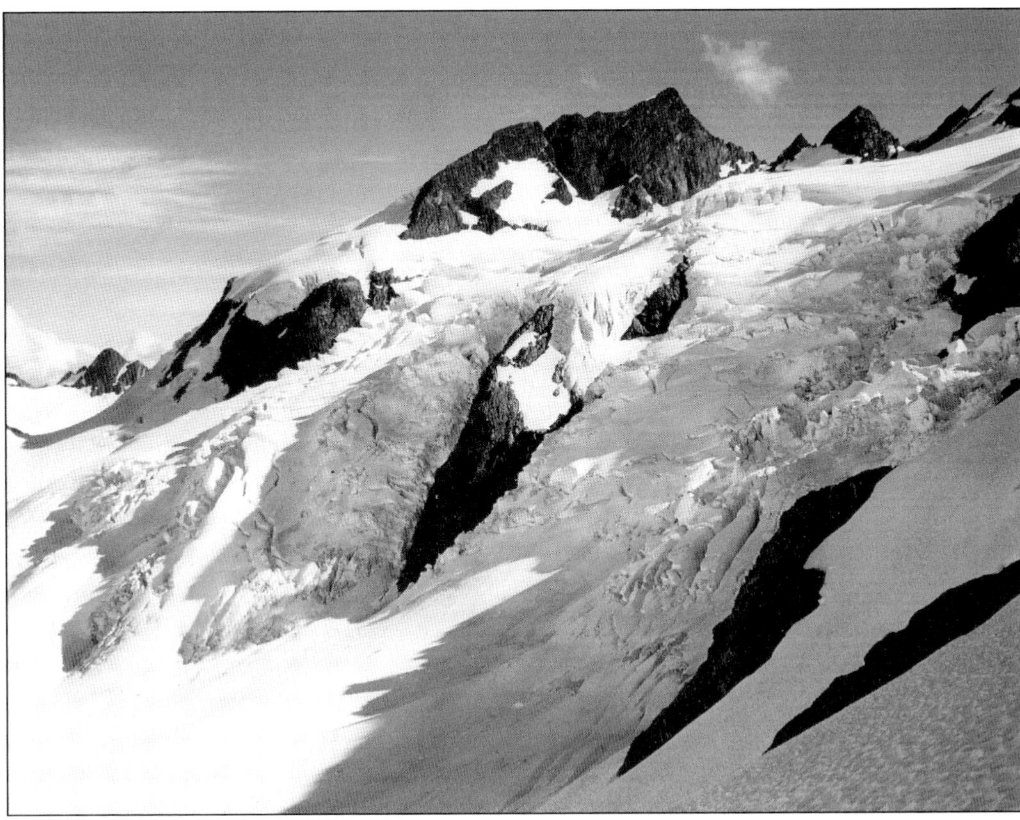

Mount Deception is the second-tallest peak in the Olympics and part of the inner basaltic ring, which formed later than the outer basaltic crescent. Its sharp angles are the result of erosion of the surrounding softer rock. The origin of the Olympics has to do with oceans, ice, and water. Their geology has been relatively obscure because of their inaccessibility and lack of valuable minerals. (Photograph by Dan Hudgings.)

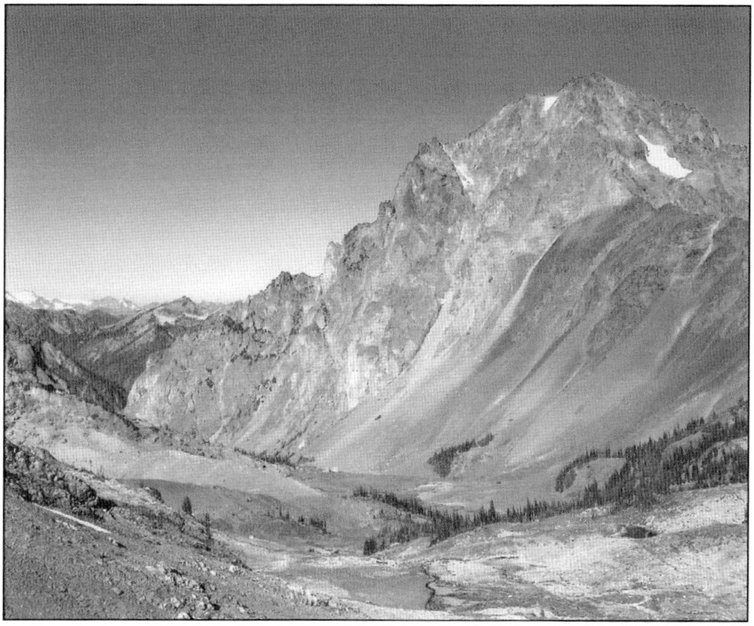

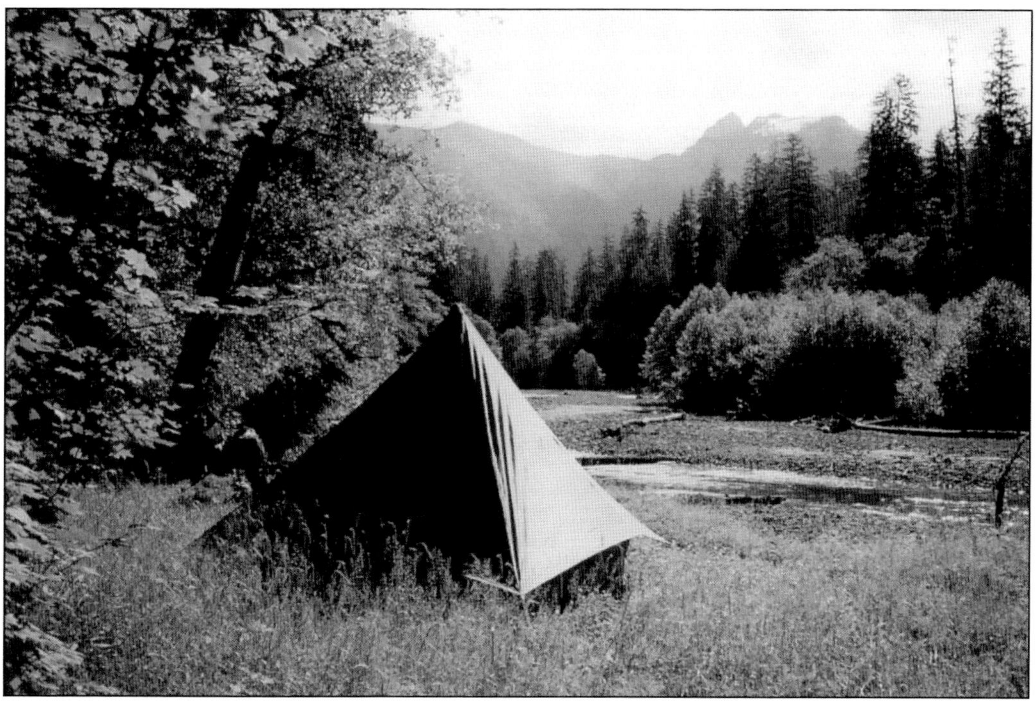

The rivers of the Olympic National Park drain into the Pacific Ocean, Strait of Juan de Fuca, Puget Sound, and south into the Chehalis River in what has been called an island of rivers. Here, a lonely tent is pitched near the bank of the South Fork of the Hoh River, a major drainage off Mount Olympus that runs to the Pacific Ocean. (Photograph by the author.)

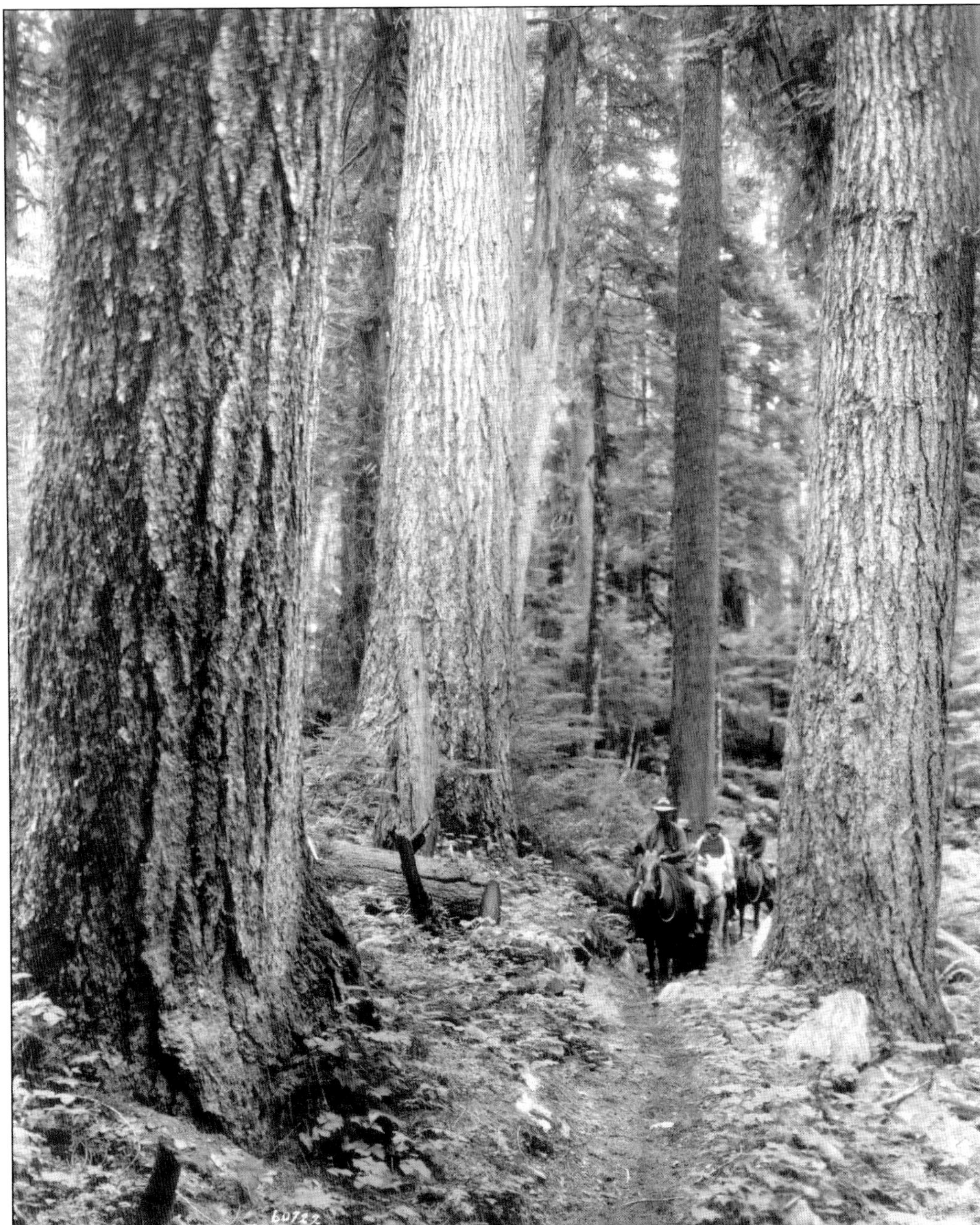

Horsemen on the East Fork of the Quinault River show the size of the Douglas fir that grow in the old-growth forests that blanket much of the western areas of the park. Olympic has several world-record trees, including the largest Douglas fir, which measures 17.5 feet in diameter and is located on the upper Queets River. (Photograph by Asahel Curtis, courtesy of ONP.)

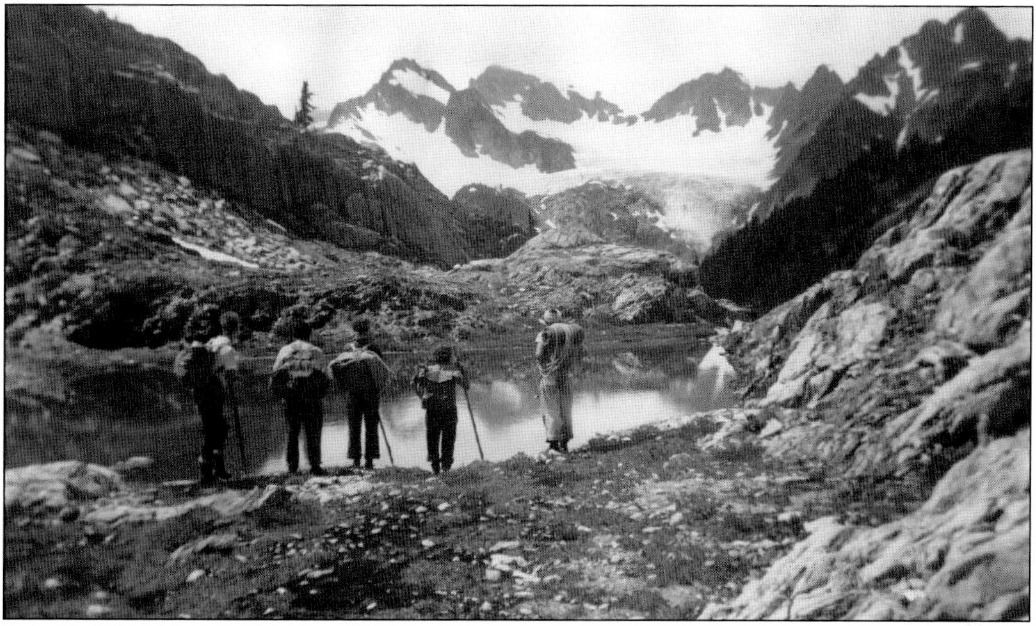

Hikers in the Olympics have endless country to explore by both well-established trails and cross-country travel, as seen here. These hikers are in the Queets Basin in July 1938. The Queets Basin is one of the most remote areas in the park and is one way to reach Mount Olympus via the Humes Glacier. (Courtesy of ONP.)

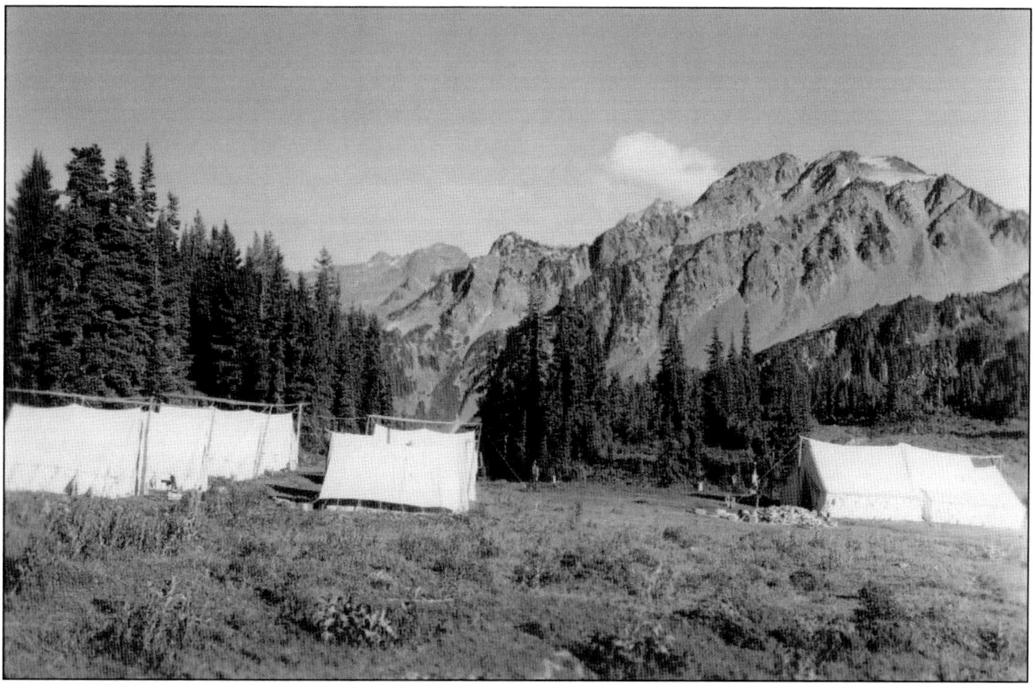

During the 1930s, the US Forest Service built many trails throughout the park with the help of the Civilian Conservation Corps. This trail crew camp is in Cat Creek Basin. The trail boss was Charles "Bud" Hanify. The men were working on the Bailey Range trail, which was never completed. Mount Carrie is in the background. (Courtesy of ONP.)

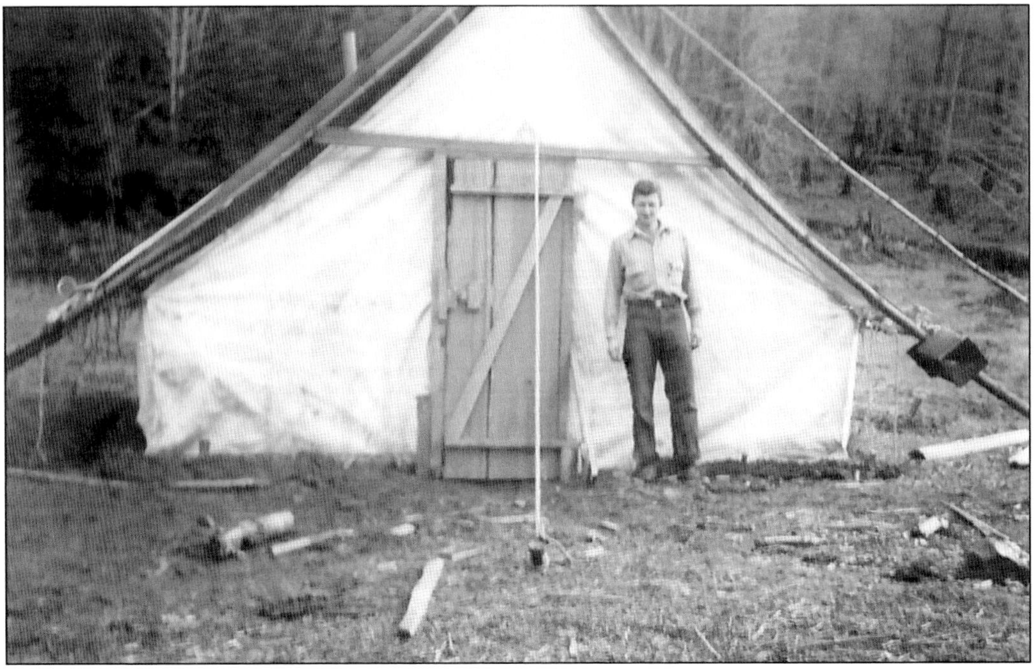

In the 1930s, the CCC established seven main camps on the Olympic Peninsula and several smaller side camps, such as Humesville (pictured here), near the ranch of pioneer Grant Humes. Above, Maynard Fields stands in front of one of the tents at Humesville. The CCC "boys" did much of the road and trail building in the Olympics before ONP was established. Below are the tents that served as the administration building and radio shack at Humesville on the Elwha River. (Both, photograph by Jim Byrne, courtesy of Bernice Byrne.)

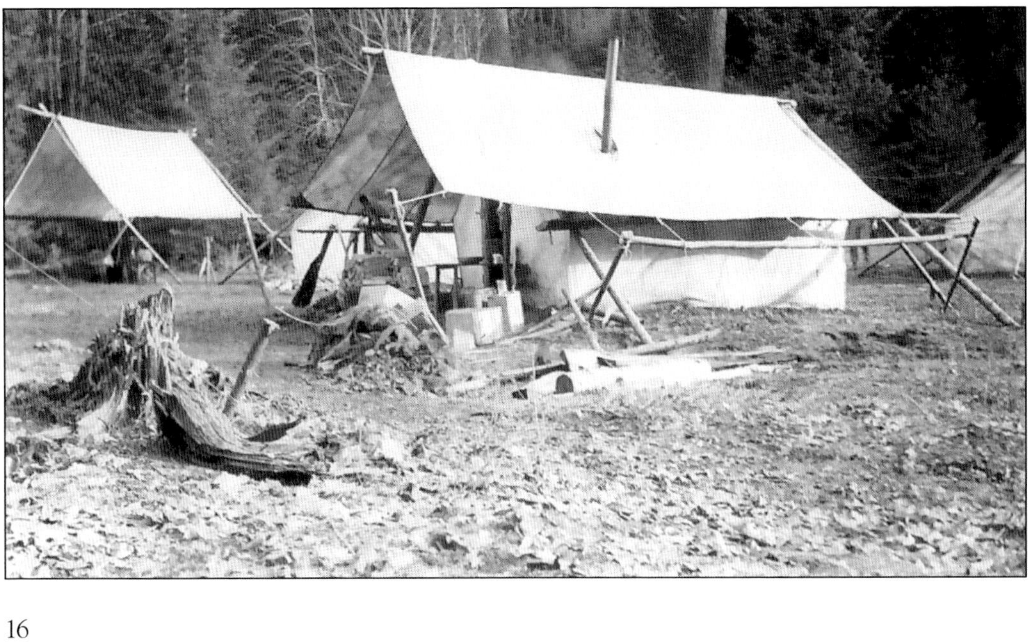

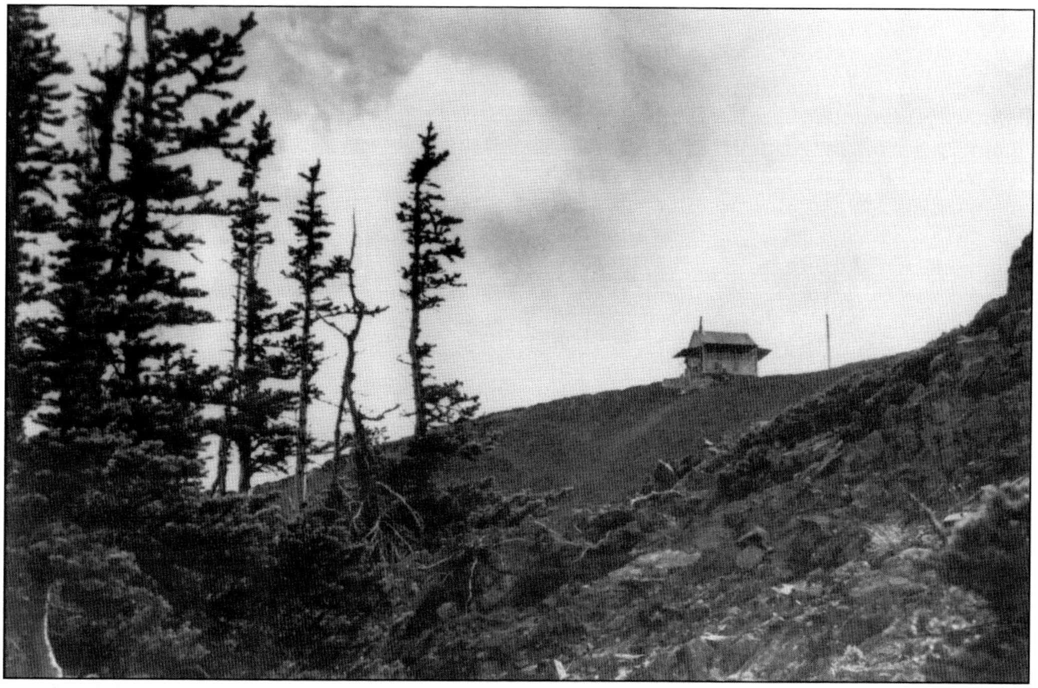

Much of the activity in the Olympic Mountains in the 1920s and 1930s centered around fire: trails to access forest fires and lookouts to detect them. Deer Park and Hurricane Hill each had fire lookouts that also served as observatories to spot enemy planes during World War II. Herb and Lois Crisler spent the winter of 1942 at the Hurricane Hill lookout pictured below. They said they were going "to the fairy's cabin in the sky." The Deer Park lookout is seen above. (Below, photograph by Herb Crisler; both, courtesy of ONP.)

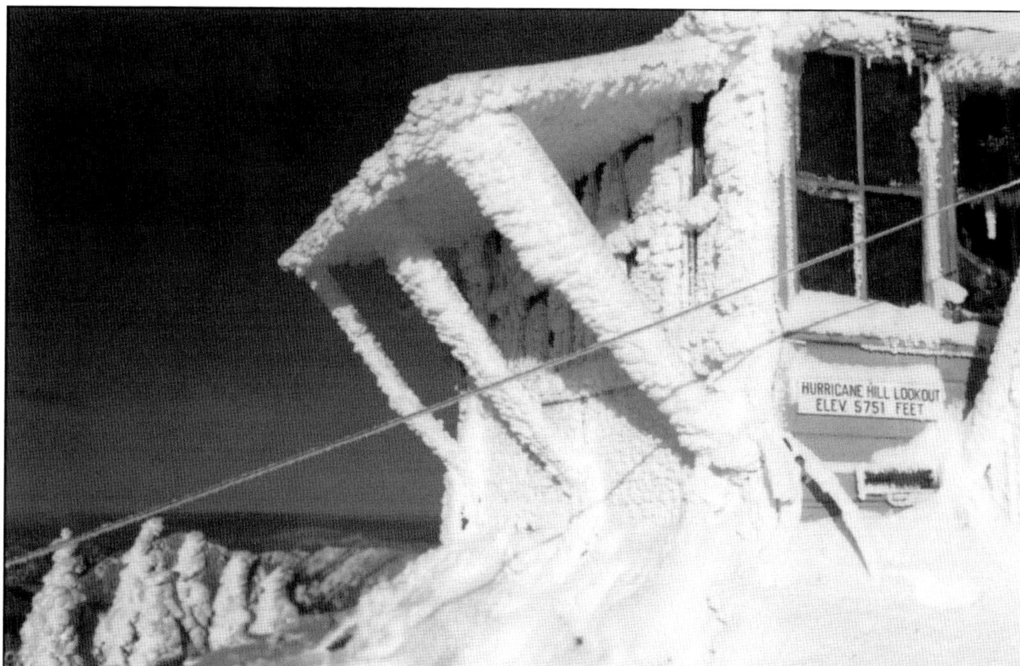

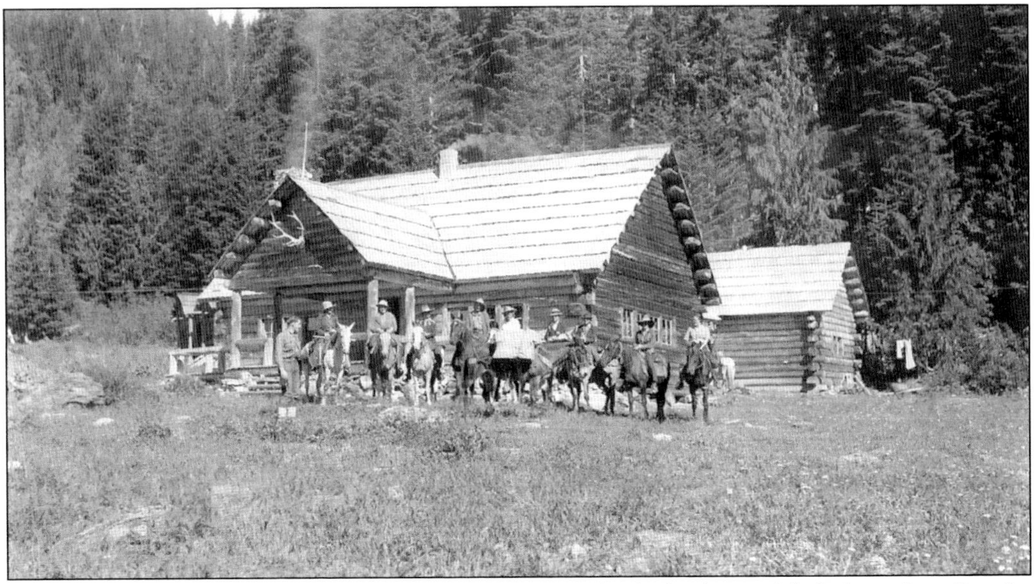

In 1926, the Olympic Chalet Company of Grays Harbor built this beautiful chalet at Low Divide, which separates the North Fork of the Quinault and the Elwha Rivers. A visitor to this remote lodge could sleep in fresh sheets. It was destroyed by an avalanche in 1944, leaving only the bathhouse. Similar lodges were built at Graves Creek and Enchanted Valley. (Courtesy of Bernice Byrne.)

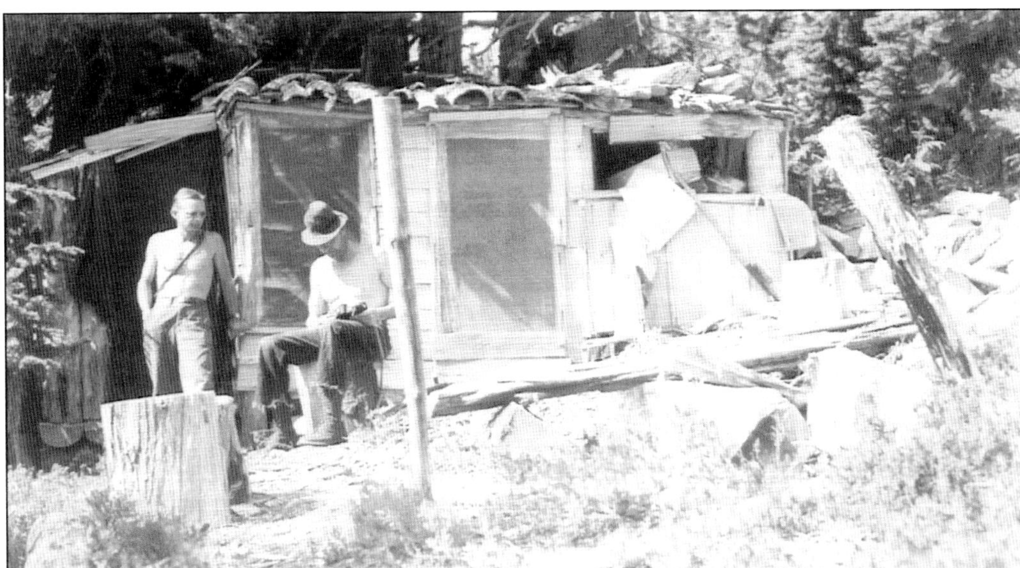

Hikers Jim Bussing (left) and Joe Hoare are at Crisler's Hot Cake Camp in Cat Creek Basin. Herb and Lois Crisler explored the Olympics extensively and had many camps and caches throughout the range. This camp got its name from the hotcake griddle that Herb packed in from the Olympic Hot Springs. (Photograph by Keith Thompson, courtesy of the author.)

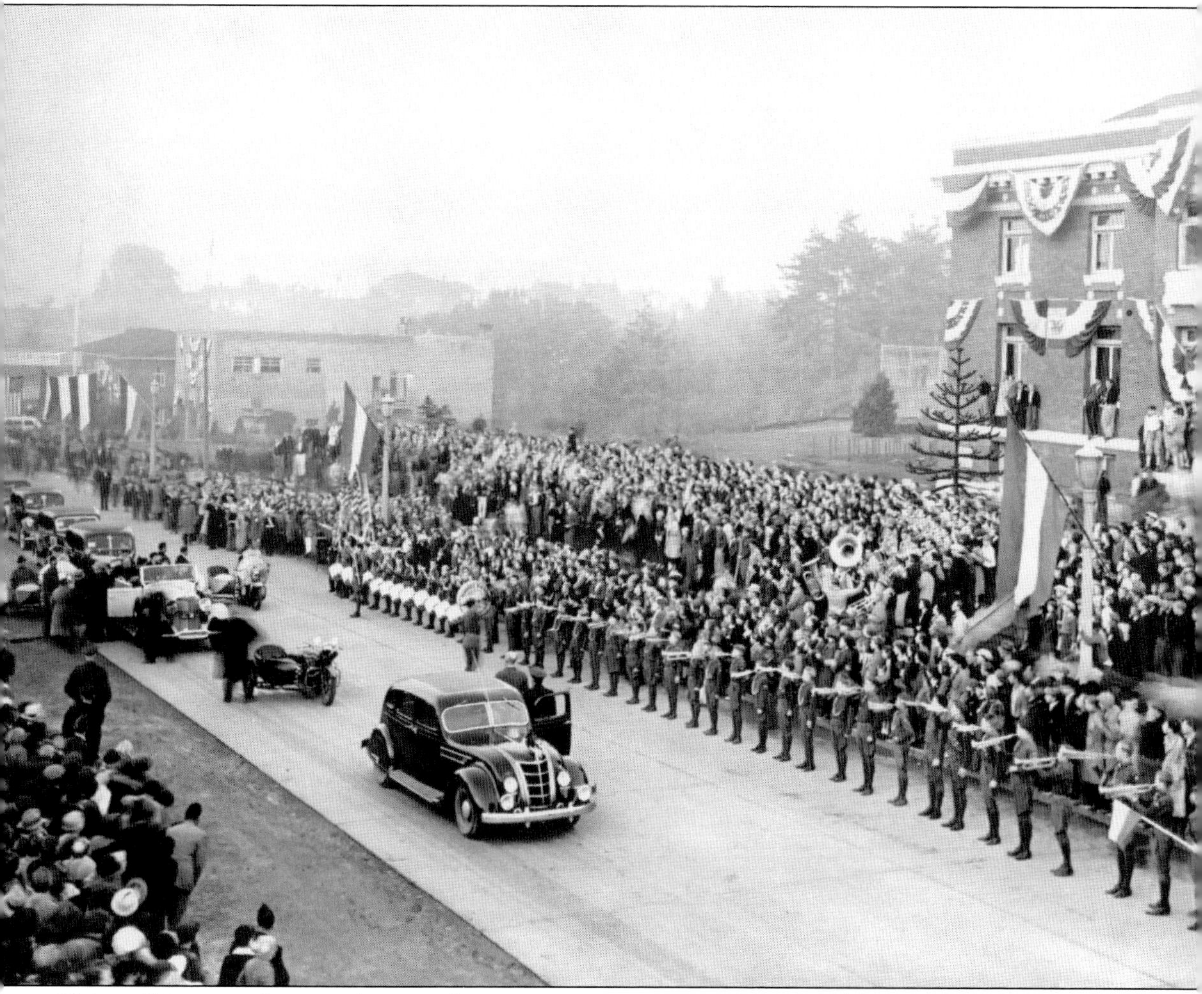

This well-known photograph is worth seeing once more since Pres. Franklin Delano Roosevelt had so much to do with creating Olympic National Park. Late in the afternoon on September 30, 1937, the president arrived from Victoria, British Columbia, on a Navy destroyer. He was greeted with the now famous sign, "Please, Mr. President, we children need your help. Give us our Olympic National Park." A day later, he famously said, "Bet your shirt, there will be a park." Olympic National Park became a reality on June 29, 1938. (Courtesy of ONP.)

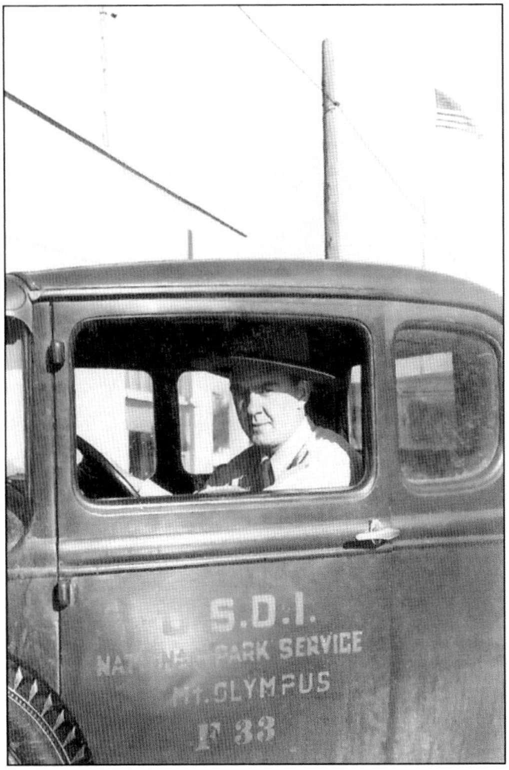

With the establishment of ONP, rangers were needed. Local youth who loved the Olympics were quick to volunteer their services. Here, Jim Byrne is seen on duty in the summer of 1938, just after the park's creation. One can see both the official uniform of the day and the rangers' official transportation. Jim later became a bank officer in Port Angeles. (Both, courtesy of Bernice Byrne.)

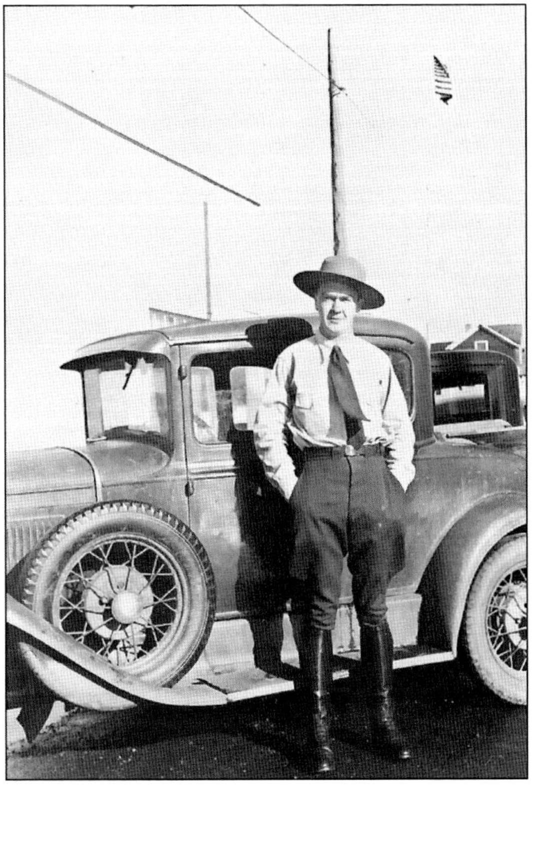

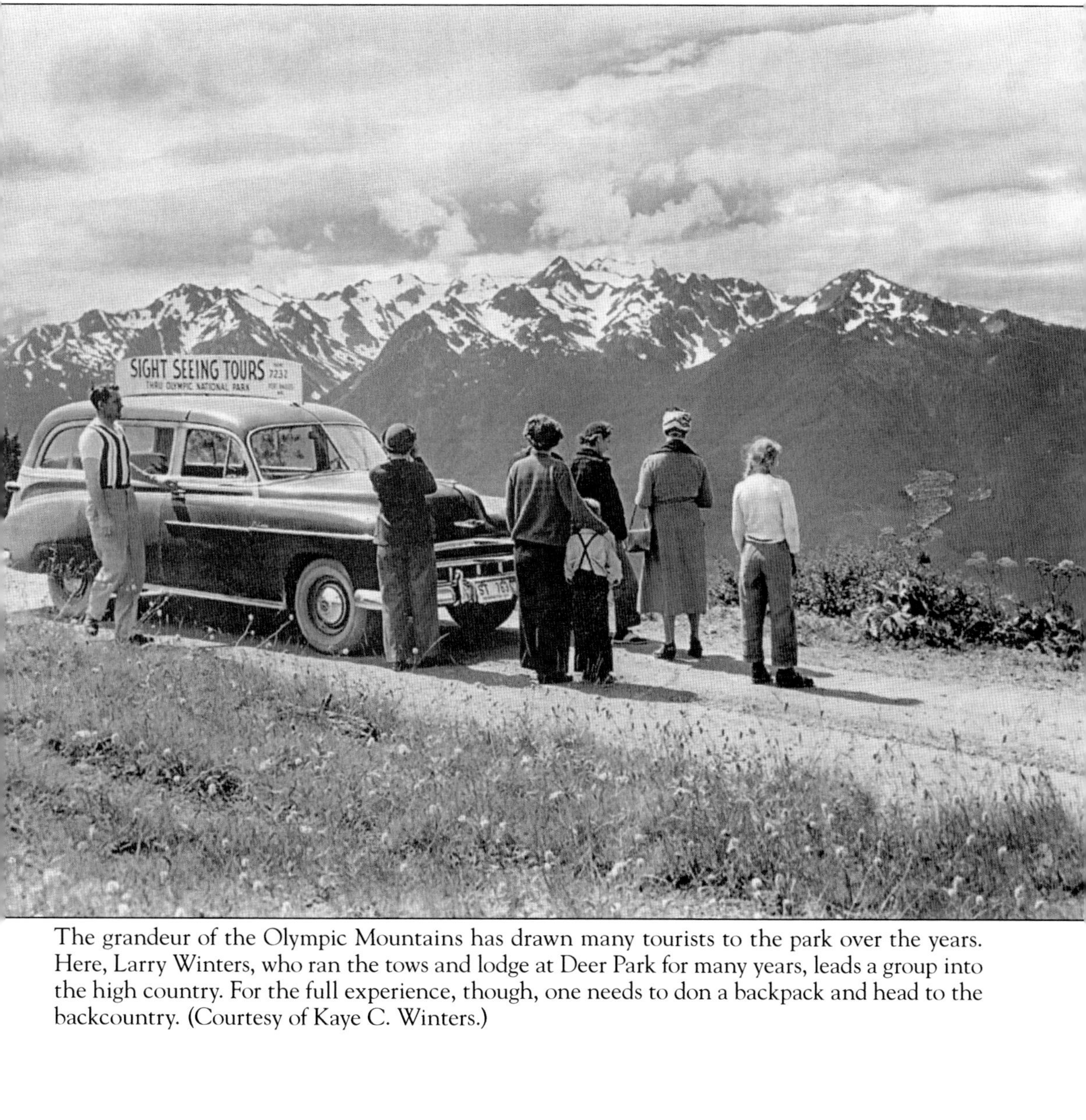

The grandeur of the Olympic Mountains has drawn many tourists to the park over the years. Here, Larry Winters, who ran the tows and lodge at Deer Park for many years, leads a group into the high country. For the full experience, though, one needs to don a backpack and head to the backcountry. (Courtesy of Kaye C. Winters.)

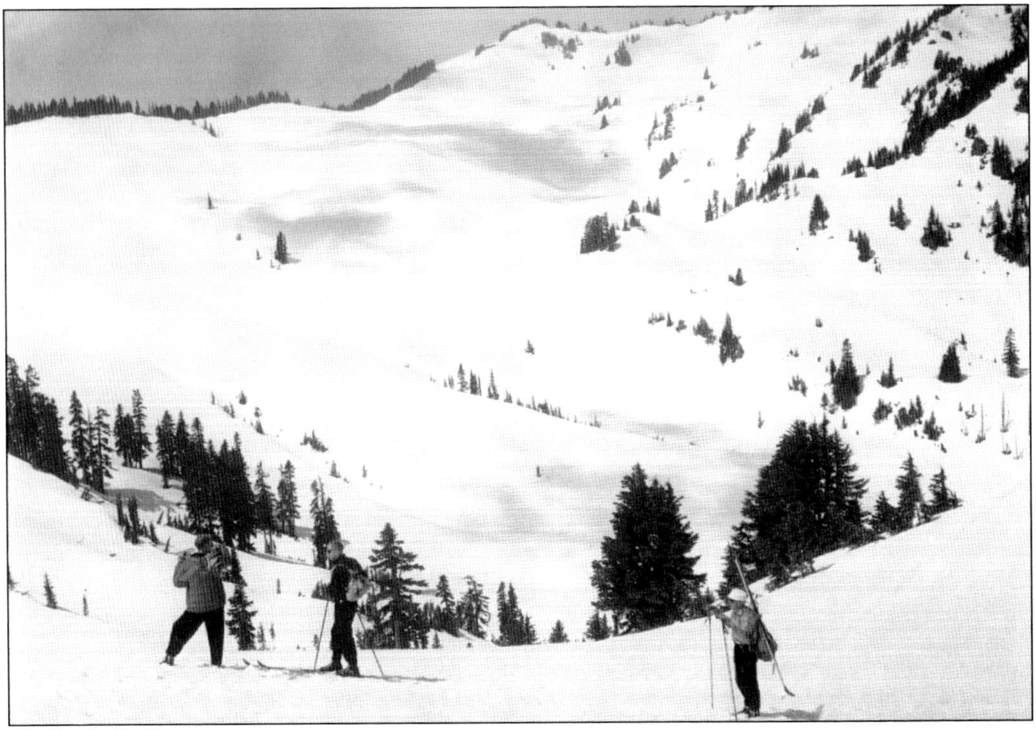

Before the ski area moved to Hurricane Ridge, skiers were exploring other potential ski areas in the Olympics. One of the most attractive was Soleduck (now Sol Duc) Park and the nearby Seven Lakes Basin. The area had plentiful snow and was north facing, so the snow kept late into the spring and summer. These skiers are in Soleduck Park in April 1960. The plan was to extend the road farther up the Sol Duc Valley and then place two gondolas, as seen in this topographical map. However, the plans never came to fruition, and the area has been preserved as a beautiful wilderness hiking area. (Above, photograph by Richard Owens Jr., courtesy of Peggy Owens; below, courtesy of ONP.)

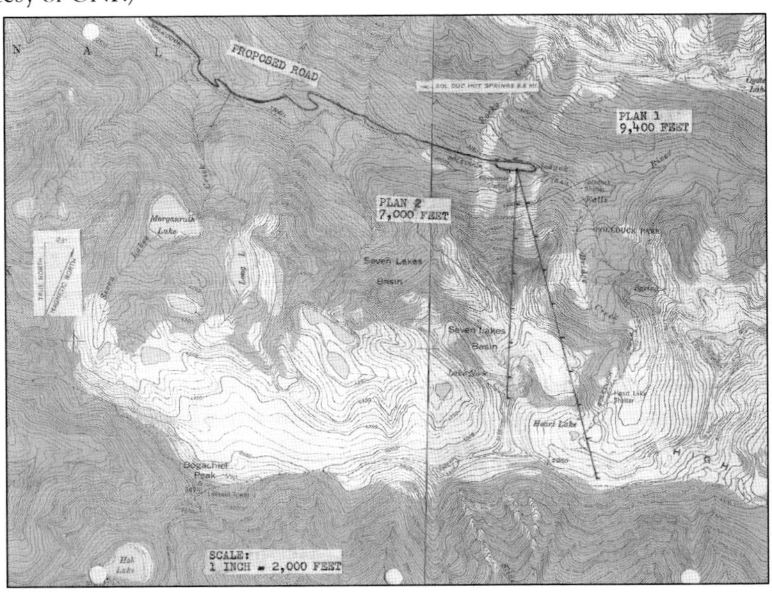

Two

Roads and Lodges
Deer Park and Hurricane Ridge

In many ways, skiing in the Olympic Mountains is a story of roads and lodges. In a national park that is today largely preserved as wilderness, it was a bygone era of road and facility construction that afforded skiers a limited but rewarding experience.

Early pioneer and then ranger Chris Morgenroth was an early builder of trails, including his Pacific Trail from the logging town of Forks to the Queets River that was started in 1892. But it was not until the 1930s that road and trail building really hit its stride. The western section of the Olympic Peninsula highway was completed in 1931, the original road to Hurricane Ridge up from the Elwha in 1933, and the road to Deer Park in 1934. It was only with the onset of World War II that a more expansive road-building program was abandoned.

The next surge in road and facility construction occurred in the 1950s when the National Park Service launched its Mission 66 program (so named because it was to be completed in 1966, the 50th anniversary of the Park Service), a $1 billion effort to improve recreational tourism in the parks. Mission 66 funds were used to complete the Hurricane Ridge in 1957, although the initial funding was not part of Mission 66. Also planned was the completion of the Deer Park road to Hurricane Ridge, creating a loop highway into the park's high country; however, the road was never completed.

Local skiers were quick to take full advantage of these periods to enjoy their sport in the Olympics. The New Deal's Civilian Conservation Corps not only built the road to Deer Park, but also left behind a former barracks and cookhouse that became a quaint ski lodge. At Hurricane Ridge, Congressman Henry Jackson, who later served as a US senator, saw his vision of a lodge come to fruition, although not as the grand overnight facility for which he had hoped.

So, this pictorial story of Deer Park and Hurricane Ridge skiing will start with a look at these roads and lodges.

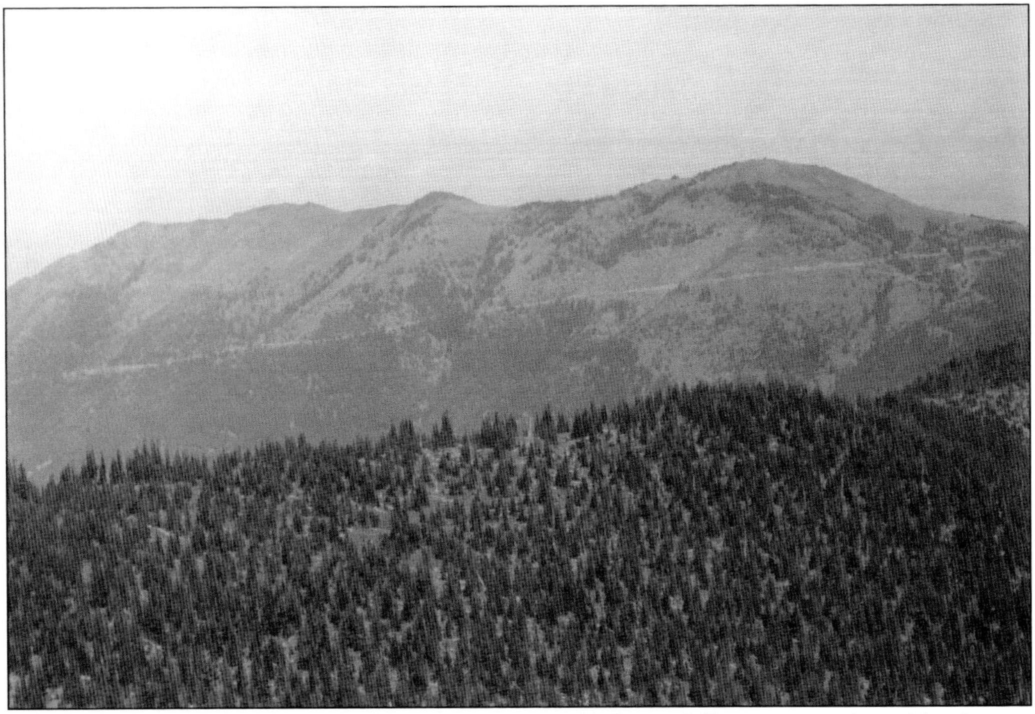

Seen across the western flank of Blue Mountain is the beautifully engineered road leading to Deer Park and the summit of Blue Mountain. It was completed in 1934 by the US Forest Service with considerable help from the CCC. The Forest Service envisioned a winter-sports paradise with a ski way to Deer Park. The grade line was accomplished with a surveying transit, contour maps, and control points. The road did have some steeper pitches (25 percent grade) near the top, which were reduced to 12 percent grades in the late 1940s by cutting a new road above the old one. Viewed in summer or winter, the road is clearly seen as it ascends the mountain. (Above, courtesy of ONP; below, photograph by USFS, courtesy of ONP.)

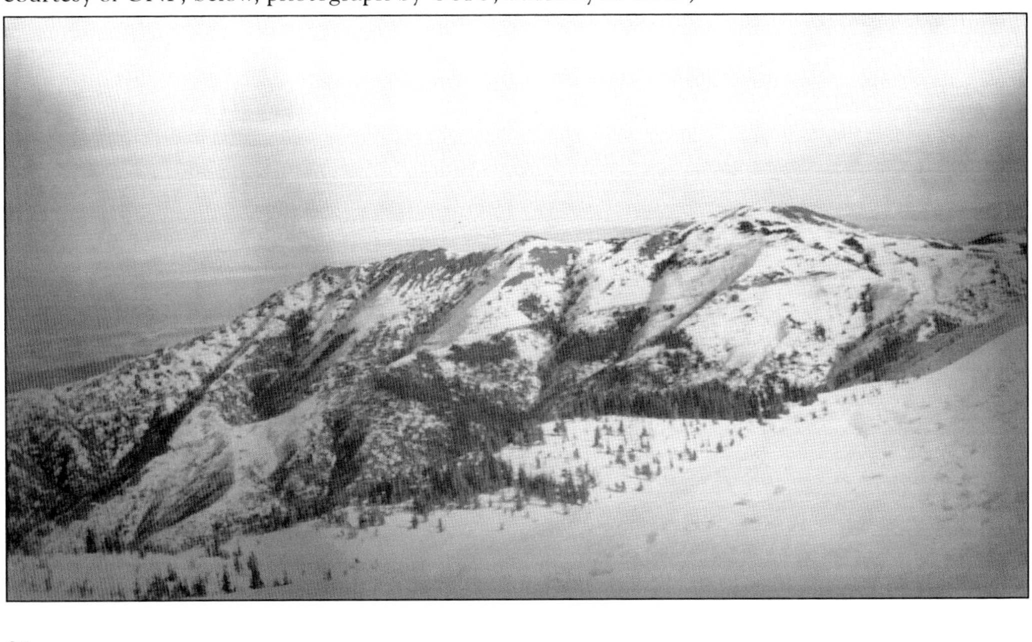

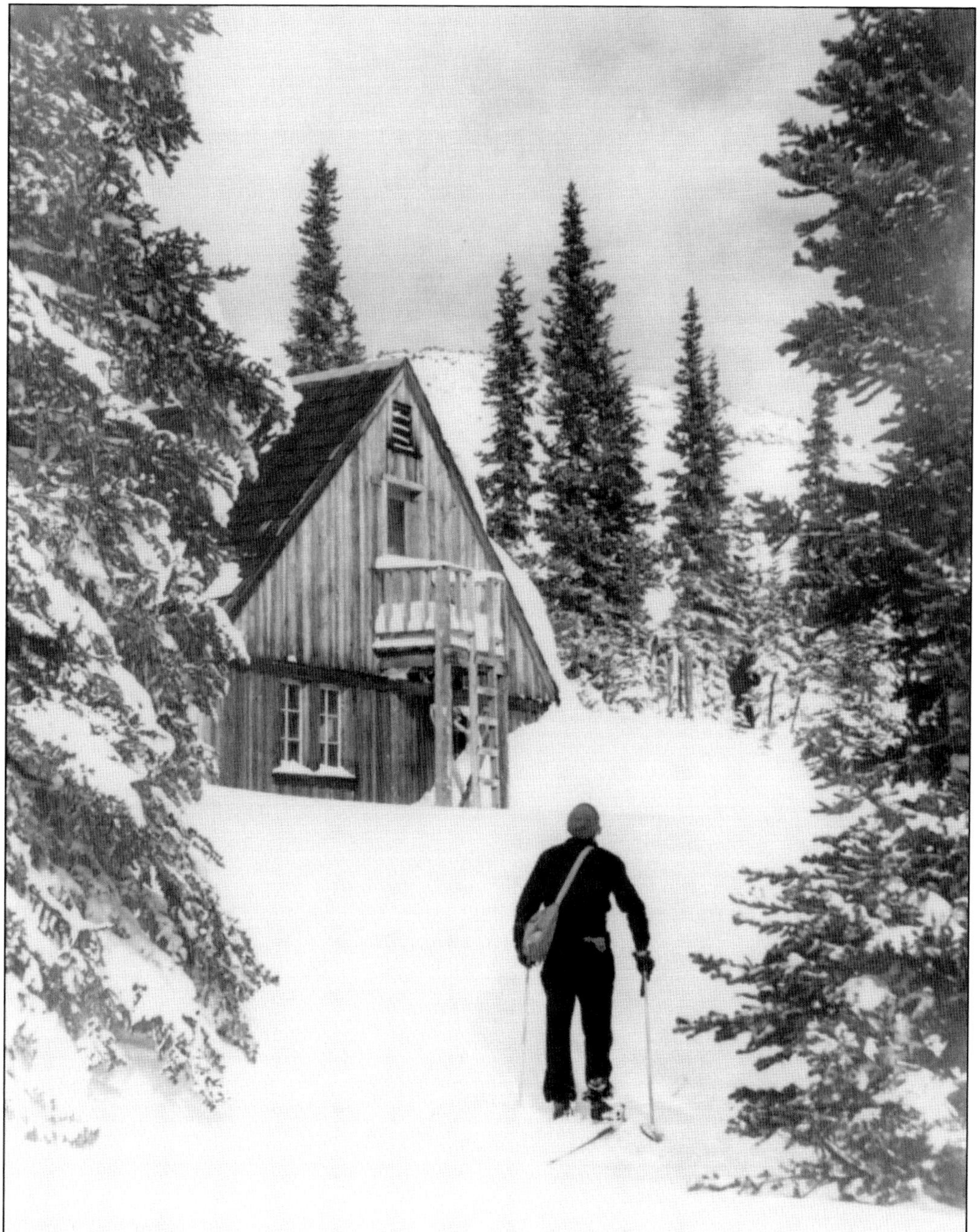

A skier approaches the Deer Park ski lodge in the 1930s. The CCC was formed in 1933 and soon became active on the Olympic Peninsula. This building served as a barracks and cookhouse and was remodeled to serve as a ski lodge for use by the public by 1937. (Courtesy of ONP.)

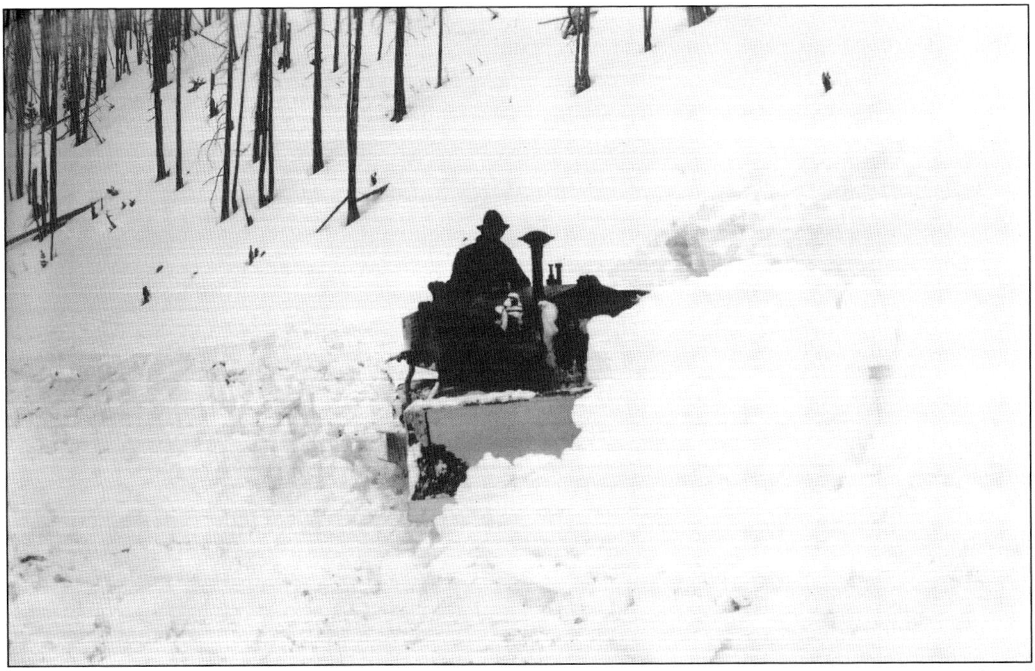

This Cletrac bulldozer is at work on the new road to Deer Park. Ernie Byers cleared the road and performed many other functions at Deer Park starting in the 1930s and again after World War II. These photographs were taken near Angeles viewpoint, which is near the top of road. This was a high avalanche area. Snow was shoved over the side, creating a protective wall. (Both, photograph by Neil Mortiboy, courtesy of ONP.)

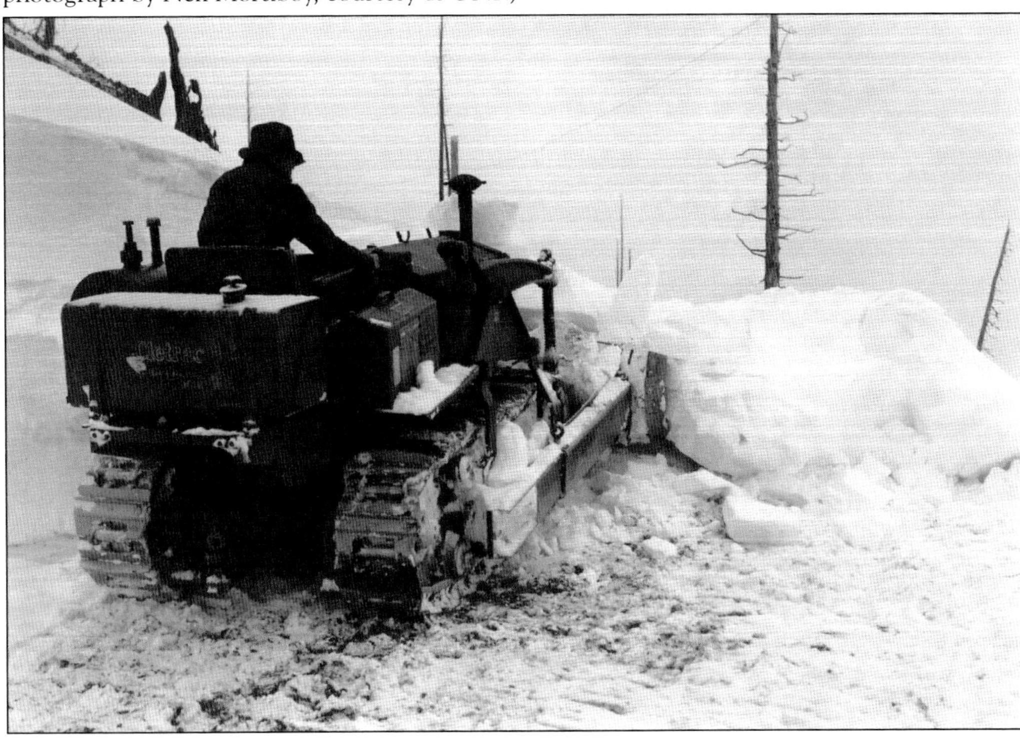

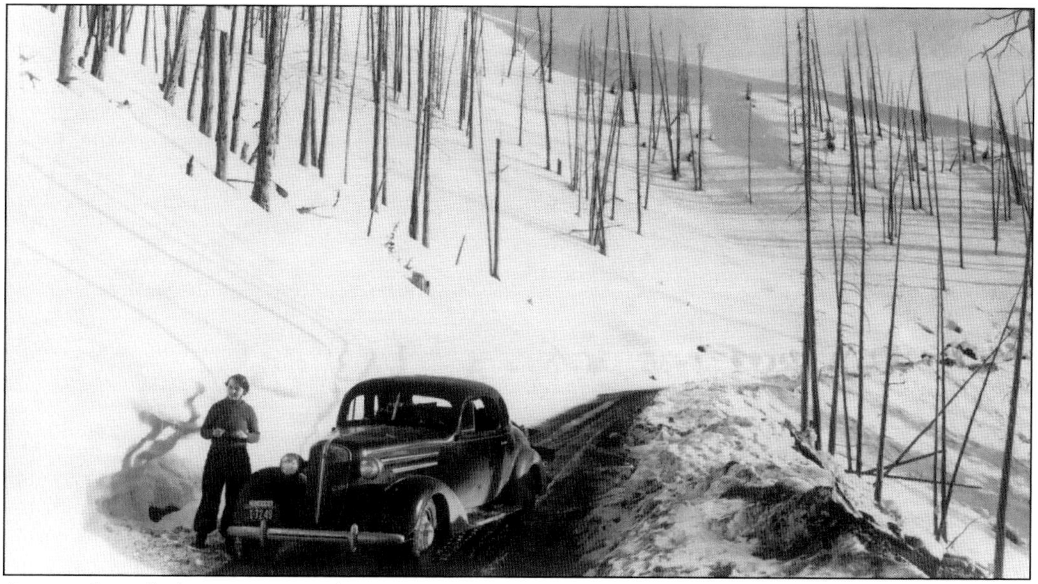

An unidentified woman stands next to a 1936 Chevrolet as it descends the Deer Park road. Clearly demonstrated is the one-way nature of the road. The rule was uphill until 2:00 p.m. and downhill starting at 3:00 p.m. Note the dead trees—fires were known to sweep through the area fairly often. (Photograph by Jim Cahill, courtesy of ONP.)

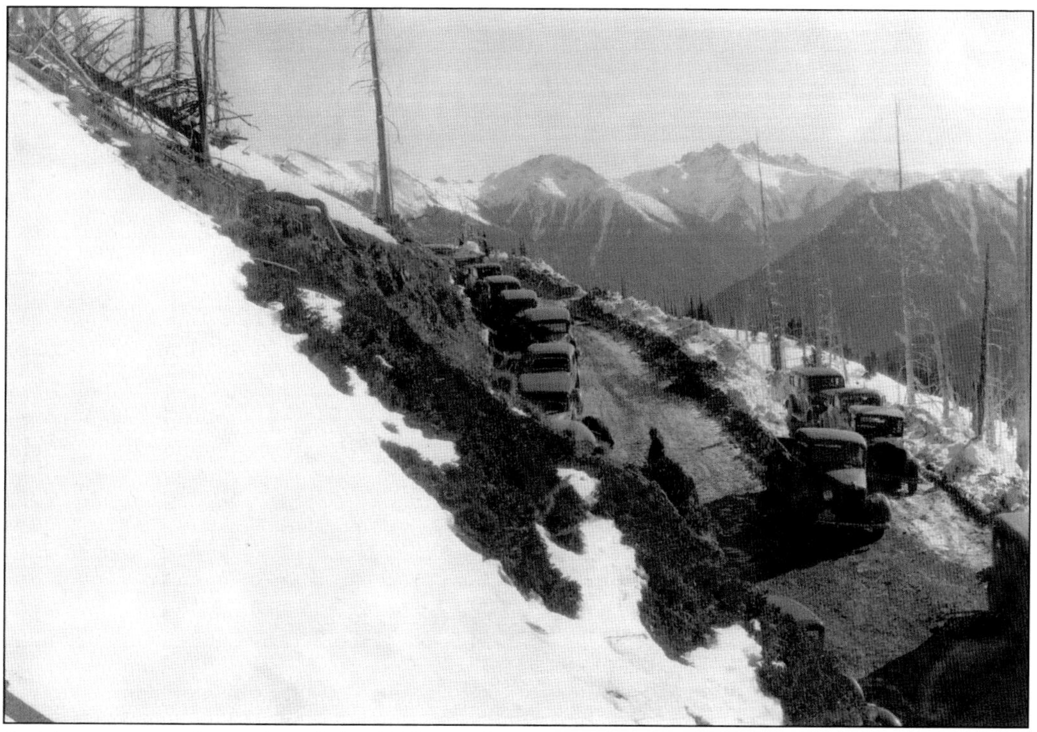

Parking was very limited, and the 1930s saw huge crowds as Deer Park was the premier ski area in the Northwest. Several men often used the bouncing method to turn the cars around. Here, cars are parked for a ski festival on February 2, 1936. (Courtesy of ONP.)

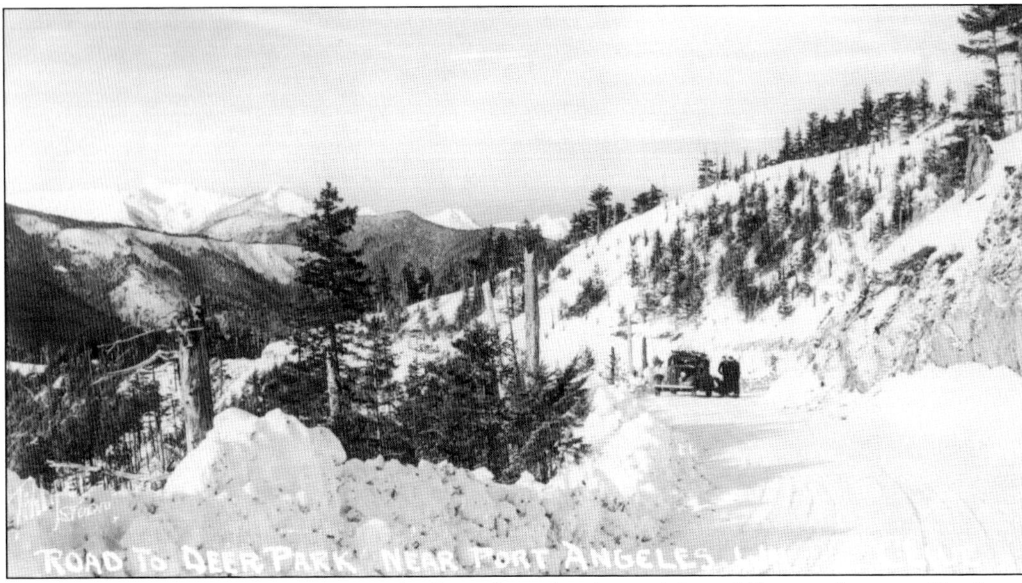

The ride up the hill was often more thrilling than the skiing. Many folks simply turned back—if they could. The road had a 25 percent grade near the top, and people often stood on the back bumper for traction. According to *Olympic Leaders: The Life and Times of the Websters of Port Angeles*, local artist, writer, and community leader Esther Webster wrote: "You learned to know and value every mile your struggling car accomplished." (Courtesy of ONP.)

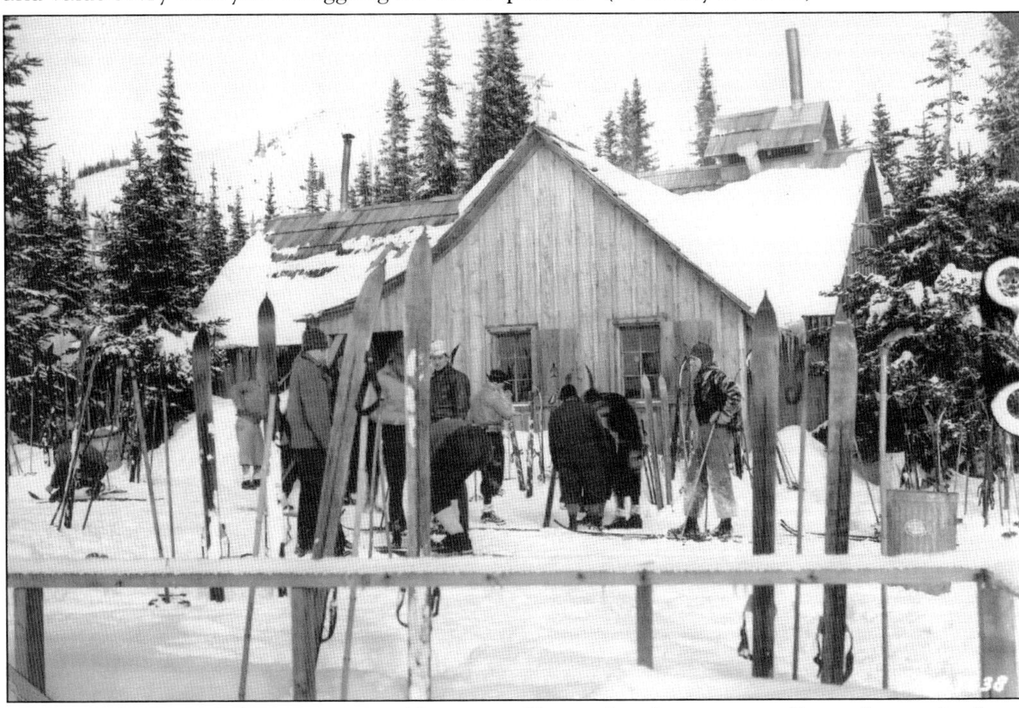

Most people carpooled to save gas and because of limited parking spaces. Once they arrived and found parking, they were greeted by this friendly ski lodge. Pictured in February 1937, this CCC building was remodeled that year to accommodate overnight guests dormitory-style. (Courtesy of ONP.)

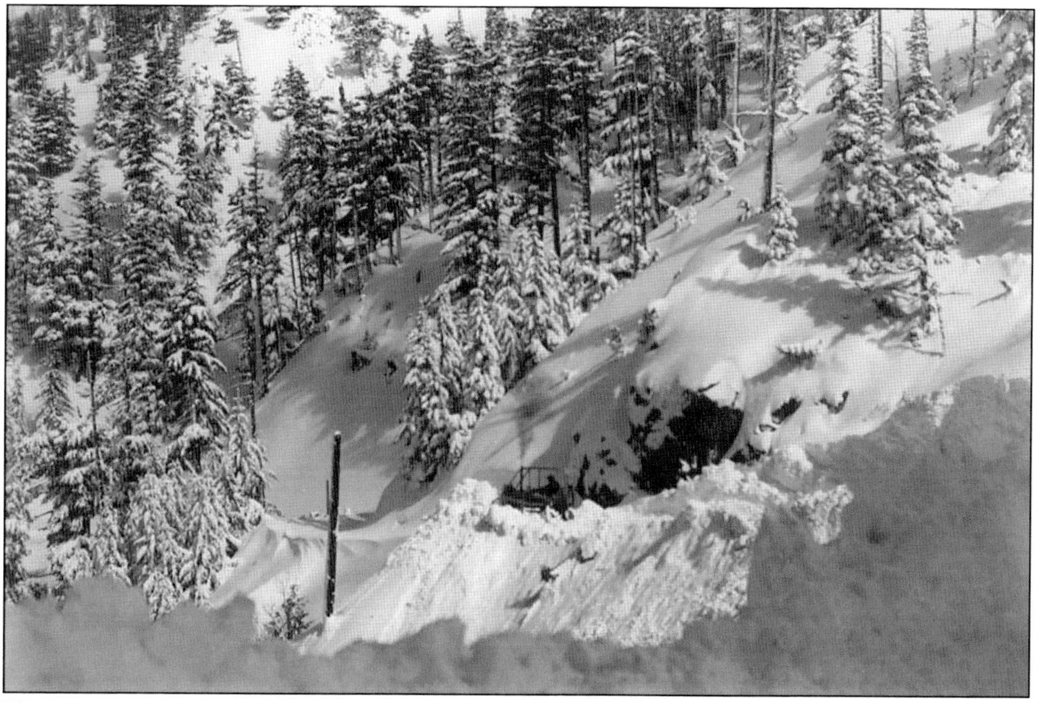

Plowing a snowy, mountainous road was a difficult task. Note the barely visible bulldozer in this photograph. Ernie Byers was called out at all hours to begin the work of clearing the roads. When this one-way road was improved in the late 1940s, some spots were widened enough to allow two cars to pass. (Photograph by Neil Mortiboy, courtesy of ONP.)

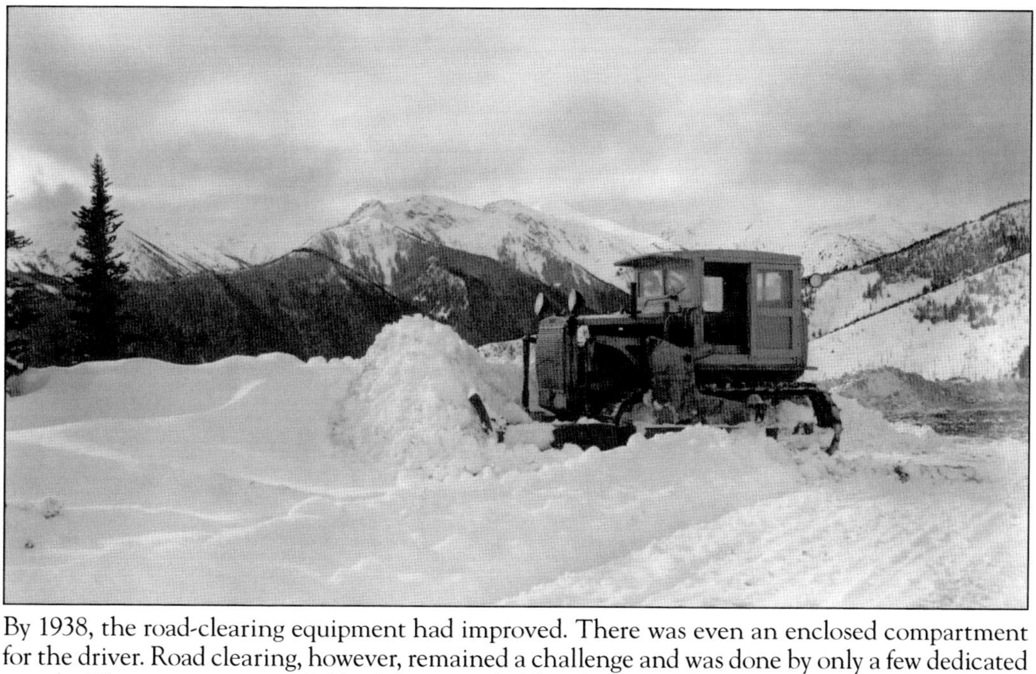

By 1938, the road-clearing equipment had improved. There was even an enclosed compartment for the driver. Road clearing, however, remained a challenge and was done by only a few dedicated people. The equipment available did a remarkable job. Later, the larger Hurricane Ridge road required much more heavy equipment. (Photograph by USFS, courtesy of ONP.)

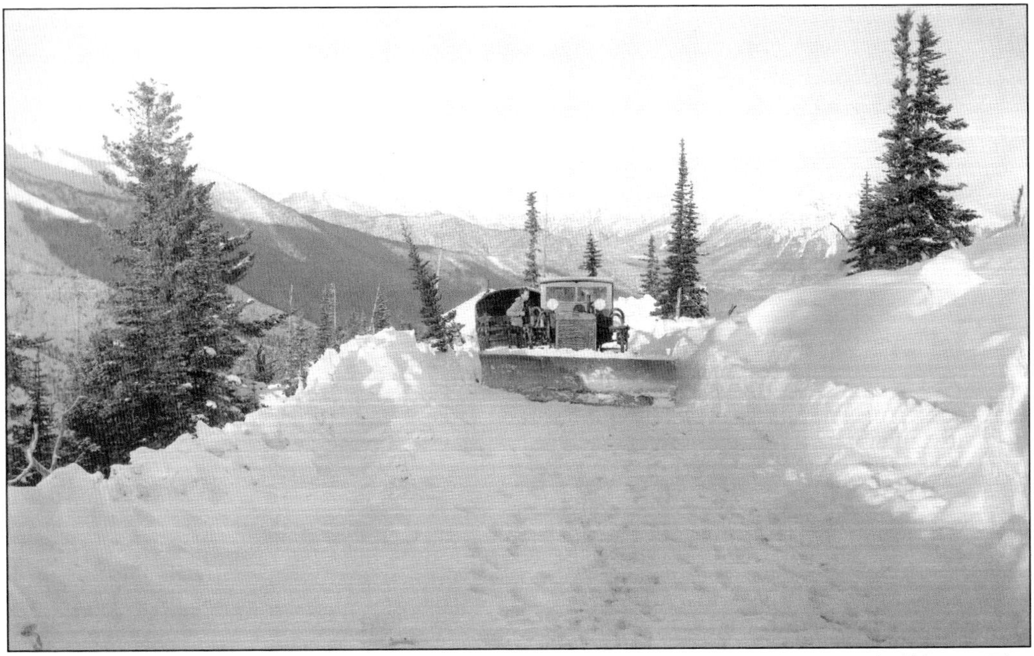

The plow seen here on February 10, 1938, was an improvement over the open bulldozer. The operator is likely Ernie Byers, who worked clearing roads and did other jobs at Deer Park for three years before World War II and for several years afterwards. (Photograph by USFS, courtesy of ONP.)

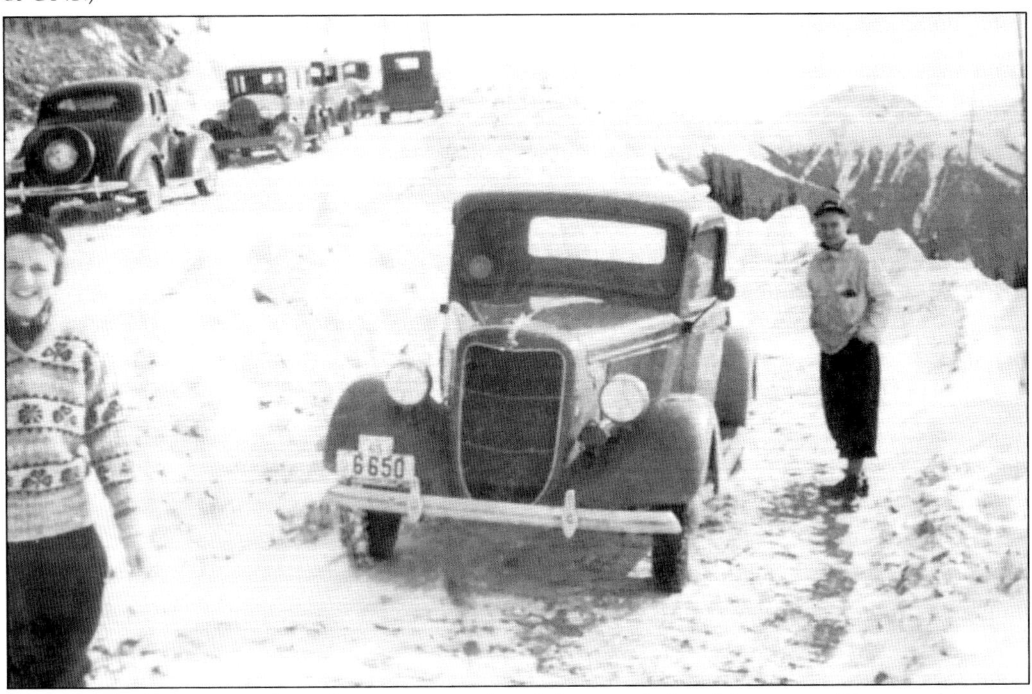

These parked cars again show the narrow road and the crowded parking areas. Since parking was at a premium, local people called into a central number to carpool. Chains were almost always required and often used. (Photograph by Jim Cahill, courtesy of ONP.)

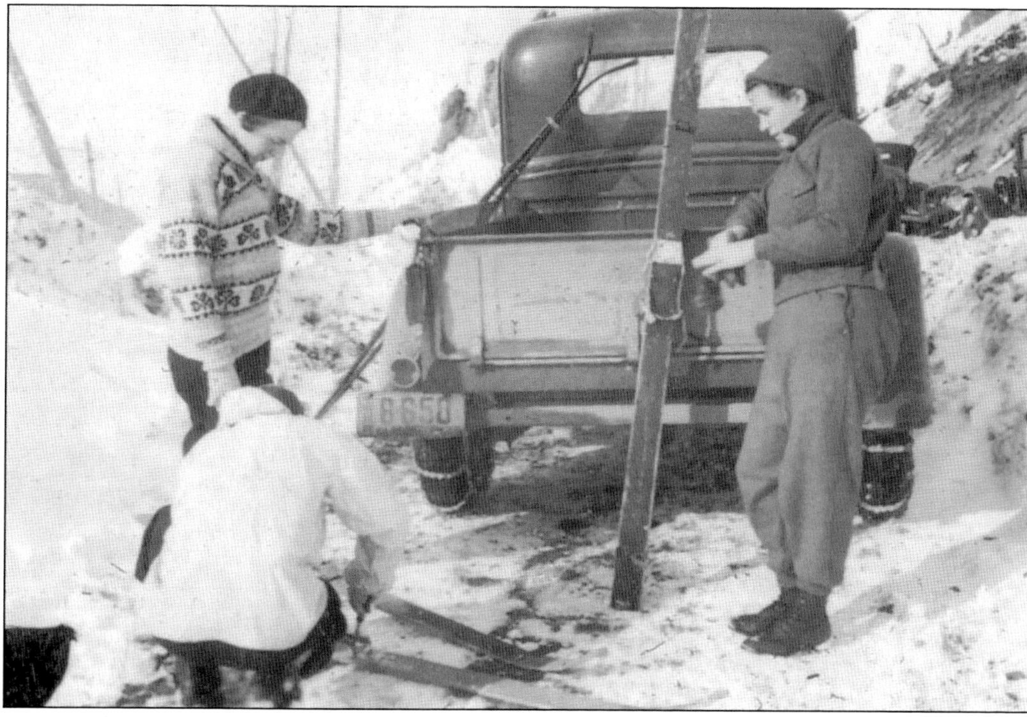

Here, a skier makes ski repairs behind a truck that has its chains in place, ready to make a downhill run. The road was often blocked by people putting chains on their vehicles, and on one occasion, it was blocked by a group of Canadians who stopped to make tea. (Photograph by Jim Cahill, courtesy of ONP.)

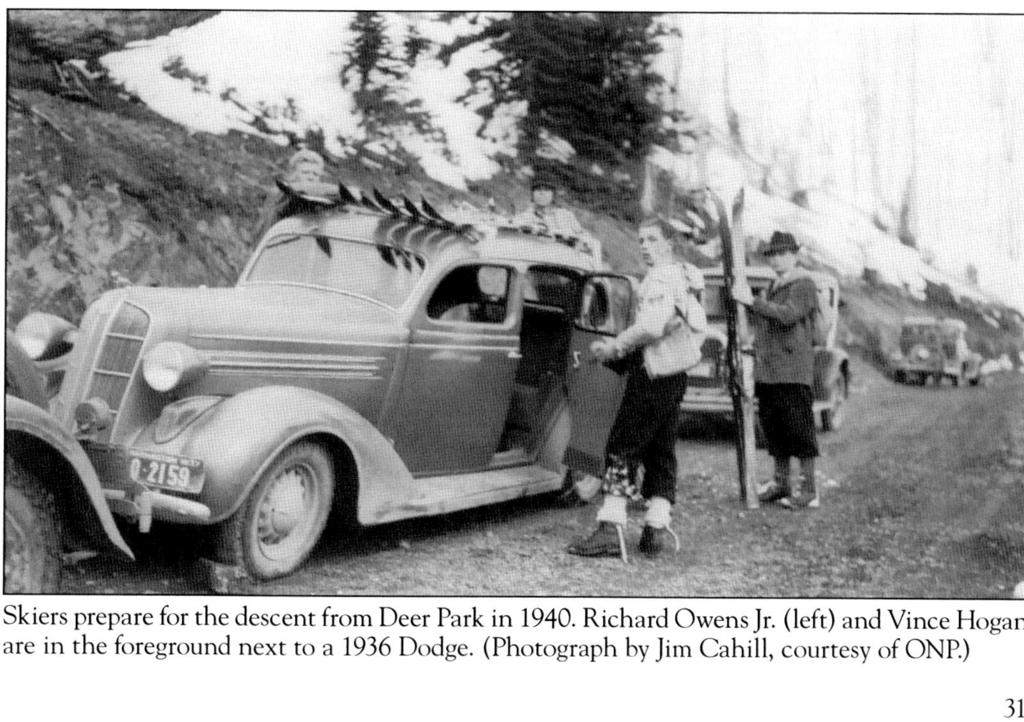

Skiers prepare for the descent from Deer Park in 1940. Richard Owens Jr. (left) and Vince Hogan are in the foreground next to a 1936 Dodge. (Photograph by Jim Cahill, courtesy of ONP.)

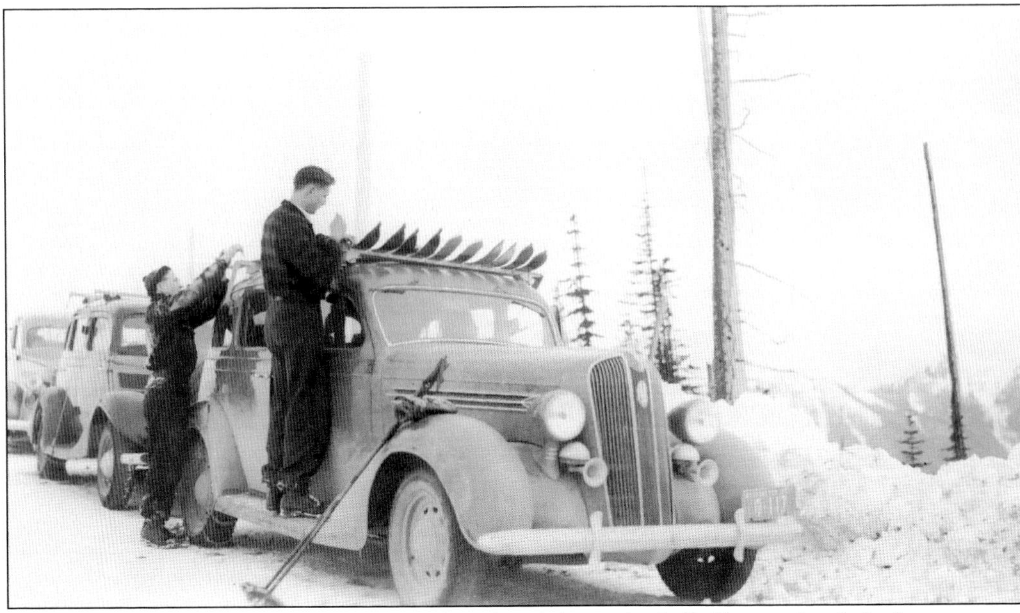

These cars have been turned and are ready to head down the hill. Skis are loaded, chains are on, and the final preparations are being done on the 1936 Plymouth in the foreground. (Photograph by Jim Cahill, courtesy of ONP.)

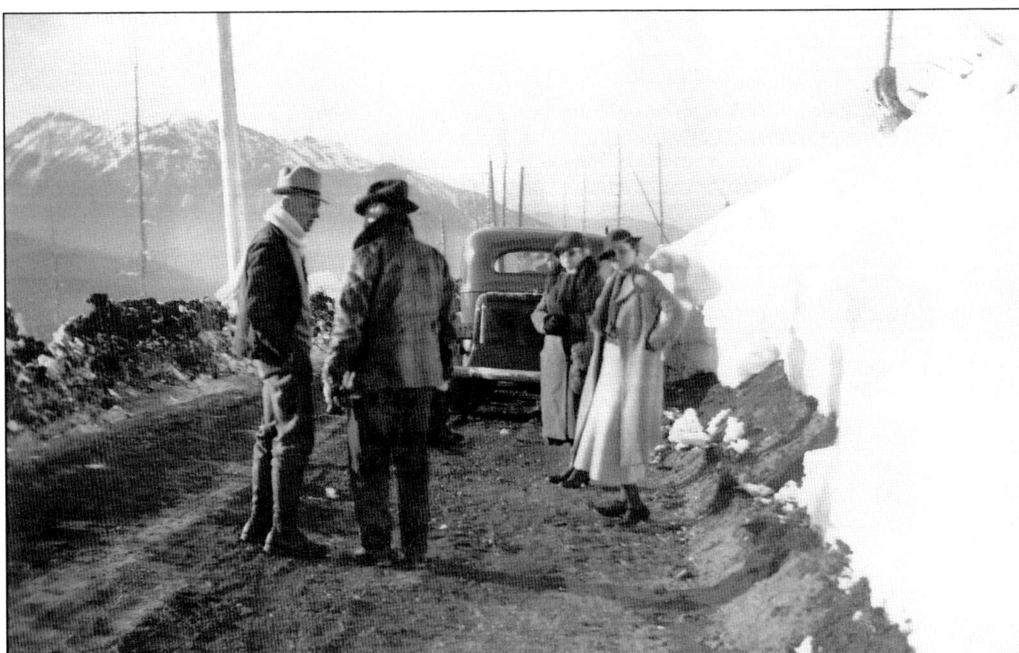

The mayors of Port Angeles and Sequim confer on the Deer Park road in February 1936. Their spouses are elegantly dressed for the outing. Because ski clothing was not something most people could afford, they came with what warm clothing they had. (Courtesy of ONP.)

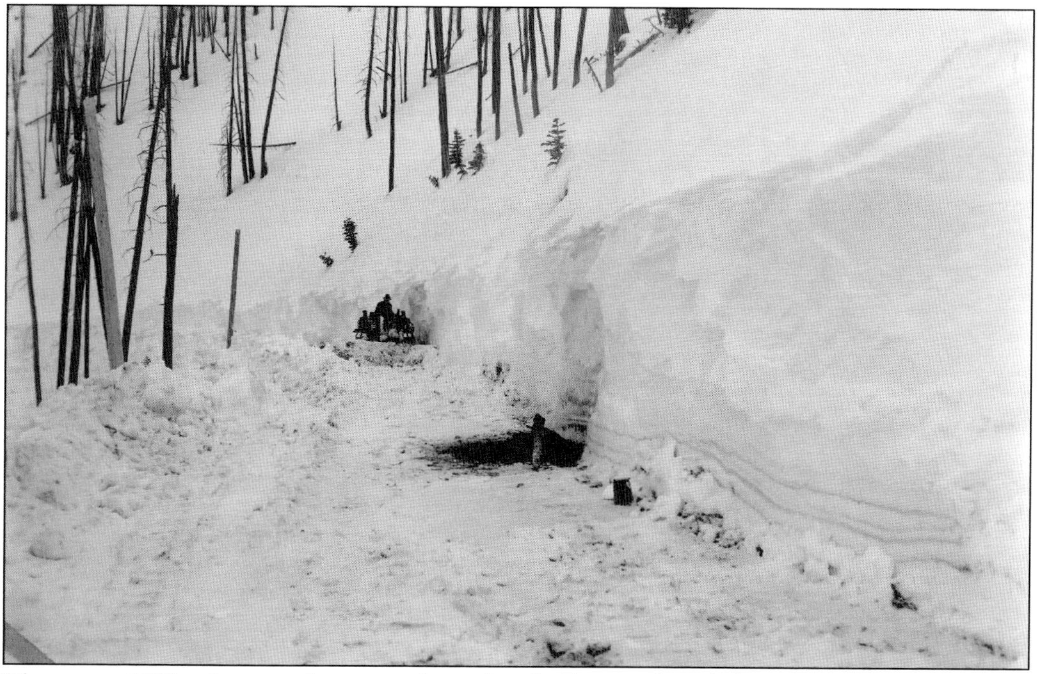

These two 1930s photographs again show the challenge of road clearing on a steep one-way mountain road ascending to 6,000 feet and often buried in deep snow. The lone plow operator had a lonely job. There were 7-to-13-foot drifts at Angeles viewpoint near the top. (Both, photograph by Neil Mortiboy; above, courtesy of USFS and ONP; below, courtesy of James Wengler.)

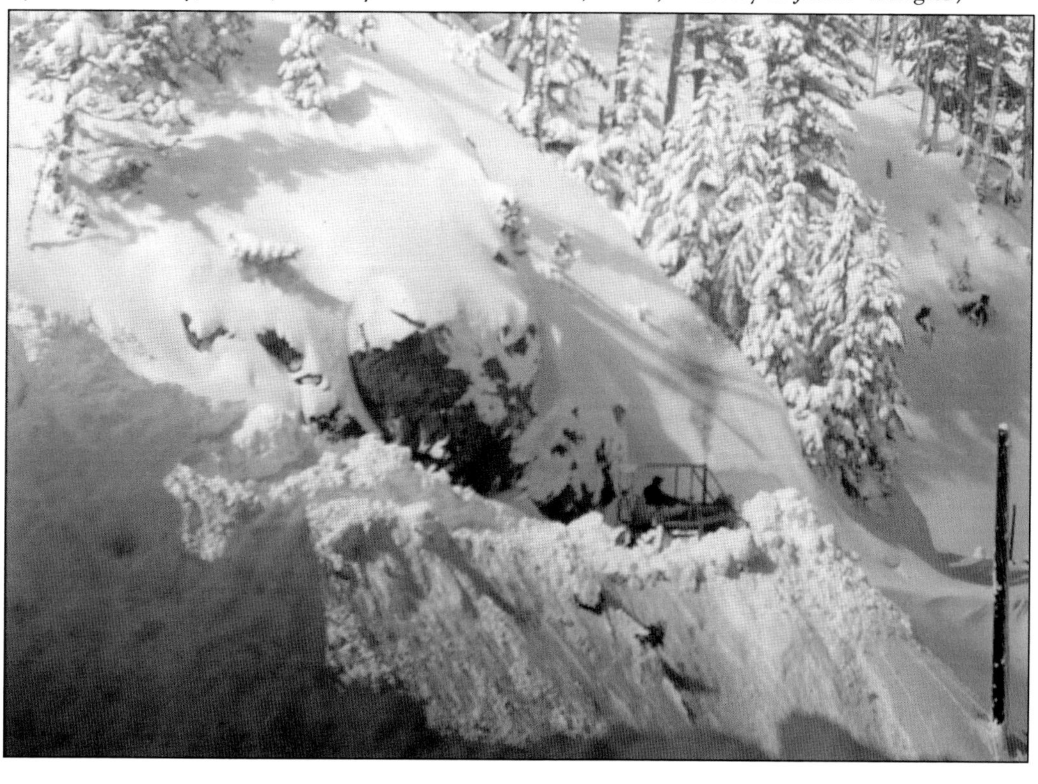

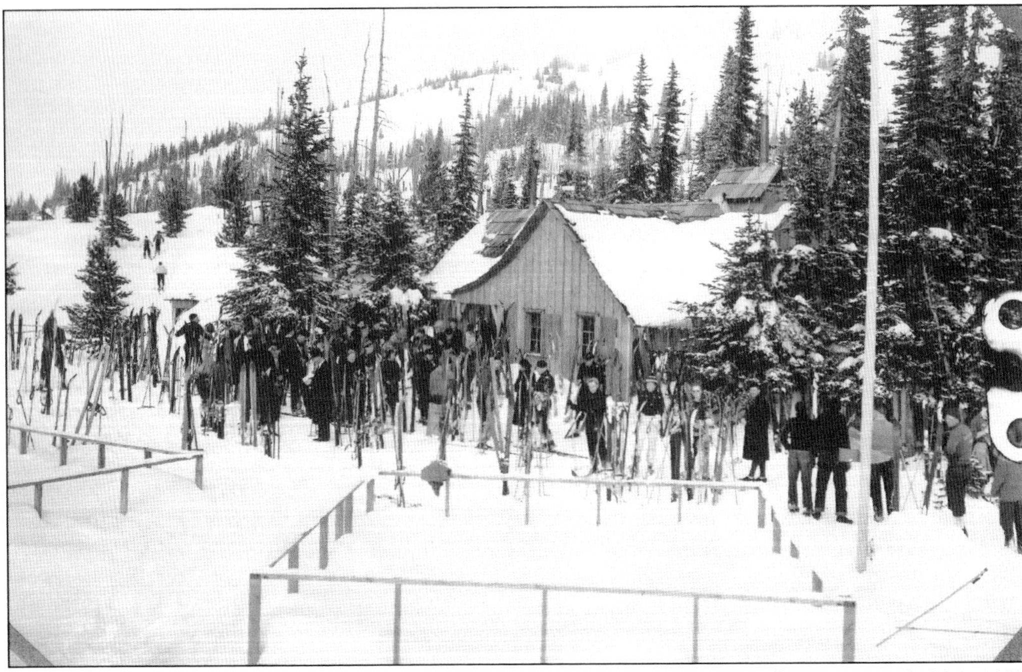

Large crowds were common at Deer Park when it opened for skiing in the winter of 1936–1937, which made for interesting travel and parking on the marginal Forest Service road. Pictured on February 2, 1937, these skiers are in front of what was known then as the "Deer Park Cook House," which would soon be remodeled and become the lodge. (Photograph by USFS, courtesy of ONP.)

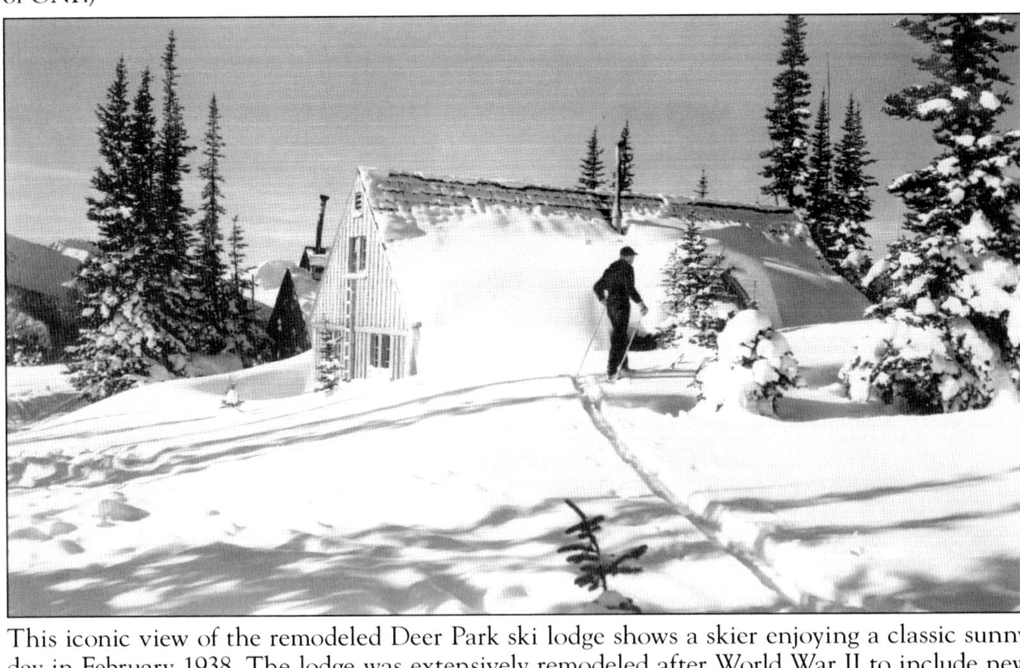

This iconic view of the remodeled Deer Park ski lodge shows a skier enjoying a classic sunny day in February 1938. The lodge was extensively remodeled after World War II to include new chimneys, cupboards, a kitchen stove, sinks, and washbasins, as well as running water and electric lights. (Photograph by USFS, courtesy of ONP.)

This photograph of the Deer Park lodge shows its location at the base of Blue Mountain. Its footings can still be seen in the current campground, although the lodge was demolished in the early 1960s. There were several outbuildings, including a storage building (pictured here), an outhouse, and a ski-rental shack. (Photograph by Art Jackson, courtesy of ONP.)

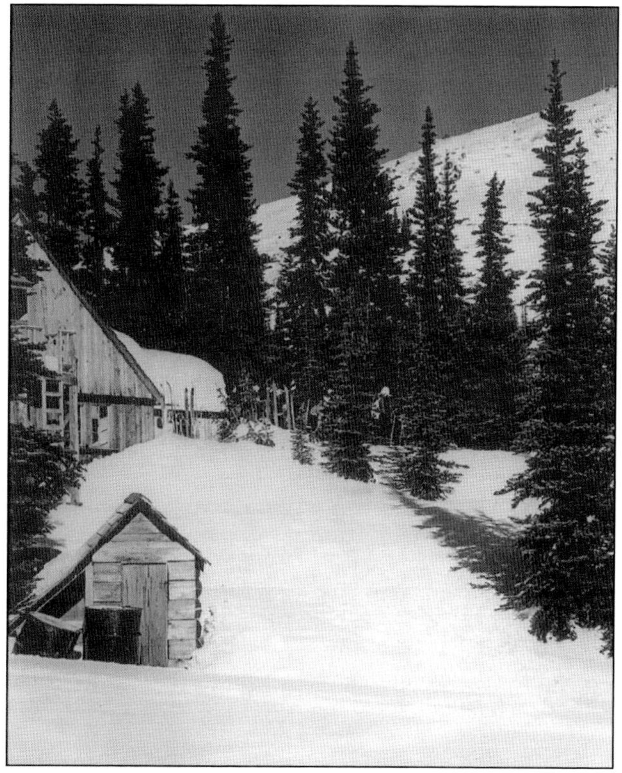

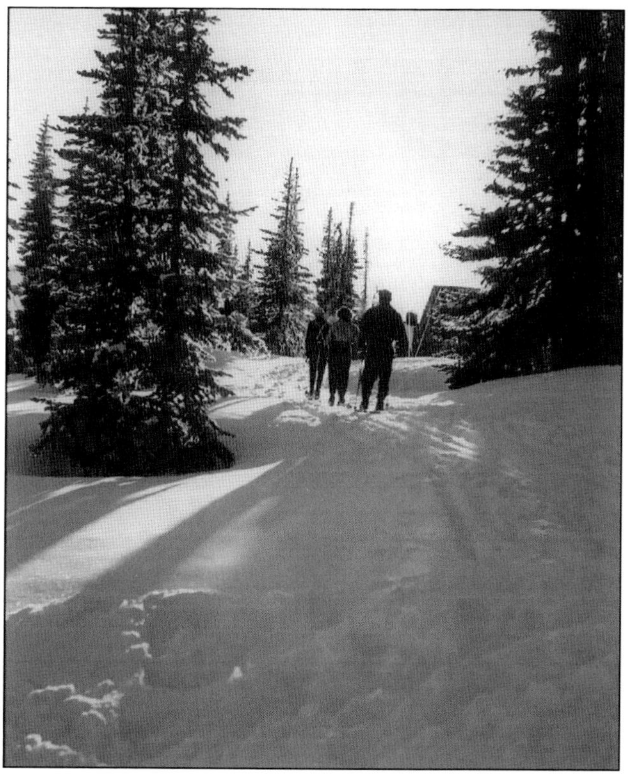

This photograph captures the idyllic nature of a winter ski day at Deer Park. Known for its rain shadow, sunny southern exposure, and panoramic mountain scenery, Deer Park offered a winter experience like no other. (Photograph by Art Jackson, courtesy of ONP.)

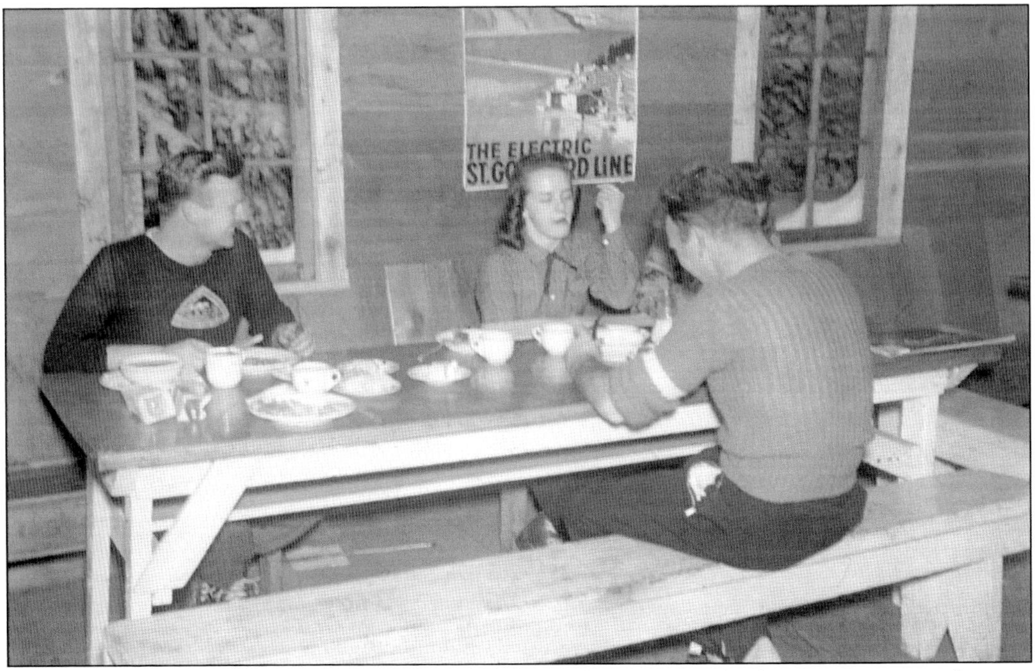

The Deer Park lodge offered family-style dining and dormitory-style sleeping accommodations. Prices were reasonable. In 1940, dinners were 50¢, and lodging was 50¢ with one's own bedding. Skiers warmed themselves with a large potbellied stove and warm drinks from the kitchen. In the late 1940s, lodge renovations included red-plaid curtains against powder-green walls and a waterproof vestibule entrance. (Photograph by Jim Cahill, courtesy of ONP.)

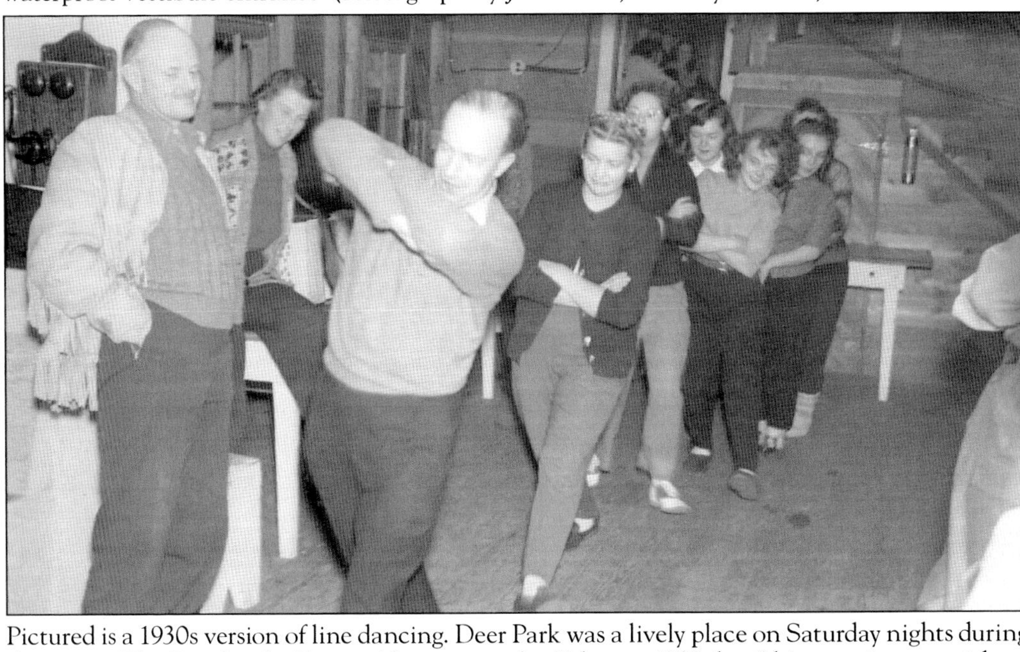

Pictured is a 1930s version of line dancing. Deer Park was a lively place on Saturday nights during the winter. The *Port Angeles Evening News* reported in February 1939 that "skiers staying overnight at the Deer Park ski lodge will have a merry evening of dancing and music, with a four-piece orchestra furnishing melodies to enliven the party." (Photograph by Jim Cahill, courtesy of ONP.)

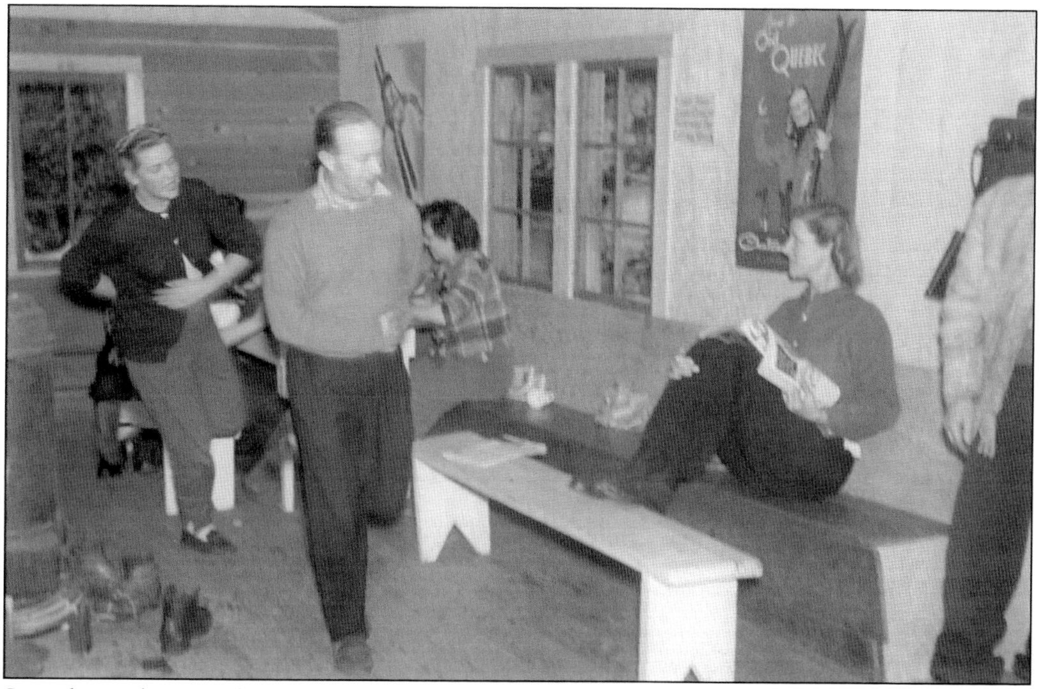

Saturday nights were lively at the lodge. Some people danced while others read or played games. Esther Webster, a local artist and community leader, could frequently be seen sitting in a corner and sketching the whole scene. (Photograph by Jim Cahill, courtesy of ONP.)

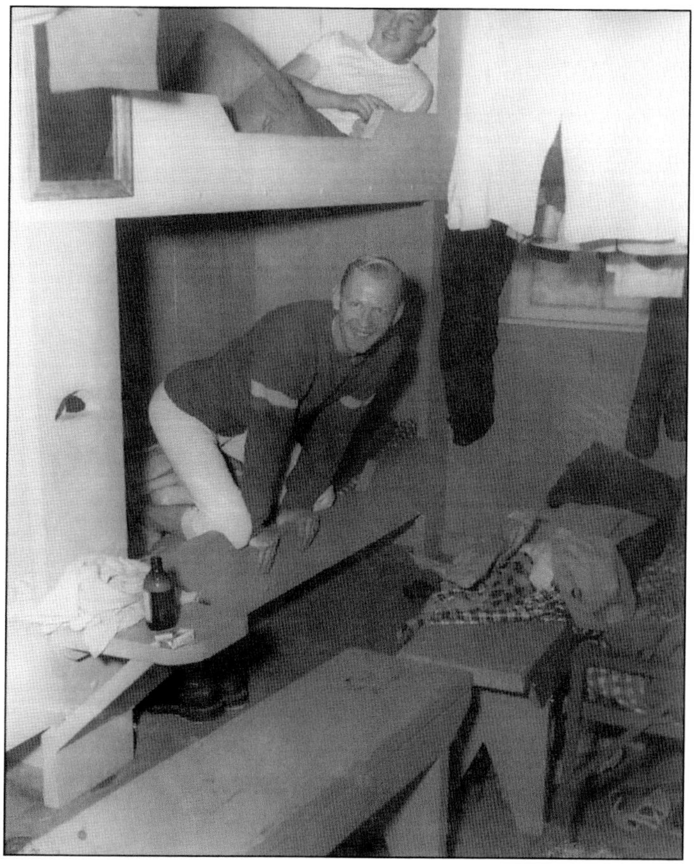

The Deer Park lodge offered separate dormitories for men and women. Bunk beds provided mattresses, but skiers brought their own bedding. A favorite evening activity was moonlight skiing followed by a much-needed rest before another day of skiing. (Photograph by Art Jackson, courtesy of ONP.)

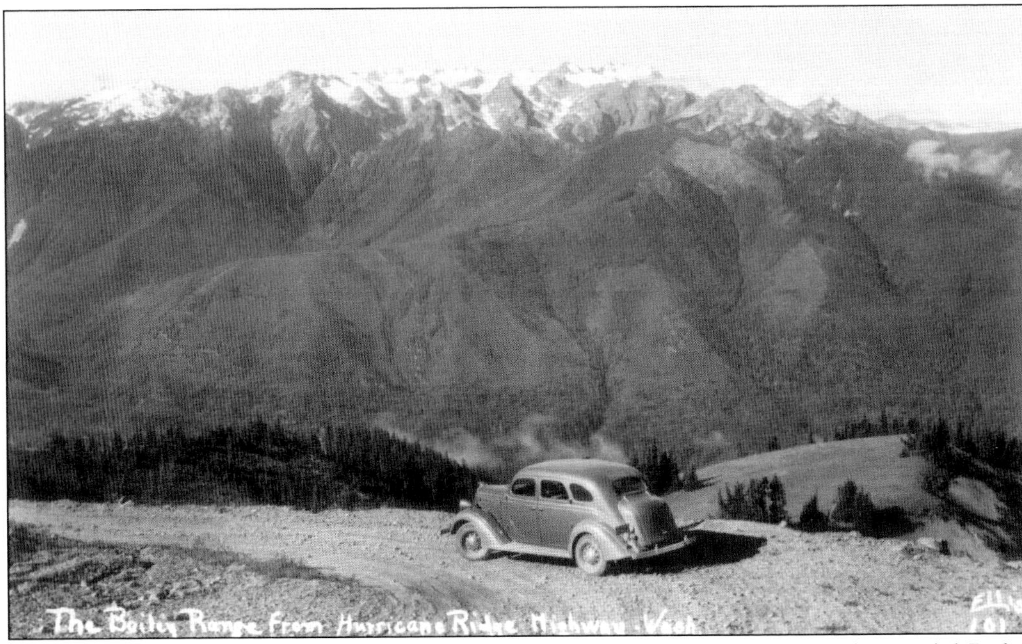

The original road to Hurricane Ridge came from the Elwha Valley, turned up Salal Ridge at Whiskey Bend, and eventually ran 23 miles to Obstruction Point. Access for building the Hurricane Ridge lodge and the upper part of the new road was via this old, winding, narrow dirt road. (Courtesy of ONP.)

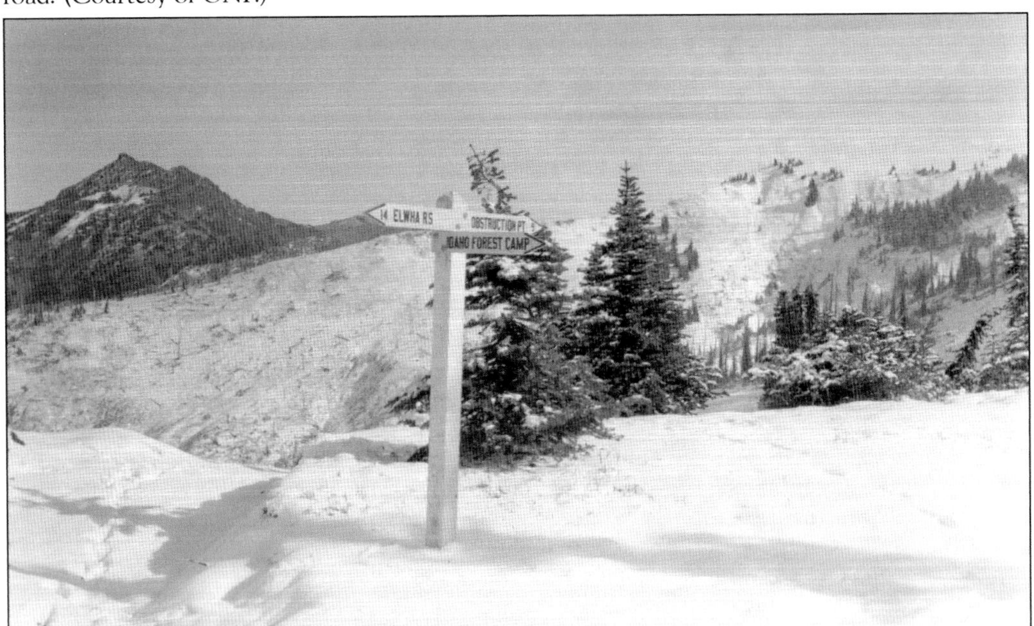

This signpost at Hurricane Ridge points to the Idaho Forest Camp, which was located 14 miles up the old road and served as a staging area for the lodge construction. It also points to Obstruction Point, which was the terminus of the old road. Mount Angeles is in the background. (Courtesy of ONP.)

This road to Obstruction Point is a continuation of the original road to Hurricane Ridge built by the CCC in the 1930s. In the winter, it serves as a good route for cross-country skiers. Plans to extend this road to Deer Park were suspended because of World War II. (Courtesy of ONP.)

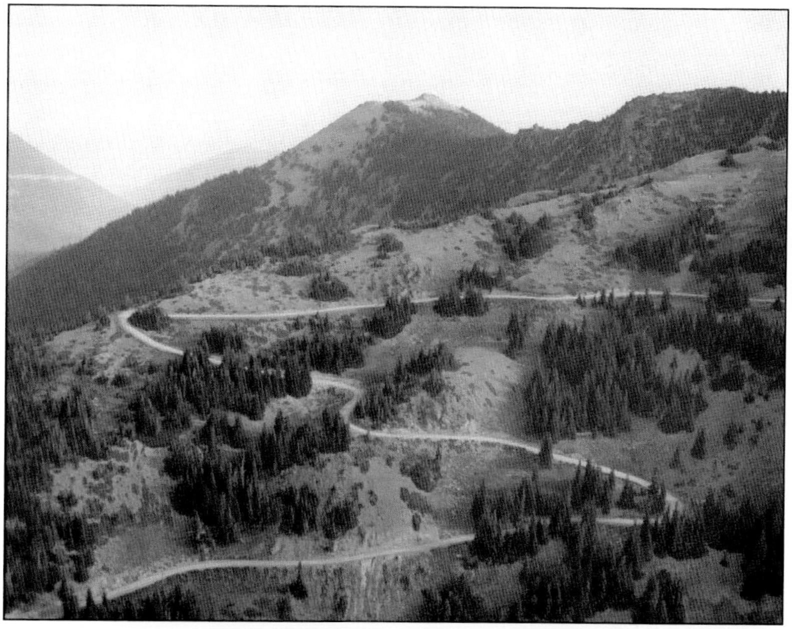

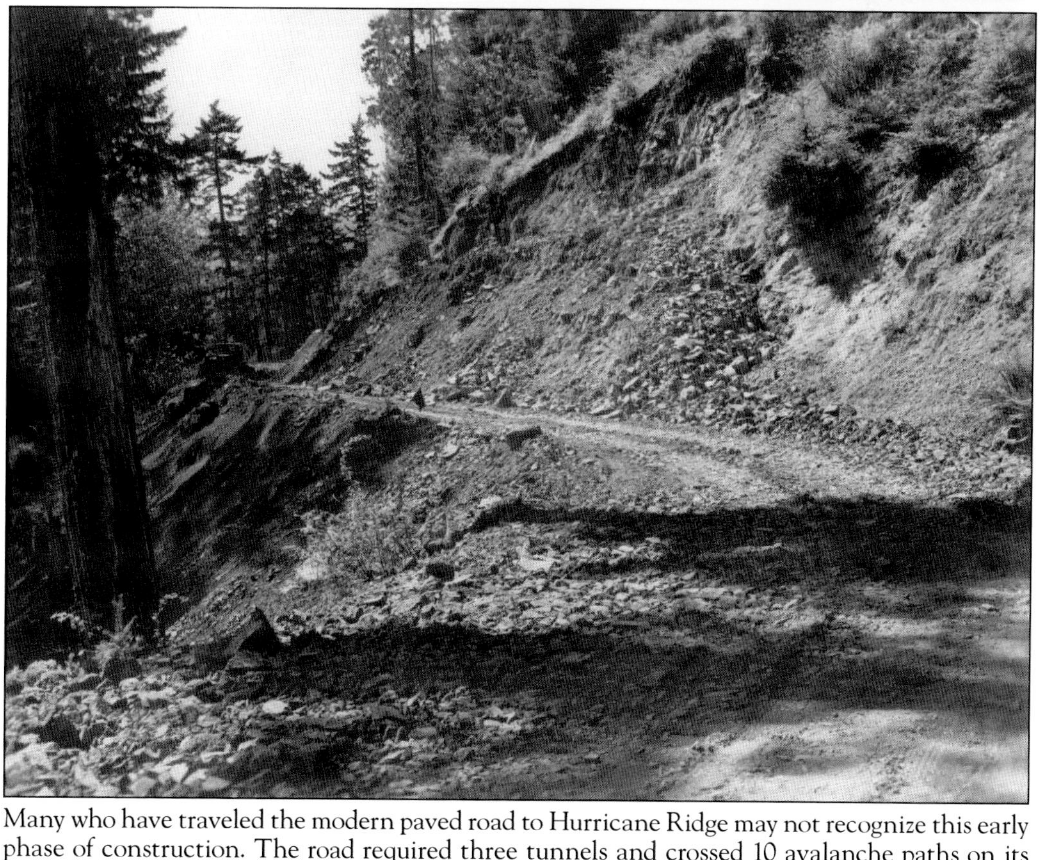

Many who have traveled the modern paved road to Hurricane Ridge may not recognize this early phase of construction. The road required three tunnels and crossed 10 avalanche paths on its way to the ridge. Two men were killed during construction of the top seven miles, which were constructed from the top down to the tunnels. (Courtesy of ONP.)

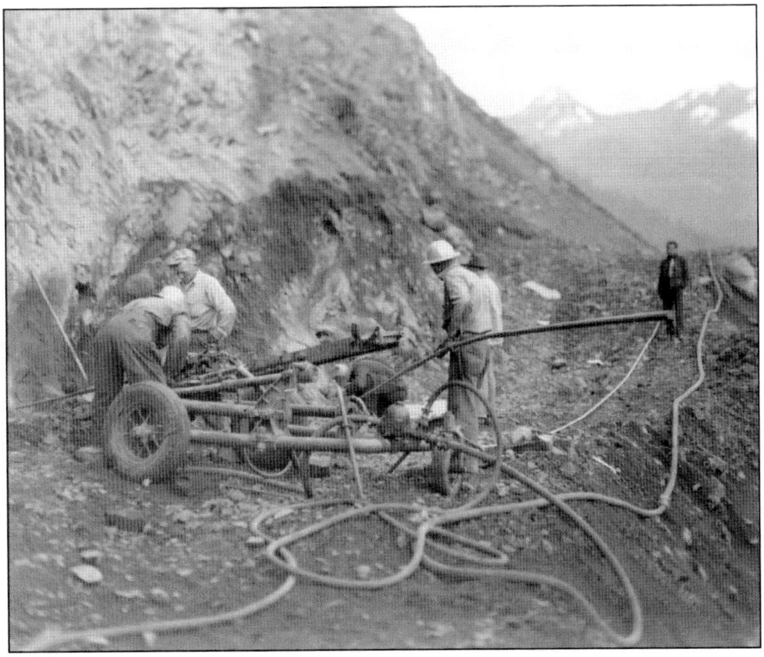

In the 1950s, work on the new road to Hurricane Ridge was in full swing. Keith Engelson, who also plowed the Deer Park road, said this road work involved drilling, blasting, an incredible amount of dynamite, logging, and moving tons of dirt. The rock was largely basalt, which is the strongest rock in the Olympics. (Courtesy of ONP.)

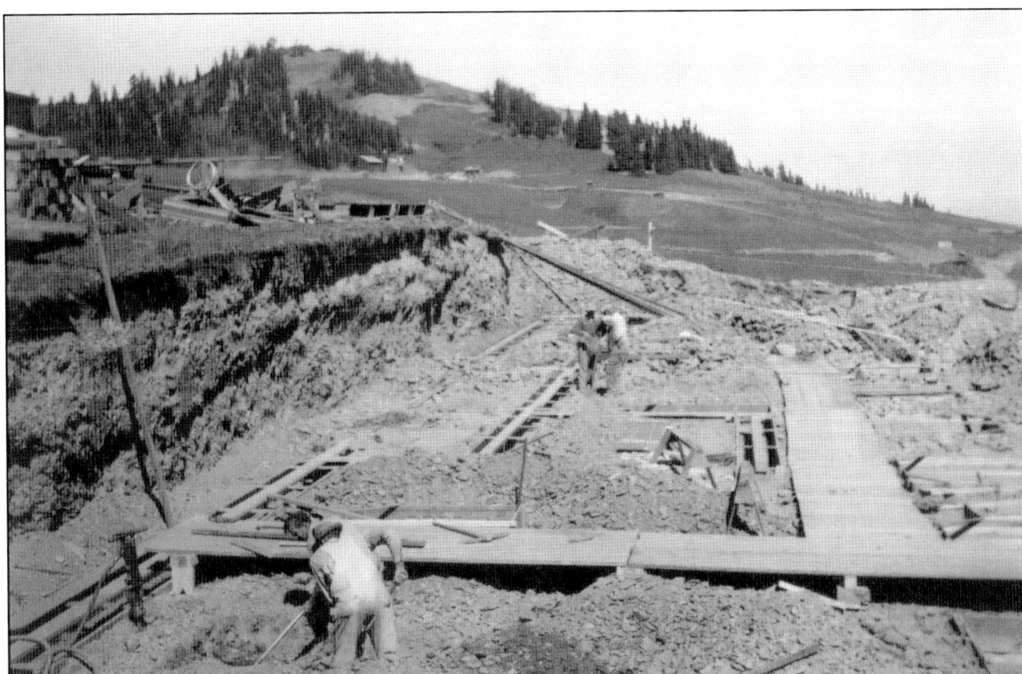

Long before the new road to Hurricane Ridge was completed, construction began on a new lodge. Here, workers for Owens Brothers of Port Angeles lay the foundation on July 26, 1951. Future ski slopes are seen in the background. Arvie Smith used his West Coast logging truck to transport materials up the old CCC road, which was a remarkable feat. Completed by 1952, the lodge was only used during the summer until the new road was completed in 1957. (Courtesy of ONP.)

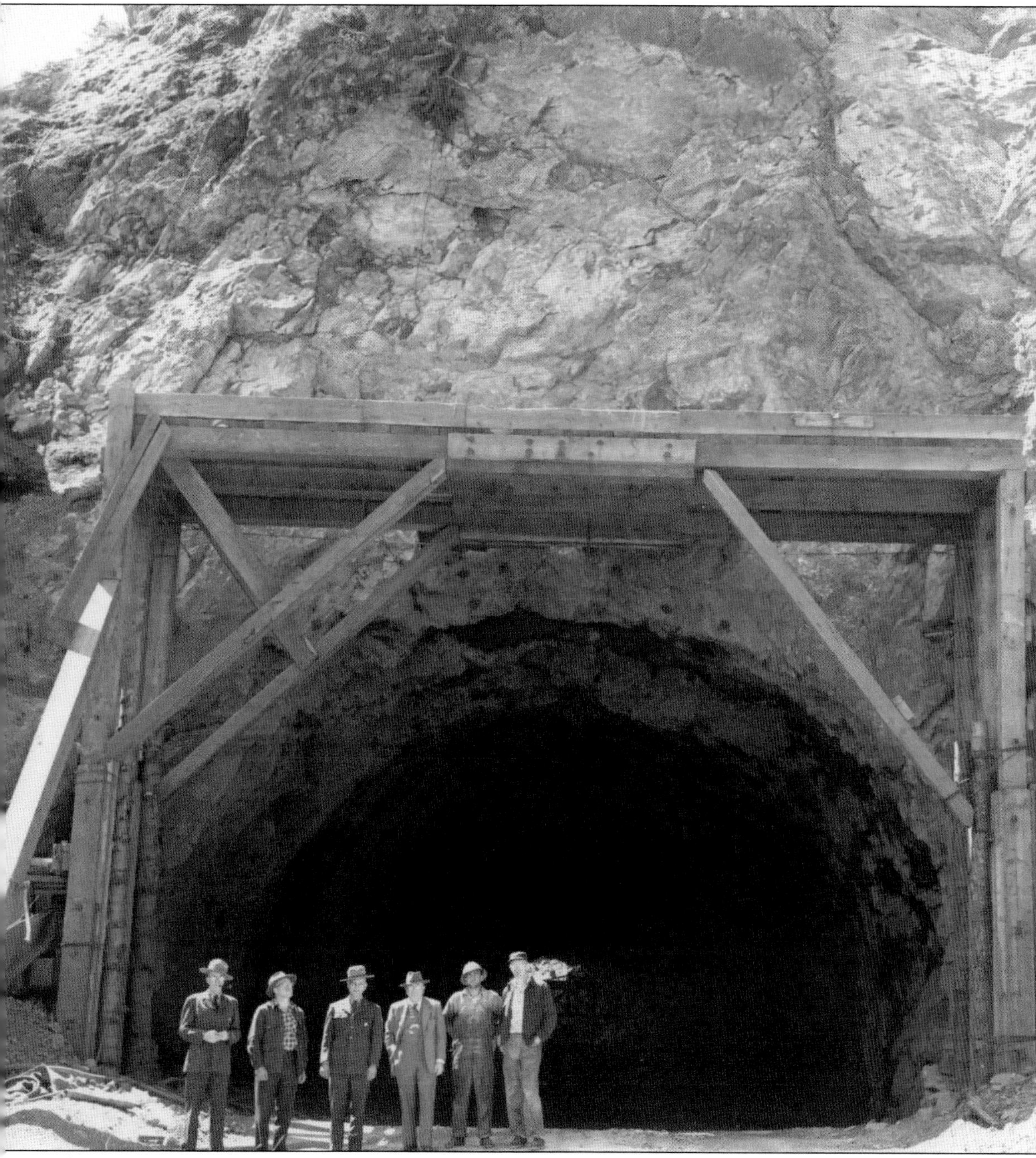

These men stand at the new entrance to one of the three tunnels required to allow the road to skirt the east end of Klahhane Ridge. Once through the tunnels, the road traversed the south side of the ridge across 10 avalanche chutes. Park ranger Jack Hughes, who studied geology in college, pointed out that because the tunnels were dug through pillow basalt, which tends to have multiple fracture lines, they required lining. (Courtesy of ONP.)

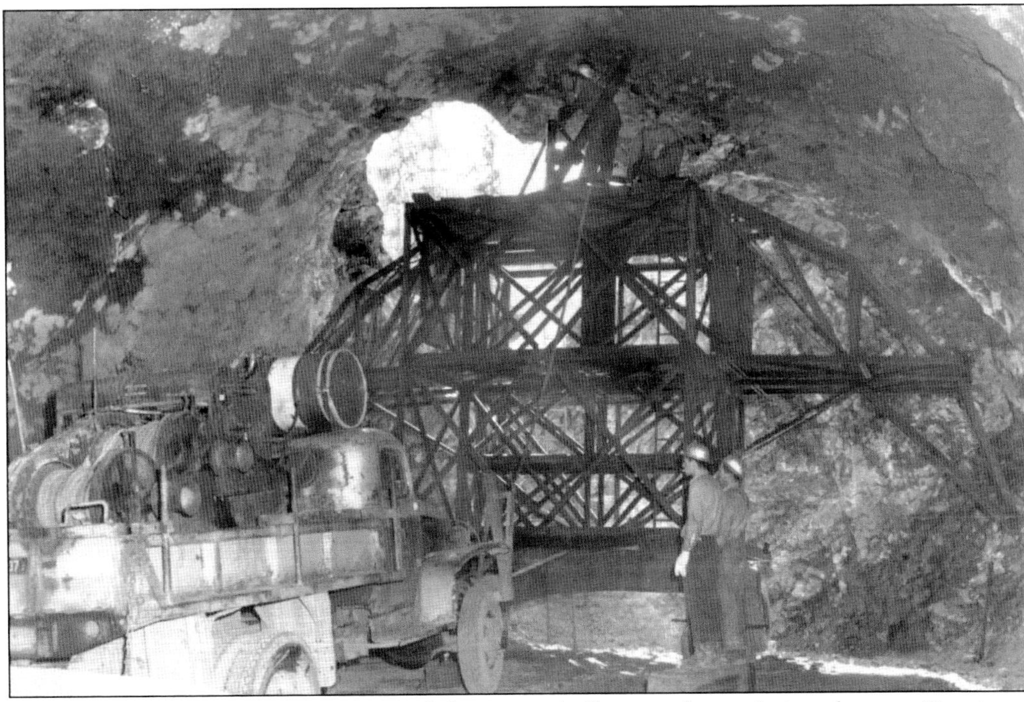

These photographs demonstrate one of the main challenges of completing the new Hurricane Ridge road. Three tunnels were excavated in total. The tunnel work was dangerous, but was accomplished without loss of life. (Above, courtesy of ONP; below, photograph by Deines Studio, courtesy of ONP.)

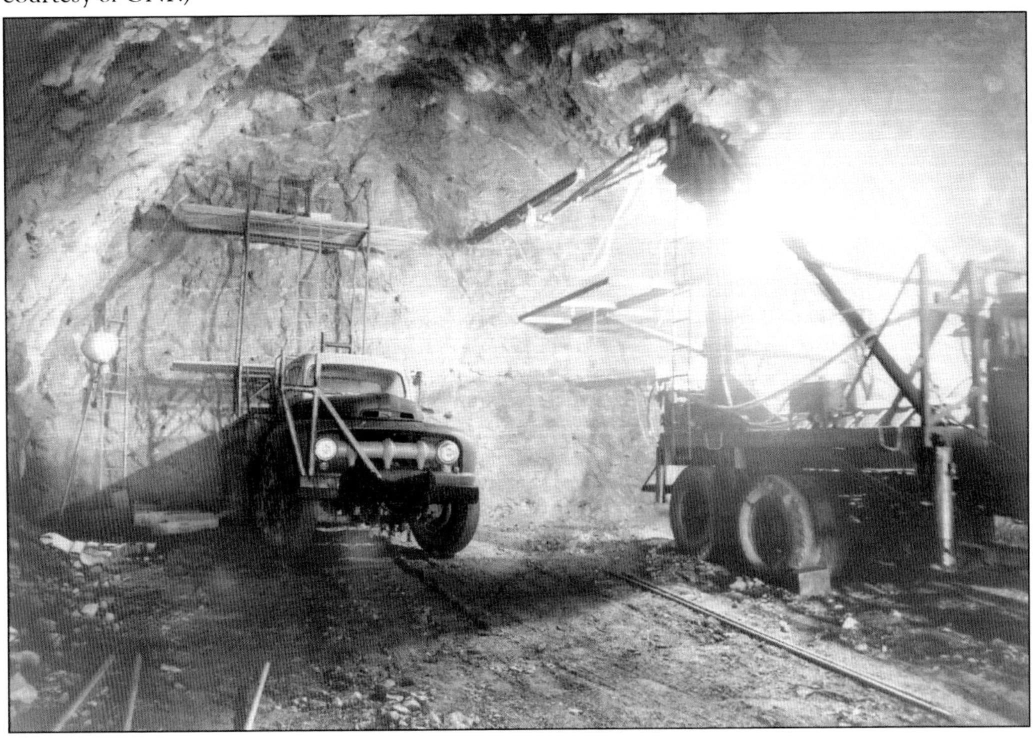

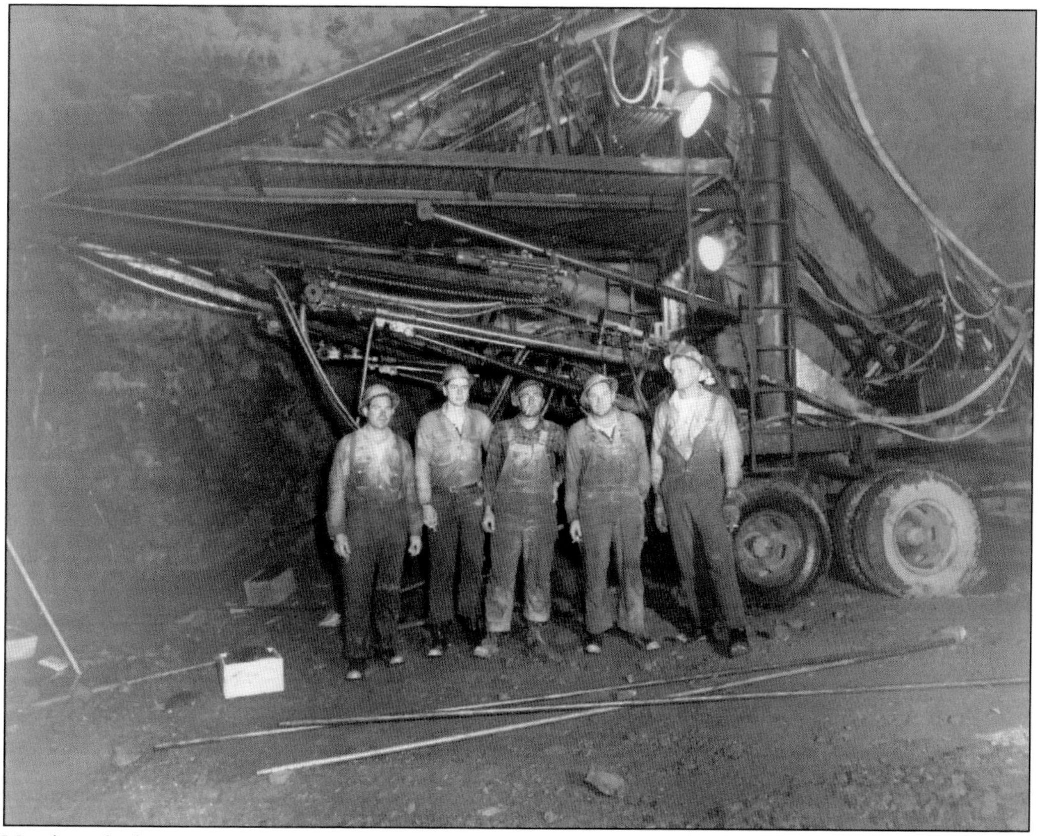

Unidentified construction workers pose in one of the three tunnels on the road to Hurricane Ridge in the 1950s. These tunnels were dug through basalt on the east end of Klahhane Ridge. (Photograph by Deines Studio, courtesy of ONP.)

With newly completed paving, a beautiful and safe modern highway now takes visitors the 17 miles from Port Angeles to mile-high Hurricane Ridge. Here, a car is about to enter the first of three newly completed tunnels. The road was opened for winter use during the winter of 1957–1958. (Photograph by Rogers Studio, courtesy of ONP.)

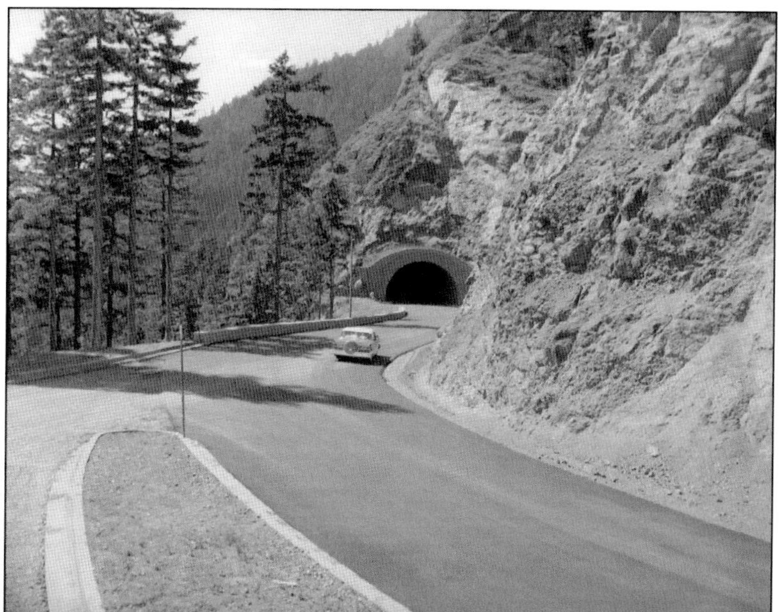

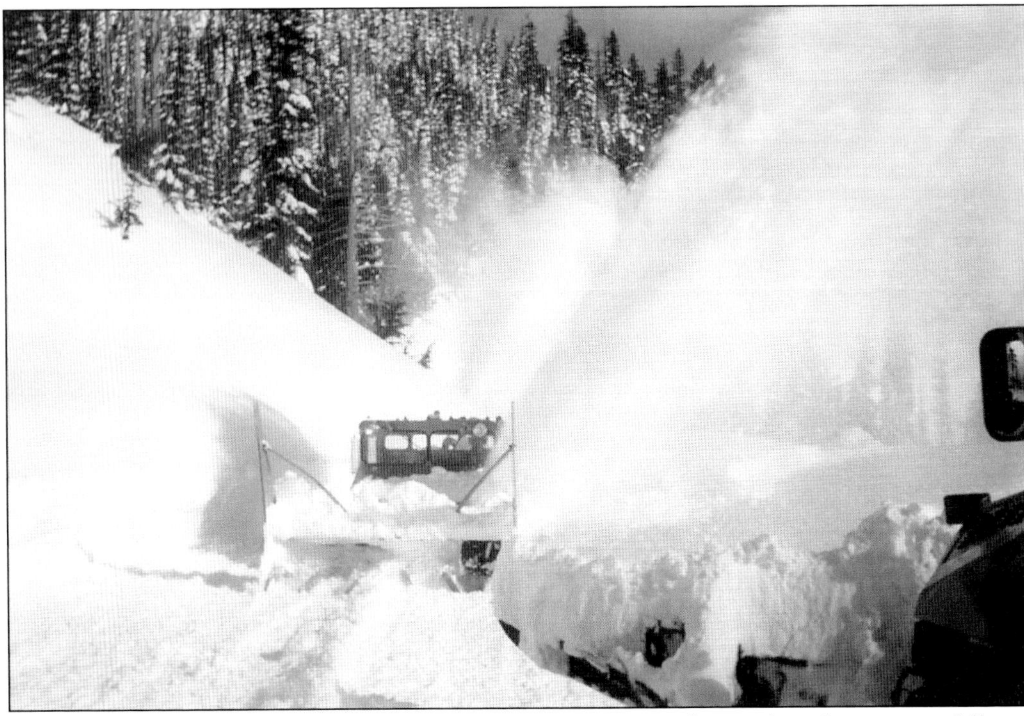

Here, one can see the challenge of winter use at Hurricane Ridge, with its heavy snowfall and mile-high elevation. With the much-improved wider road and heavier snowfall came a need for better snow-removal equipment. Above, a rotary plow is hard at work. Gordon Grall worked on road maintenance for 30 years. He said they usually had two rotary plows that worked in conjunction with a Walters Snowfreighter and, later, an Oshkosh. Below is a grader with a front blade. Many different blade setups were used to get the job done. (Both, courtesy of ONP.)

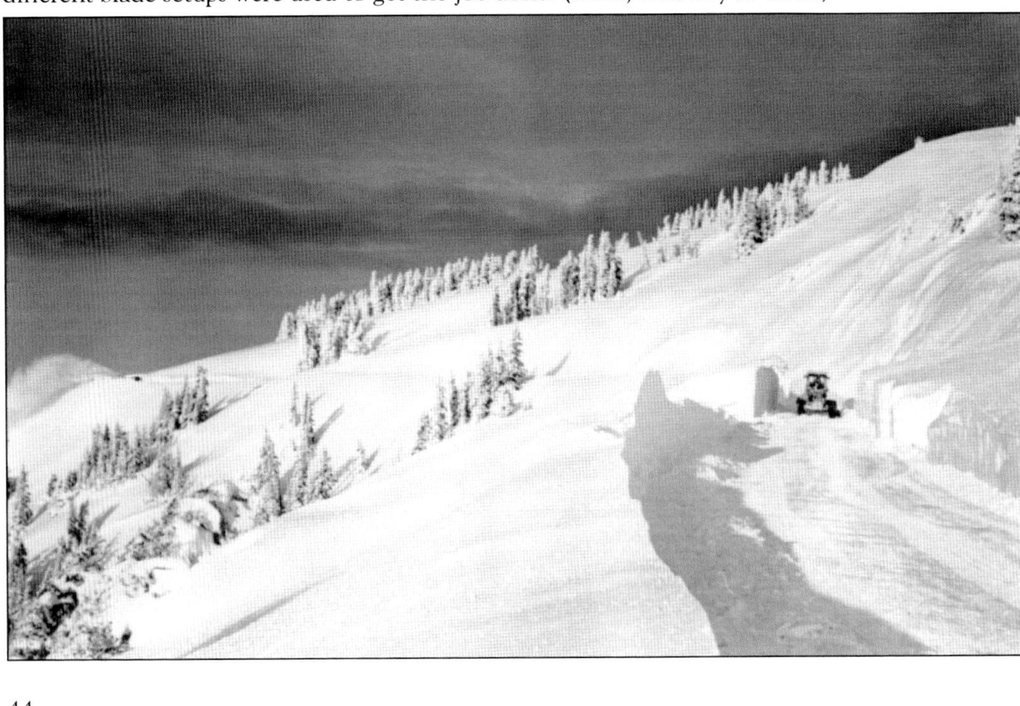

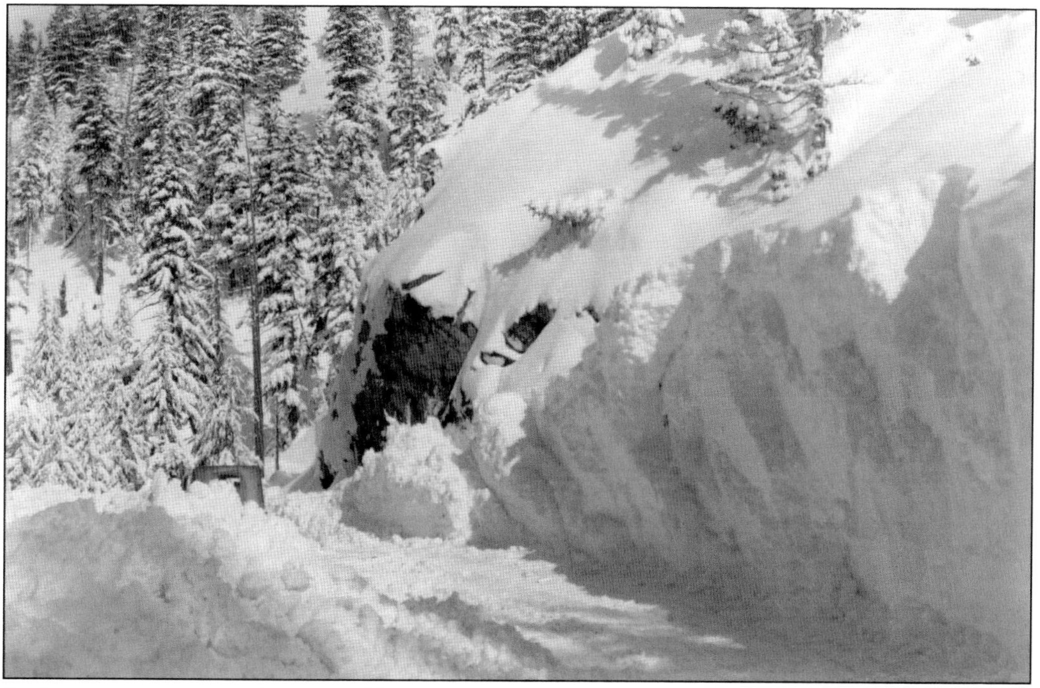

Besides steep banks and snow buildup, there are multiple avalanche chutes along the Hurricane Ridge road. The avalanche chutes have names and have always been well known to the road crews. Two of the worst are Old Faithful and Goat Creek. (Courtesy of ONP.)

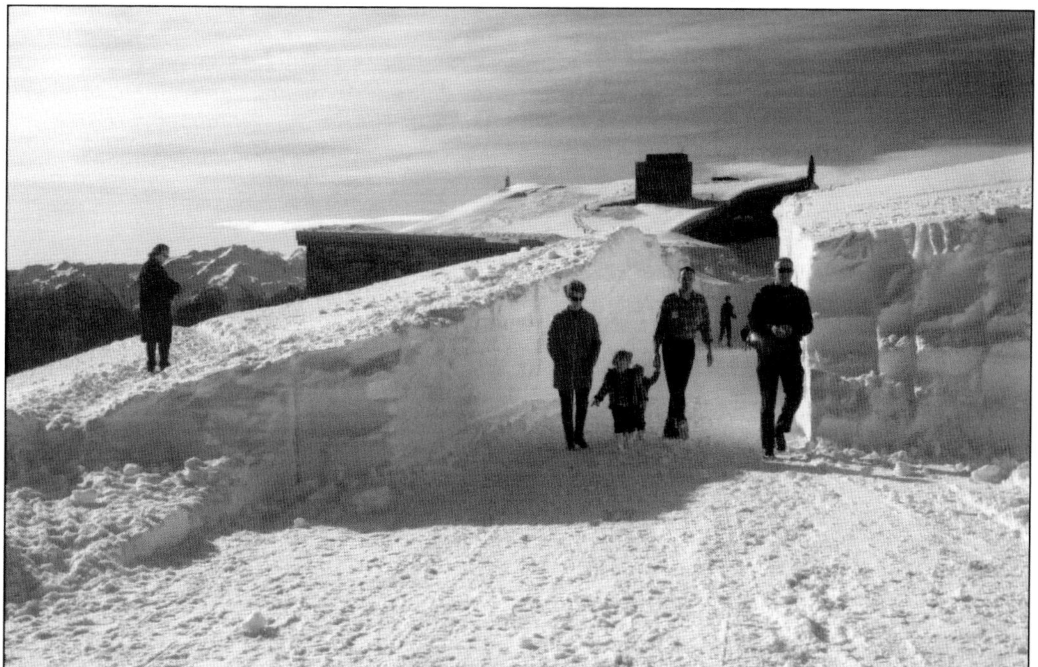

The parking area often drifts in with deep snow. Snowdrifts are common as the meadow area is subject to high winds. Here, visitors give perspective to the depth of the snow. The Hurricane Ridge lodge is in the background. (Courtesy of ONP.)

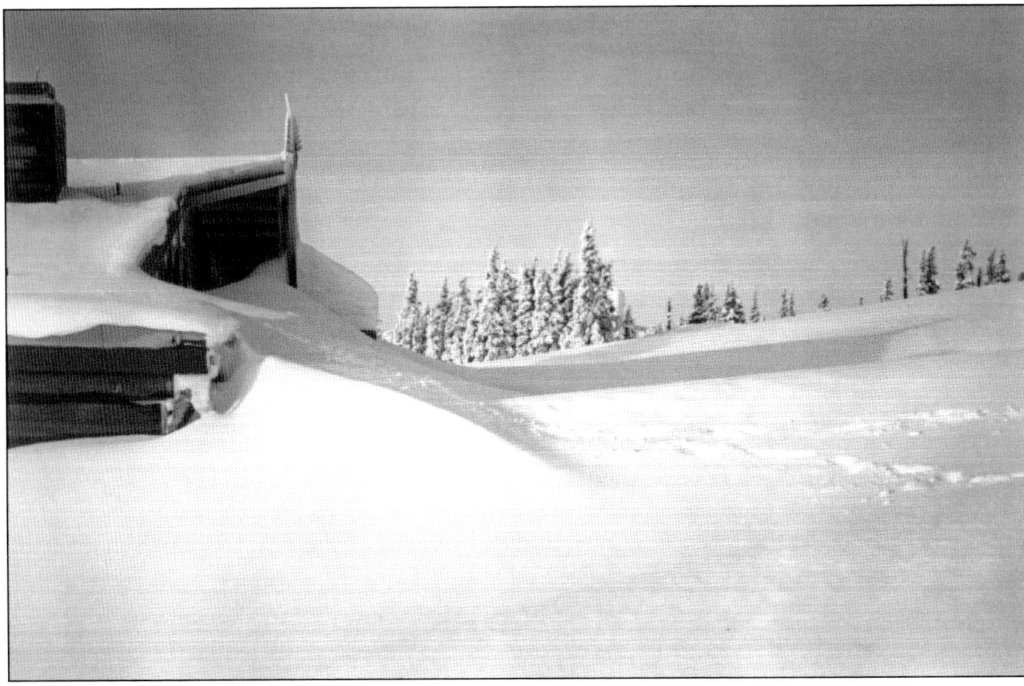

Because it is in the path of moist air off the Pacific Ocean from the southwest, Hurricane Ridge often receives very heavy snowfall. Above, the lodge is almost buried under a deep blanket of snow. Snow can drift in quite rapidly, with drifts of 12–15 feet not uncommon and often trapping visitors' vehicles in the parking lot. (Both, courtesy of ONP.)

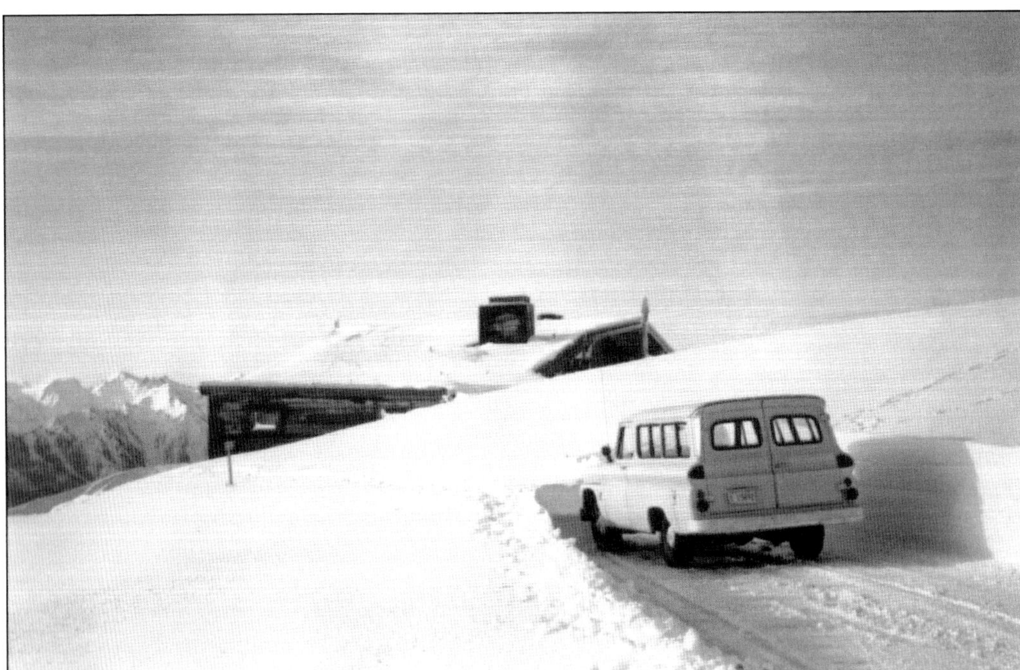

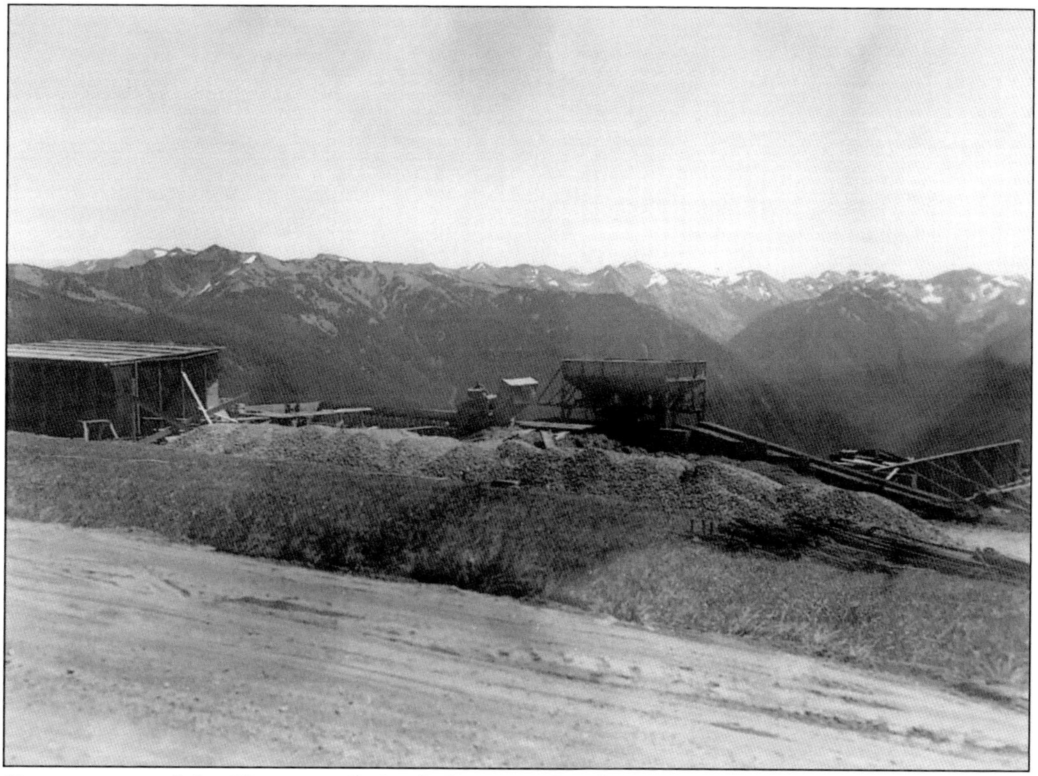

Construction of the Hurricane Ridge lodge, completed in 1952, required moving all materials up the old Forest Service road since the new road was not completed until 1957. The lodge has subsequently been extensively remodeled twice. It overlooks one of the most spectacular views in the park. (Above, photograph by Art Jackson; both, courtesy of ONP.)

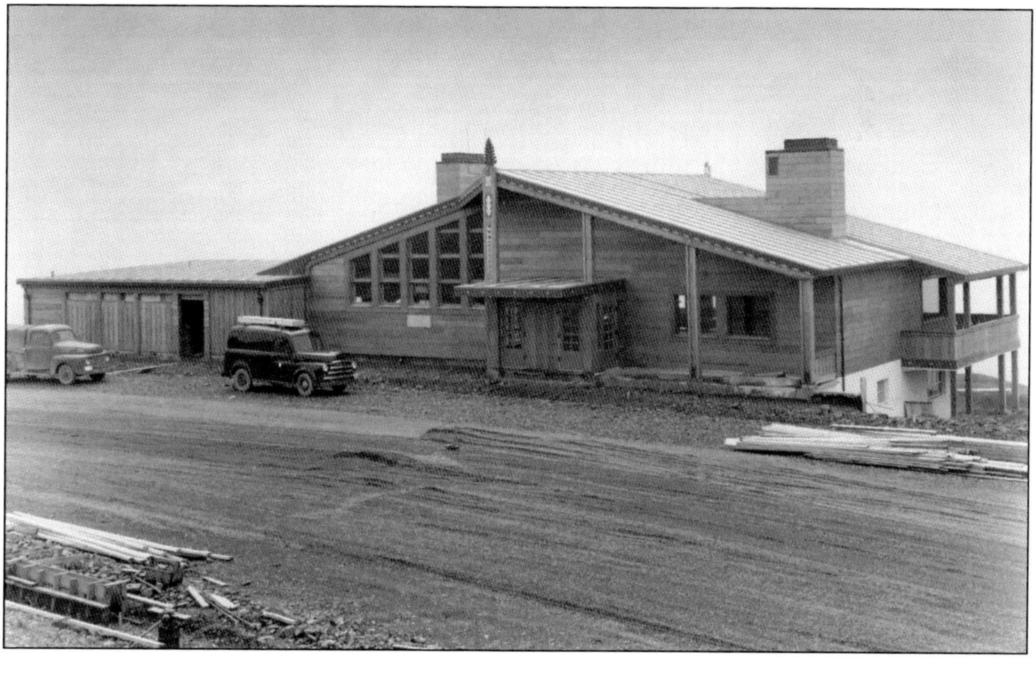

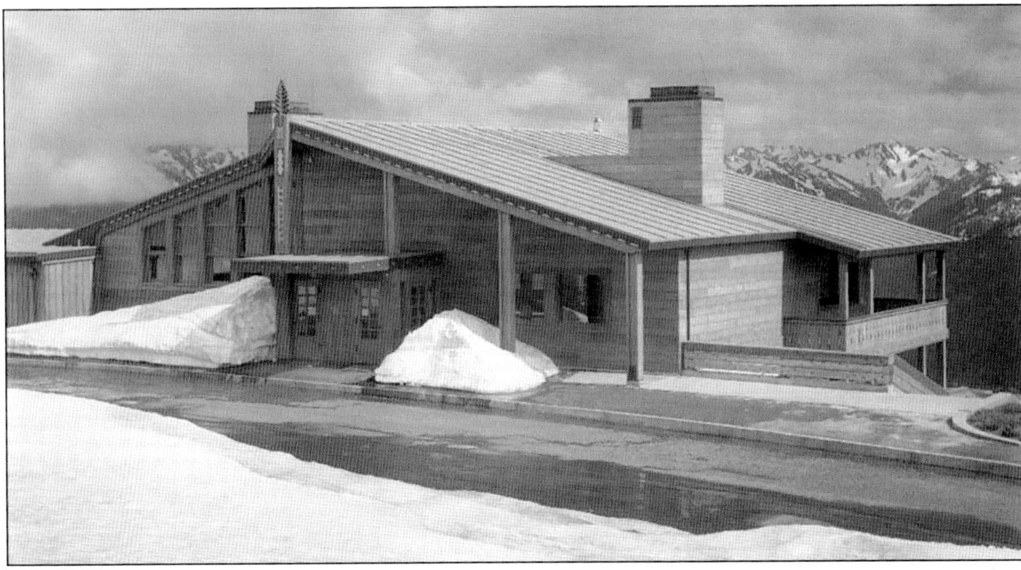

This newly constructed lodge was open only in the summers until the winter of 1957–1958, when it began serving skiers and other winter visitors. During the winter, it provided a cozy fireplace, ranger quarters, a first-aid station, skiers' lockers, ski and snowshoe rentals, and food service. As seen below, the dining area was initially upstairs, though it was later moved downstairs. Interpretive displays and a small theater now occupy the upper level. (Above, photograph by Ed Halterman, courtesy of ONP; below, photograph by W. Ray Scott, courtesy of National Park Concessions, Inc. and ONP.)

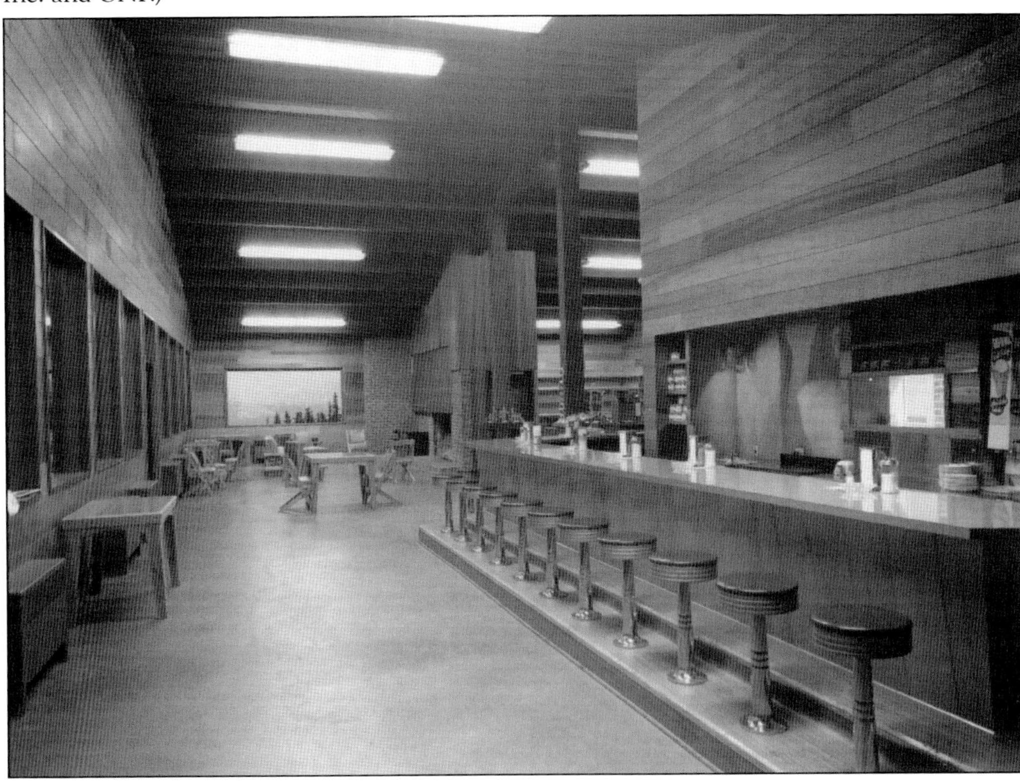

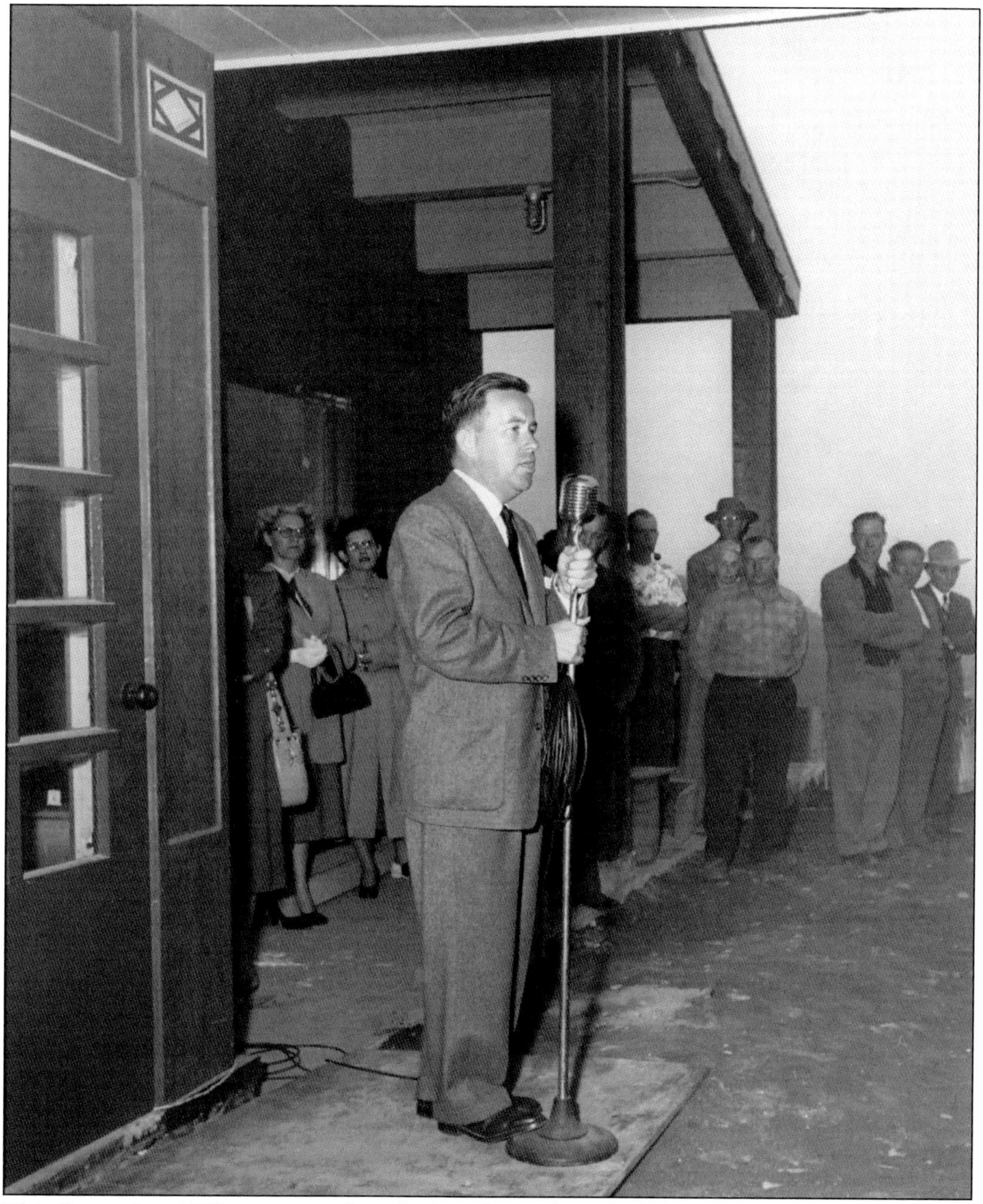

This September 1952 event was described as the "informal" dedication of the new Hurricane Ridge lodge. Congressman (later Sen.) Henry M. Jackson is speaking to a group of community leaders. The entire project of a new road directly up from Port Angeles and a modern lodge was accomplished largely through the efforts of Jackson. His goal of a rustic overnight lodge similar to Timberline Lodge on Mount Hood was not to be. The new Hurricane Ridge lodge would be for day use only. (Courtesy of ONP.)

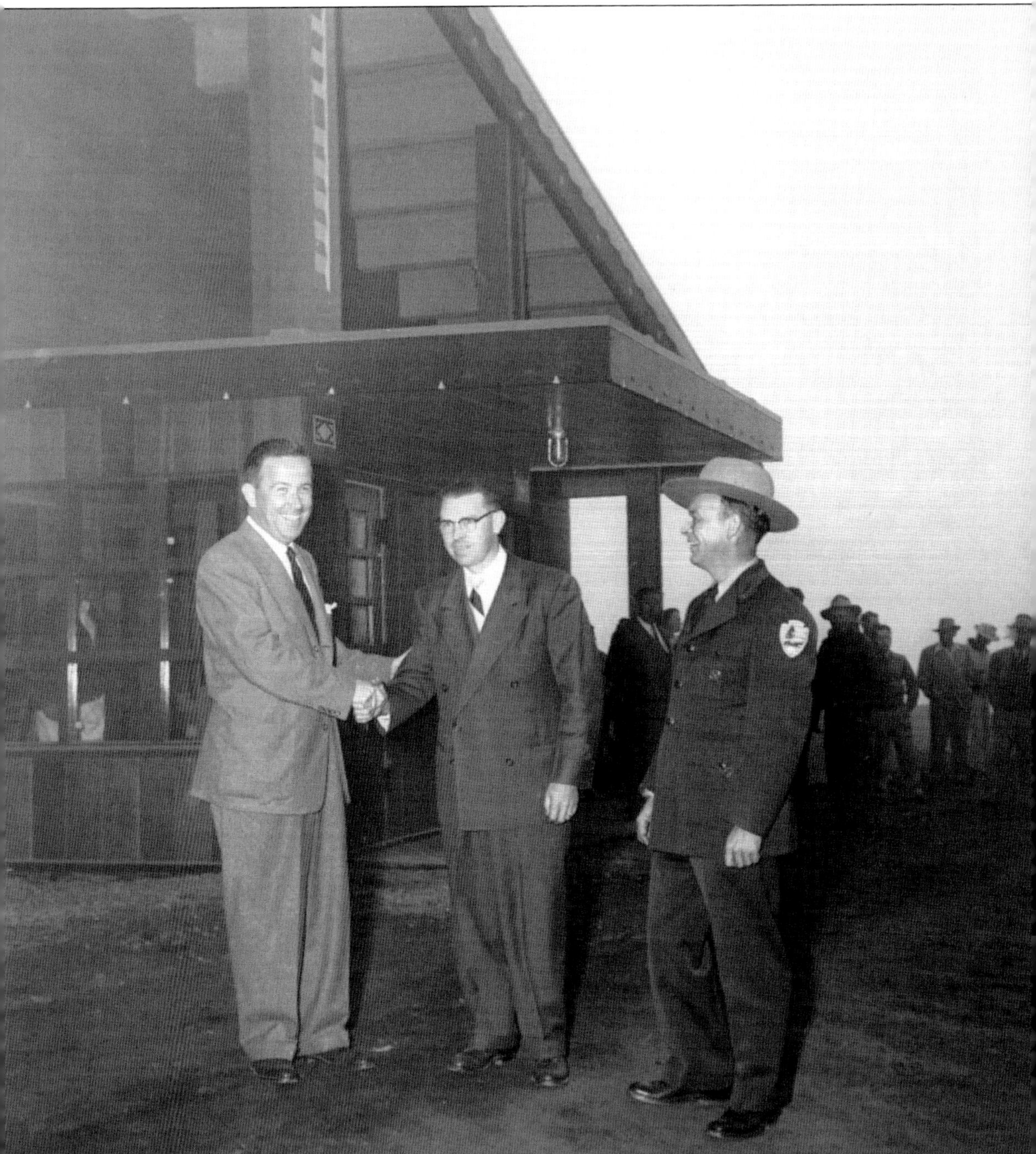

It is fitting to end this chapter with a photograph of Congressman Henry Jackson shaking hands with Leo White, president of the Port Angeles Chamber of Commerce, since White was the man who built the first ski lift at Deer Park in 1936. His leadership in the community and in the local ski scene bridged both the Deer Park and Hurricane Ridge ski areas. White also taught ski lessons at both Deer Park and Hurricane Ridge. Pictured at right is Supt. Fred Overly. (Courtesy of ONP.)

Three

Deer Park 1936–1957

A 1939 *Washington Motorist* ad enticing skiers to what was becoming one of the premier ski areas in Washington State promotes "a new, unsurpassed ski field" and a "good road to ski lodge"—never mind that the so-called good road was a dirt Forest Service road rising to 5,000 feet on steep, treacherous terrain or that the "ski lodge" was a Civilian Conservation Corps crew barracks and cookhouse with dormitory-style bunks (bring your own bedding).

Given the infancy of alpine skiing in the United States, this ad was relatively accurate at the time. After all, the first chairlift in this country had just been installed at Sun Valley in 1936, so it was a rather astonishing feat when Leo White, a local businessman, borrowed a motorcycle engine and installed a small rope tow at Deer Park that same year. While it would never become a major ski area, Deer Park would be an important part of early skiing in the Pacific Northwest.

Deer Park is located on a beautiful alpine bench formed by erosion of sedimentary rock trapped between two ridges of volcanic basalt on the south side of Blue Mountain. Blue Mountain, named for the bluish tint that is visible from the Dungeness Valley it overlooks, stands 6,000 feet above sea level. Viewed from the north, it really does not stand out from the surrounding peaks. When viewed from the west, one can see its broad expanse and get a feeling for its geologic origins—a mass of sedimentary rock given shape and form by the streaks of basalt running through it. One can also see the road cut through its western flanks as it perfectly contours up the hillside.

As outlined in the introduction, Deer Park has a rich geological, archaeological, and cultural history.

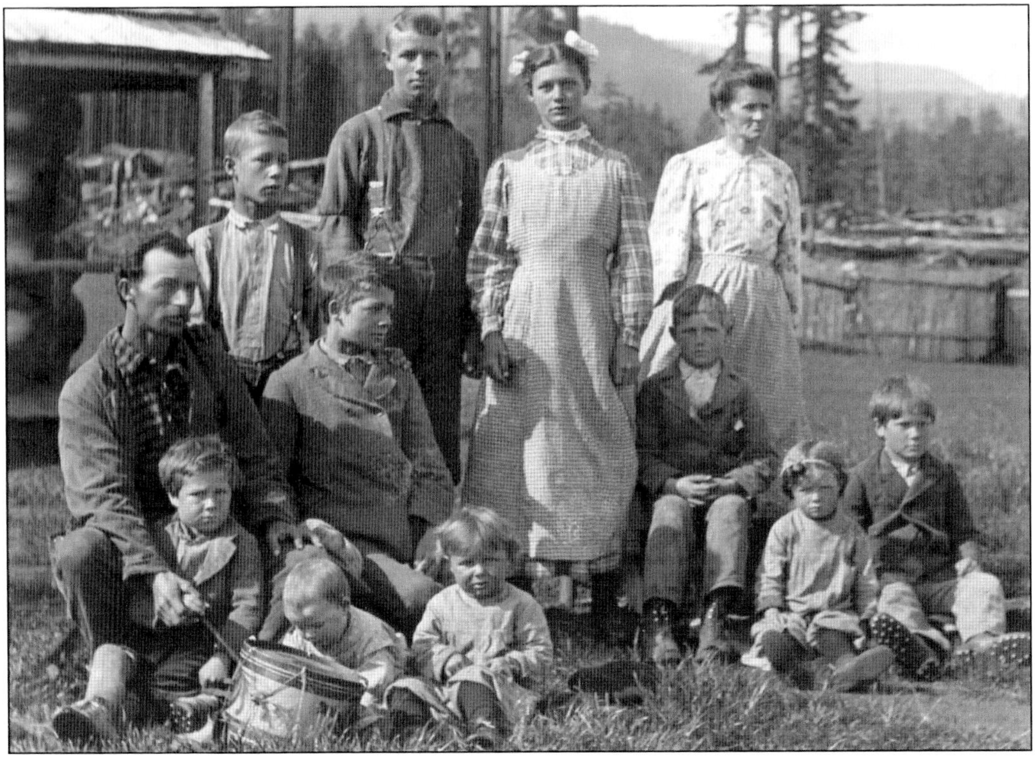

Long before skiing became popular at Deer Park, the Blue Mountain area was settled in 1898 by the Amos Cameron family. Amos and Sarah proceeded to have 14 children, 10 of whom are pictured here. Amos hunted the area extensively. He also built a trail from his place east of Blue Mountain up to Deer Park, paralleling the current road and continuing on down to Three Forks, where Grand Creek and Cameron Creek converge and then meet the Graywolf River. Cameron Creek, located below Deer Park, is named for the family. Deer Park was named so at the turn of the century because the deer were so plentiful there. The hunter in the below c. 1910 photograph of Deer Park might be Amos Cameron. (Above, courtesy of Joan Morrish; below, courtesy of Rex Gerberding.)

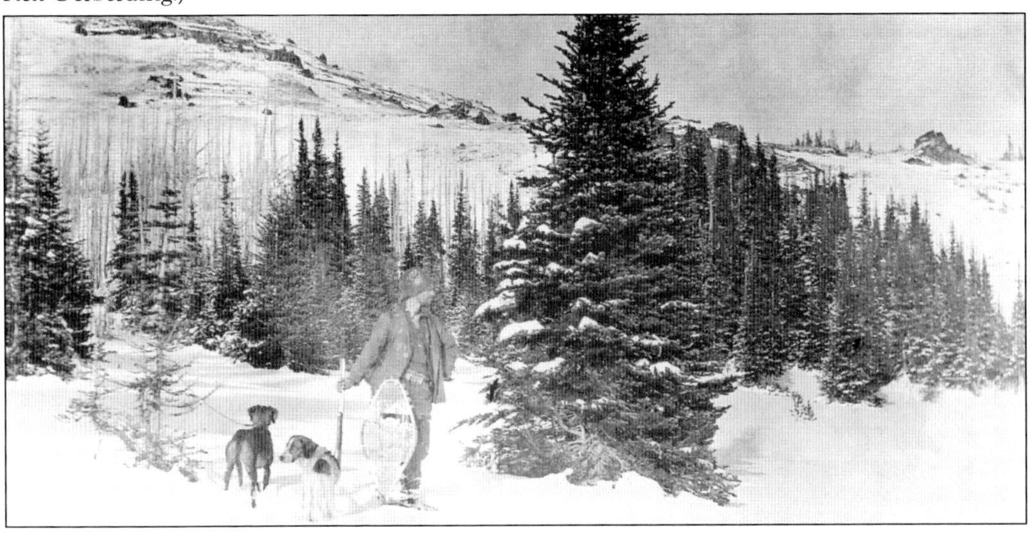

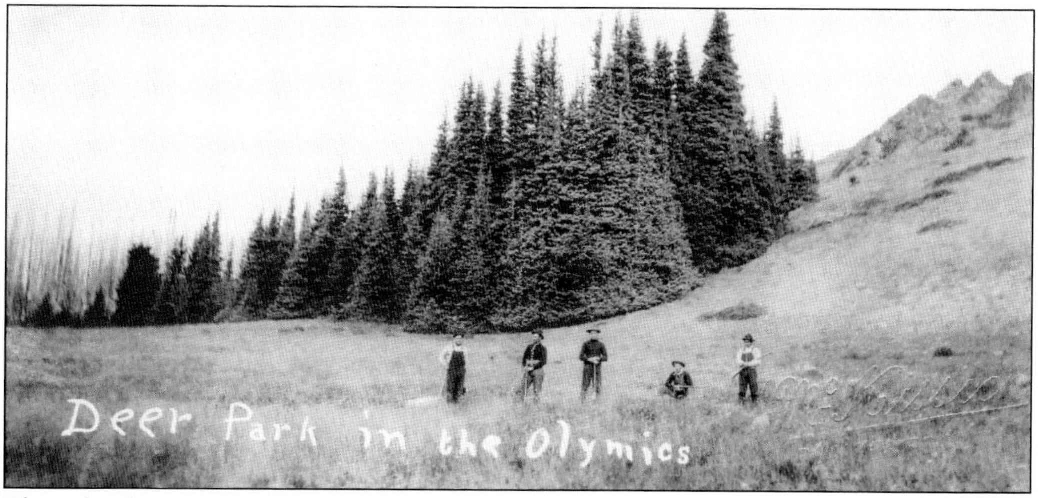

These five hunters are seen hunting for deer around 1910 at what would become Deer Park. Sheepherders later became competitors of the hunters as their sheep reduced deer forage. However, deer were plentiful and easier to find here than in the densely forested lowlands. The hunters in this image are, from left to right, Frank Knoph, ? Freeman, Ed Knoph, Oscar Sherard, and Ed Casselery. (Photograph by McKissick, courtesy of Rex Gerberding.)

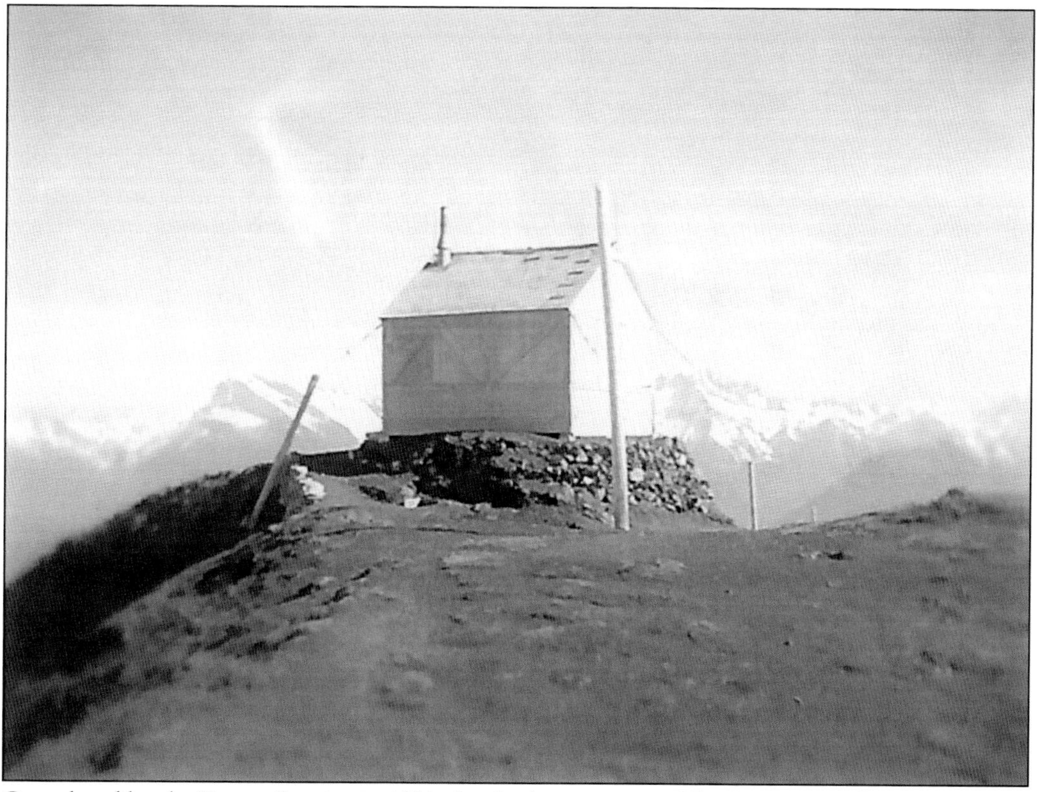

Completed by the Forest Service in 1931, this lookout sits atop Blue Mountain above Deer Park. There is a vast view of the interior range. It was used as a lookout for enemy planes during World War II. During at least one winter, it was staffed by Claud Johnson, who may have been one of the few skiers at Deer Park during the war. (Photograph by Jim Byrne, courtesy of Bernice Byrne.)

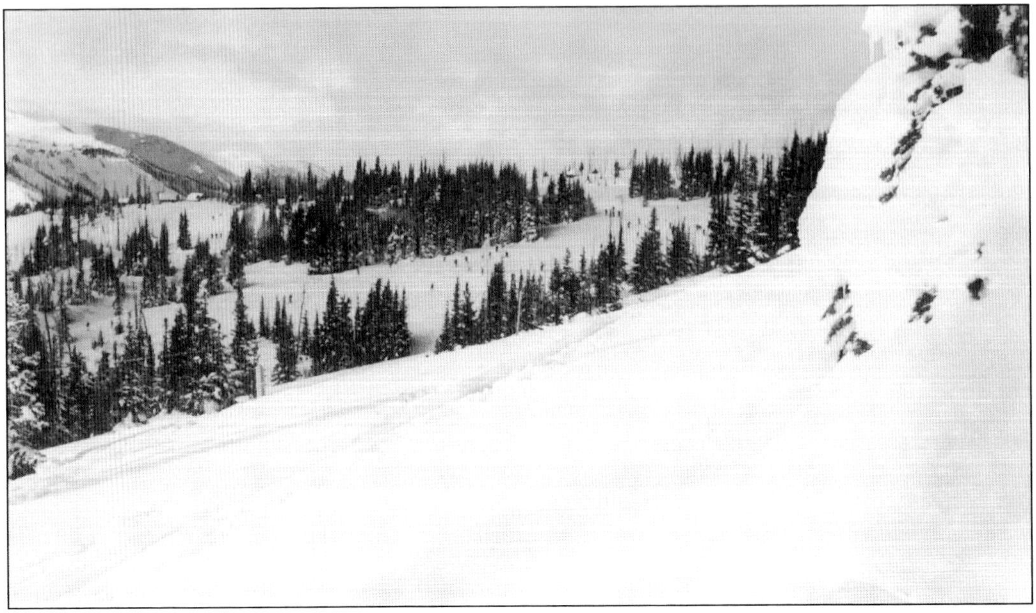

While skiing is the subject of this book, it would not be a complete story without thinking about the setting of a national park, as well as the roads and lodges that were integral to its popularity. The above March 1937 panorama shows the Deer Park area, with several buildings visible in the distance. Below is another view of the lower meadow at Deer Park, looking westward toward Hurricane Ridge. Both were taken in February 1937. (Above, photograph by Jim Cahill, courtesy of ONP; below, photograph by USFS photograph, courtesy of ONP.)

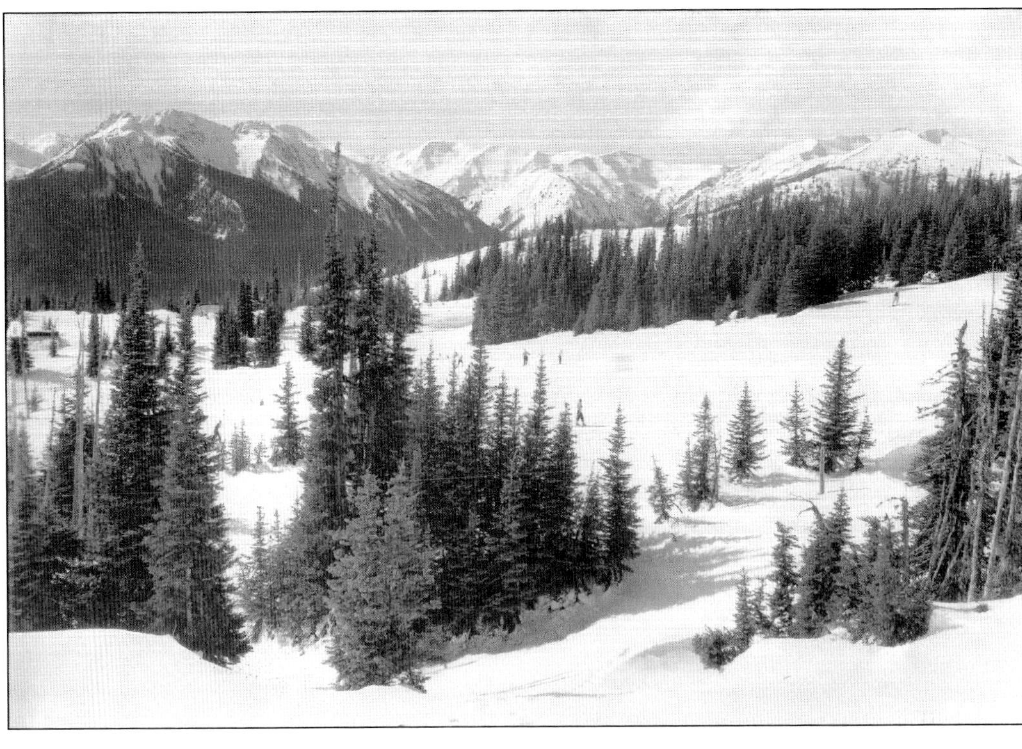

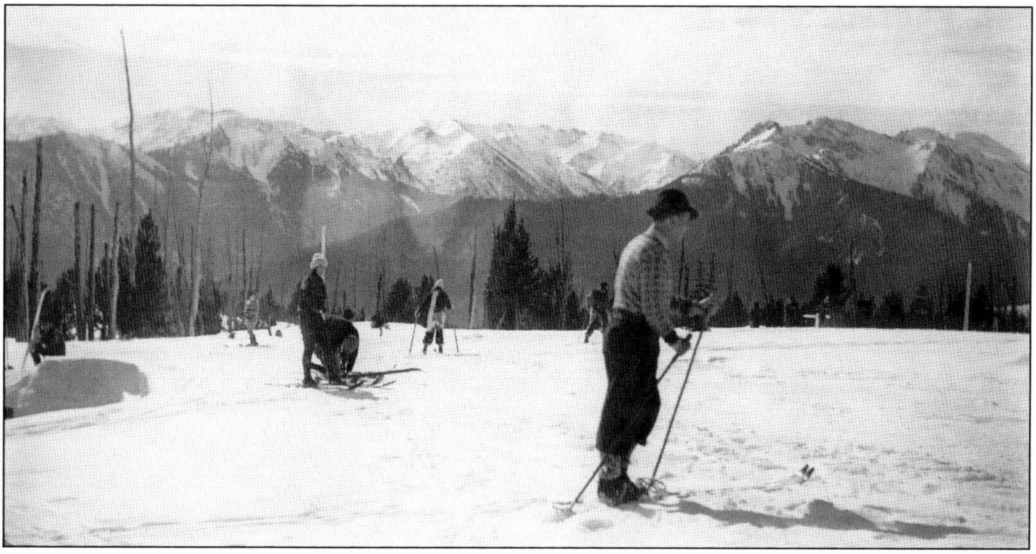

This February 1936 photograph is from the earliest days of skiing at Deer Park. It was taken the year before the first small rope tow was installed and before the CCC barrack was remodeled as an overnight ski lodge. Here, skiers dressed in garb typical of the era enjoy a classic day in the Olympics. (Photograph by USFS, courtesy of ONP.)

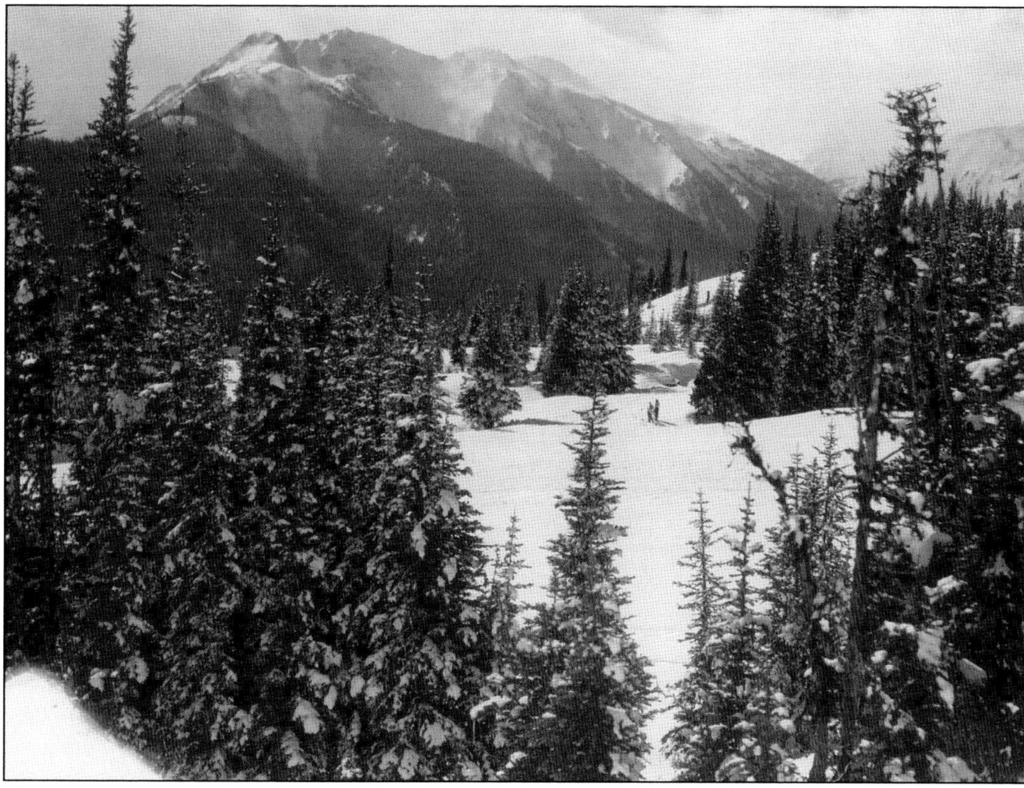

The view in this photograph from the 1930s shows not only the beauty of the Deer Park area, but also looks out toward Mount Cameron and the Cameron Glaciers. Two lone skiers are enjoying the day. (Photograph by Neil Mortiboy, courtesy of James Wengler.)

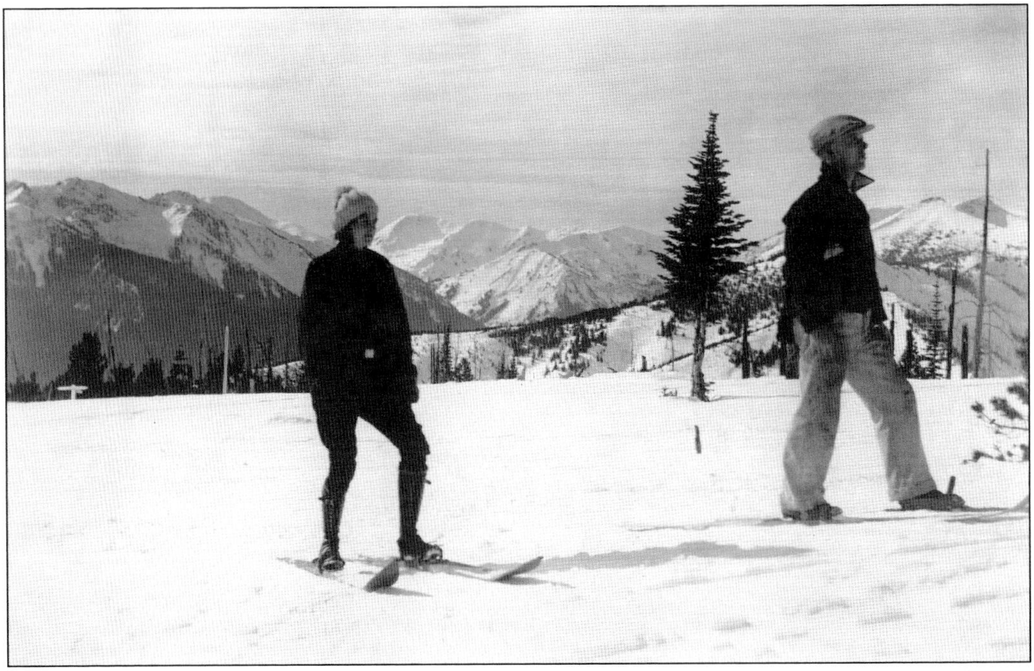

Using snowshoes rather than skis, this couple is taking a safer course. The view in this February 1936 photograph captures the beauty of the area as it looks west-southwest up Cameron and Grand Creeks. (Photograph by USFS, courtesy of ONP.)

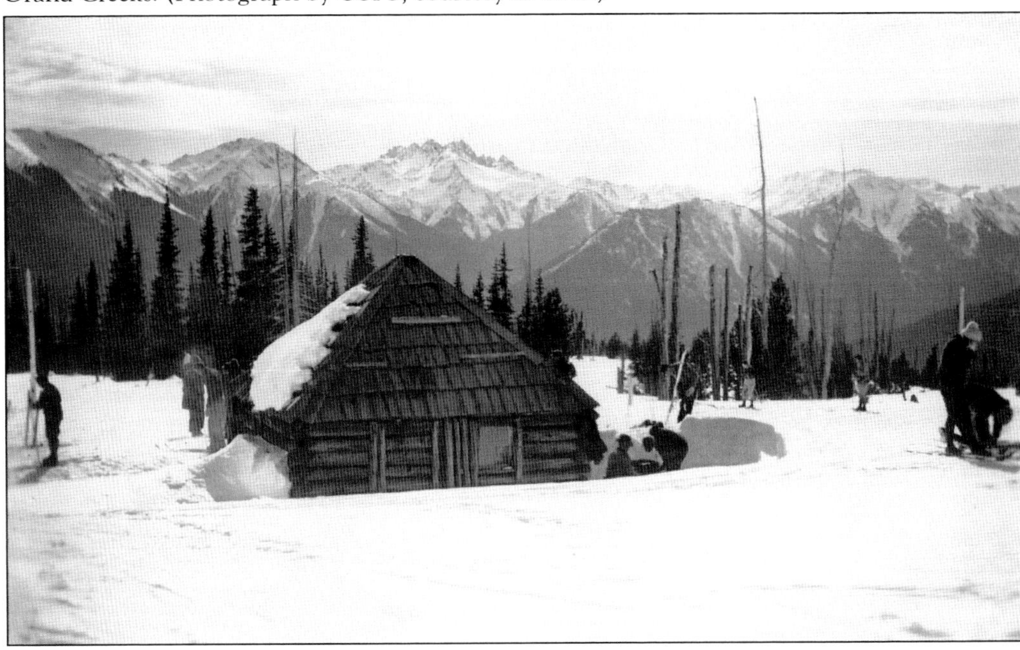

This 1936 photograph shows the sheepherder's cabin that later served as the first-aid station at the Deer Park ski area. Prior to the creation of Olympic National Park in 1938, sheepherding was done at Deer Park. Joseph Keeler was known to run his sheep at Deer Park and probably built this structure. His sheep competed with the deer for forage, which caused friction with the hunters who frequented the area. (Photograph by USFS, courtesy of ONP.)

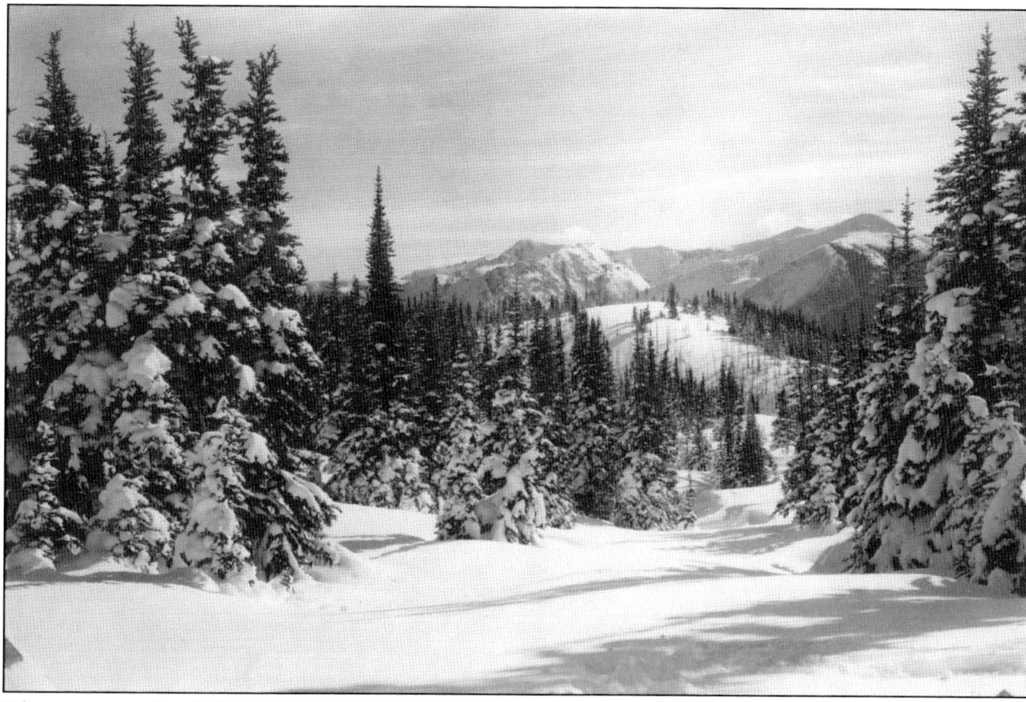

The view in this February 1938 photograph was taken from the Deer Park lodge and captures the beautiful snow cover as it looks east toward Graywolf Ridge. The mix of trees at Deer Park is different from many other areas because of the park's low rainfall and more porous soil. At 5,400 feet, it has subalpine fir and lots of pine. (Photograph by USFS, courtesy of ONP.)

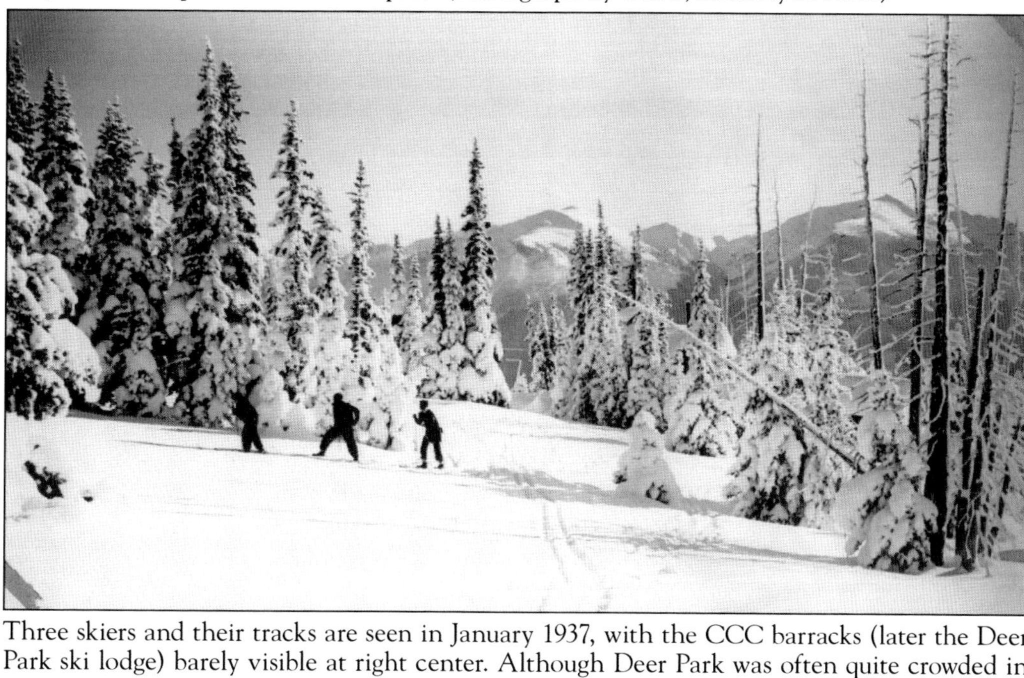

Three skiers and their tracks are seen in January 1937, with the CCC barracks (later the Deer Park ski lodge) barely visible at right center. Although Deer Park was often quite crowded in those days, one could find solitude among the trees. (Photograph by Richards, Elite Studio, Port Townsend, courtesy of ONP.)

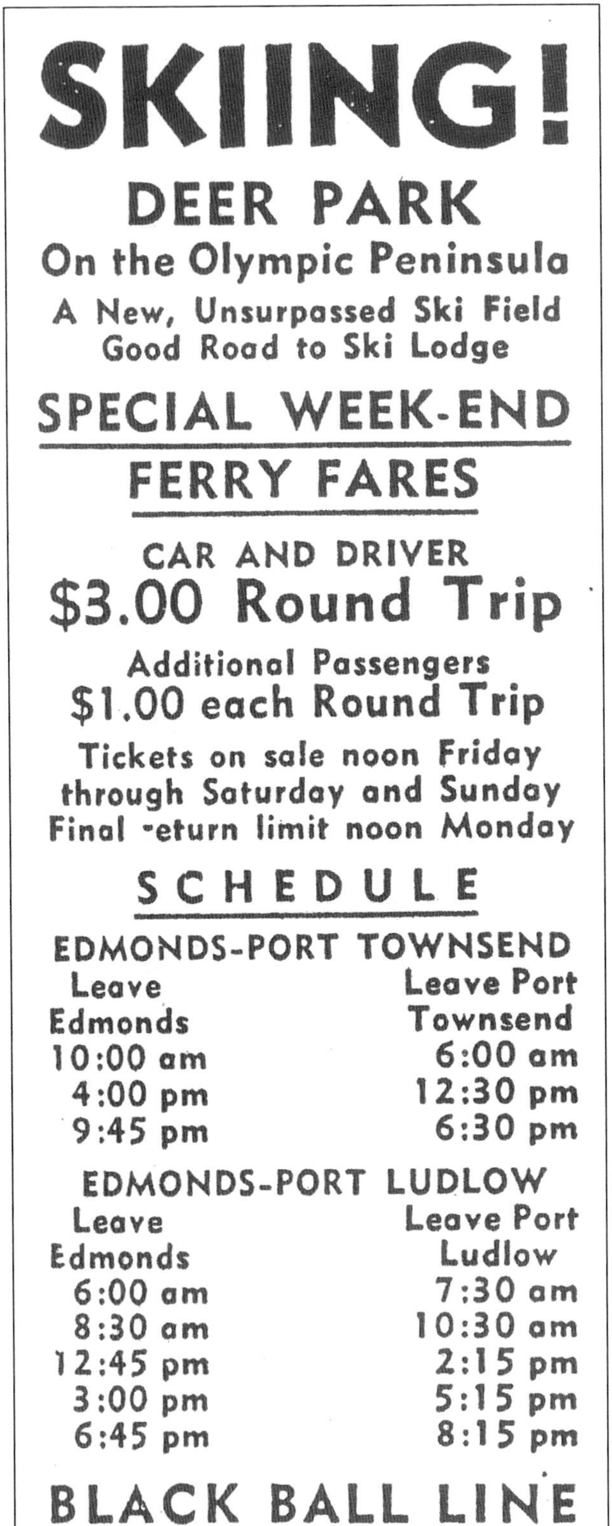

This 1939 magazine ad is actually quite accurate. Alpine skiing was just becoming popular around the country, including in the Pacific Northwest, and Deer Park was a premier ski area. It was fairly close to Seattle, especially with the availability of Black Ball Line's private ferry service, and—thanks to the US Forest Service—had a road and ski lodge. The lodge was a converted CCC barracks and cookhouse. The Forest Service was proud of its ski way. (Courtesy of the *Washington Motorist*.)

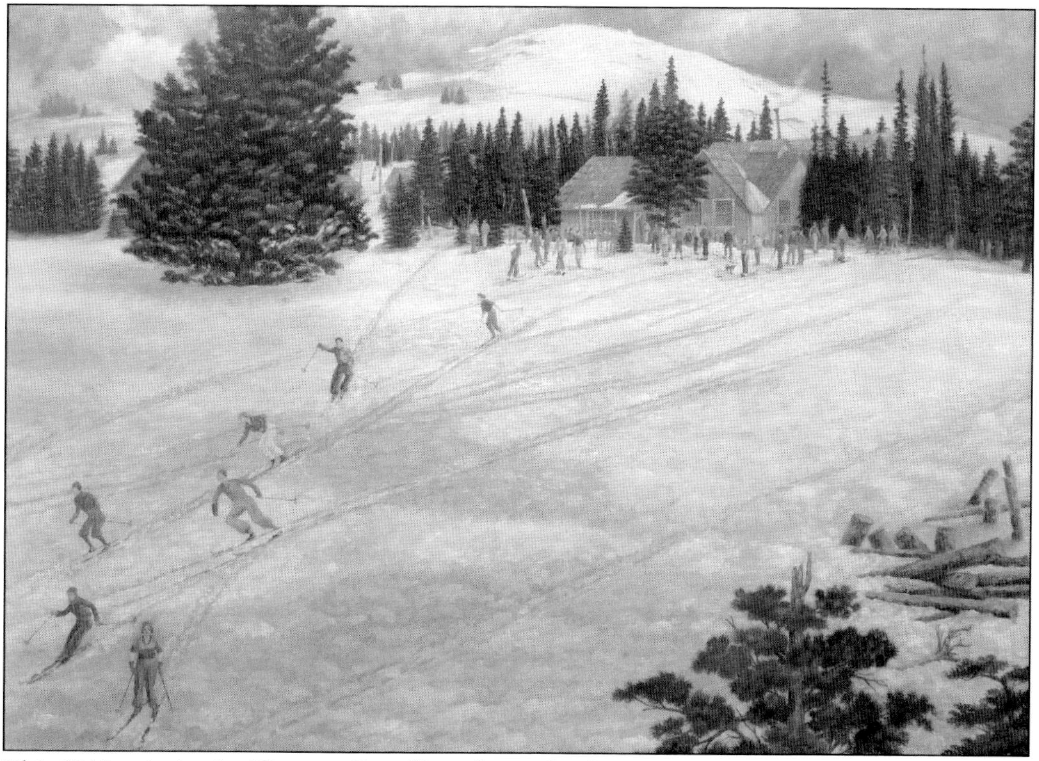

This 1940 painting by Thomas Guptill resides at the Carnegie Museum in Port Angeles. With its lodge and gentle slopes, it captures the feel of early ski days at Deer Park. However, it is not accurate in that the ski slopes were uphill from the lodge toward the summit of Blue Mountain. (Photograph by Daniel Hudgings, courtesy of Clallam County Historical Society.)

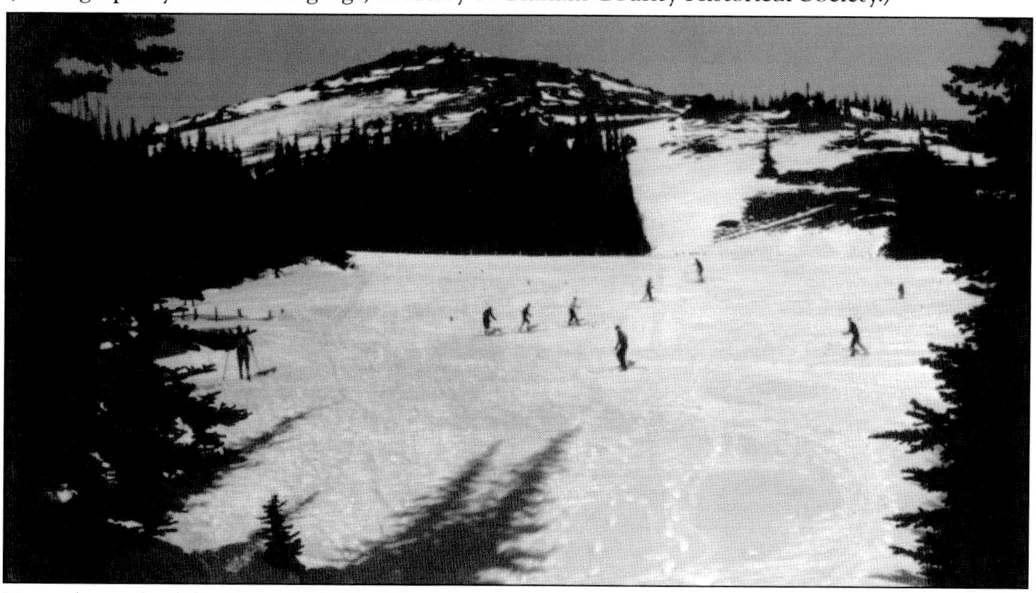

Here, skiers climb back up the hill of the lower meadow at Deer Park. Its gentle slopes were good for beginners. Later, a rope tow was installed in the meadow, but it only ran for a short time. The ski jump was directly uphill from this meadow. (Photograph by Neil Mortiboy, courtesy of ONP.)

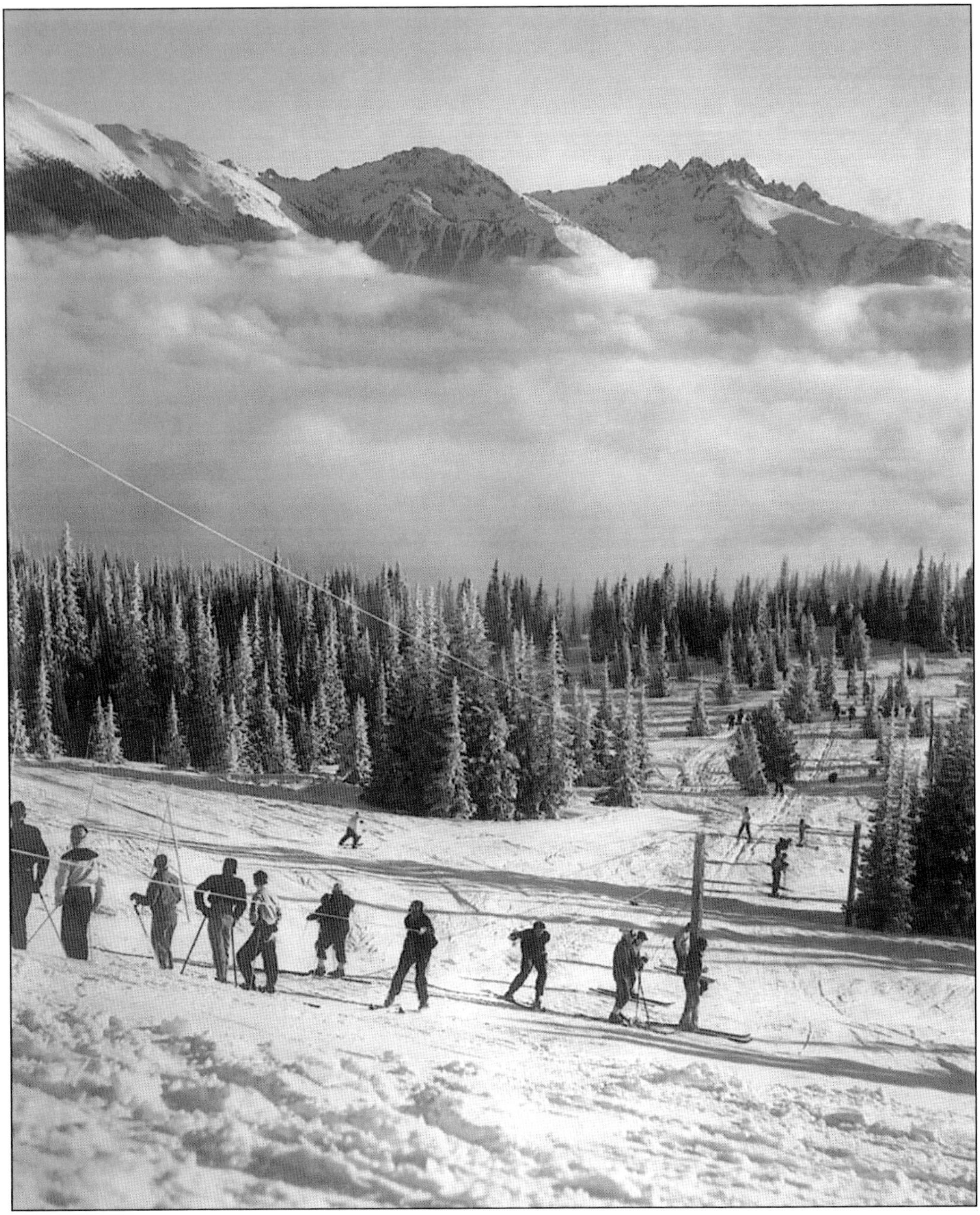

Skiers at Deer Park were used to skiing without any lifts to assist their uphill climb. Using a borrowed motorcycle engine, Leo White installed a small rope tow during the winter of 1936–1937. He thought the lift would be a way to make money. He used a half-inch hemp rope that returned downhill under the snow. White claimed that a skier could ride uphill at 20 miles per hour, but a 50-foot spacing was required. He purchased a Ford V-8 engine two years later. This new lift was installed in January 1939. Initially, it was 675 feet long (later lengthened to 900 feet) and could pull four people at a time. One could purchase four rides for 25¢ or ride all day for 75¢. (Photograph by Art Jackson, courtesy of ONP.)

The caption with this 1936 photograph describes this silhouetted ski jumper as a "Seattle expert." There was a small jump just above the lower meadow. Experienced jumpers from Seattle did enjoy the area. A Class B jump was under construction in 1941. (Photograph by USFS, courtesy of ONP.)

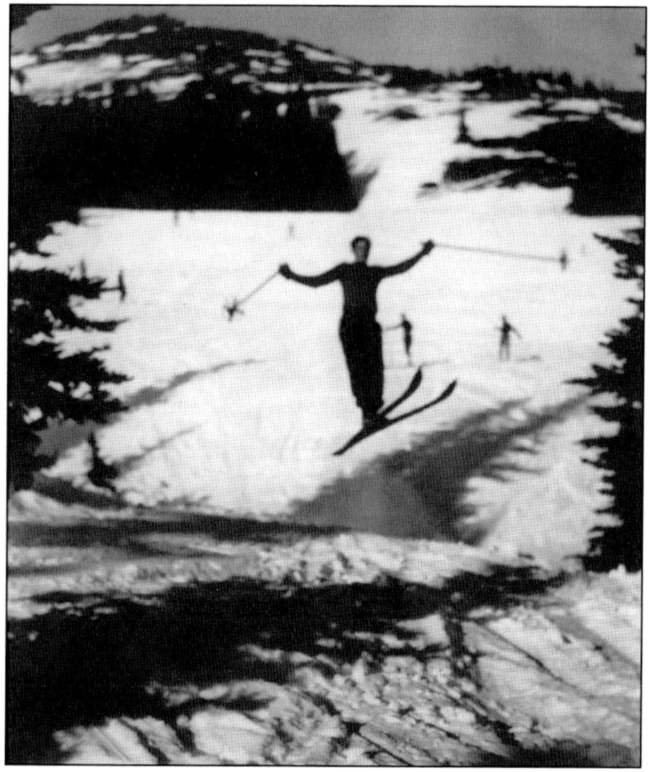

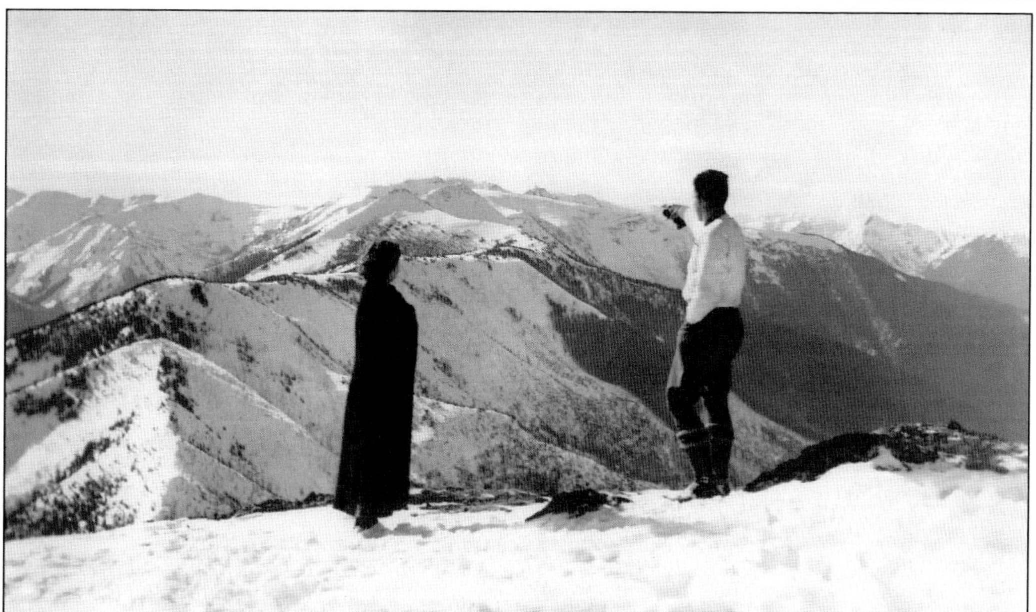

Two sightseers enjoy the view from the summit of Blue Mountain in February 1936. They are looking out to the west toward Obstruction Point and Hurricane Ridge. The trip to Deer Park was so treacherous that only the hardy made it. Chains were almost always required, and the road was a narrow, winding affair. Traffic was uphill until 2:00 p.m., and downhill traffic began at 3:00 p.m. (Photograph by USFS, courtesy of ONP.)

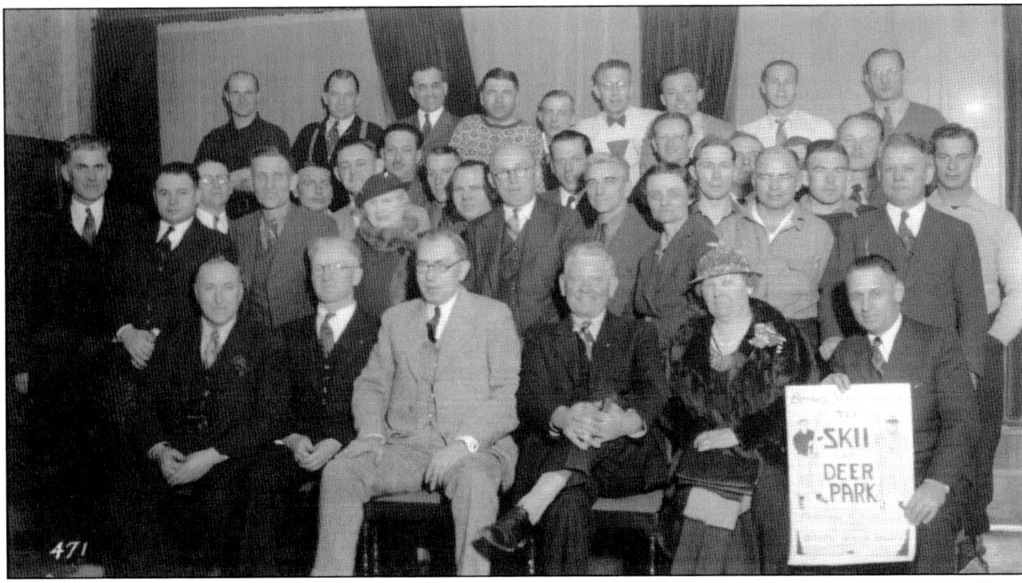

A ski festival was held February 14–16, 1936. It was more or less the formal opening of the Deer Park ski area. In attendance were 16 members of the Washington Ski Club of Seattle, who were honorees at a dinner on the night of the 14th. Deer Park had the advantage of proximity to Seattle, a road leading to an alpine area, and generally good weather with adequate snow. (Photograph by USFS, courtesy of ONP.)

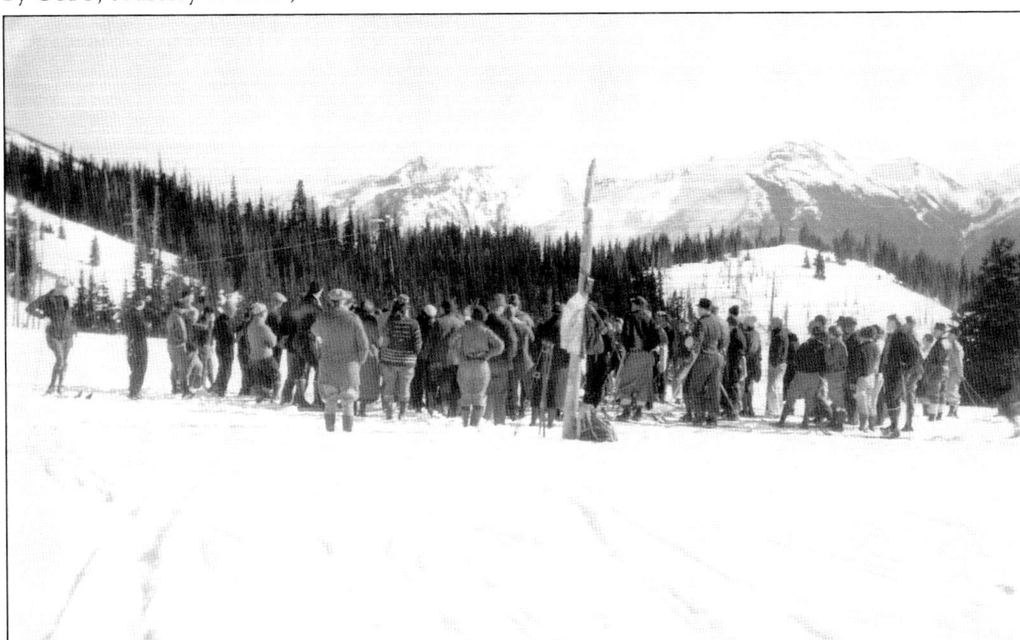

Locals were anxious to learn the sport of skiing. Here, they take full advantage of instructors from the Seattle Ski Council during a mass group lesson in February 1936. Gear was often rented from a local ski shop or from a rental service available at the ski area. (Photograph by USFS, courtesy of ONP.)

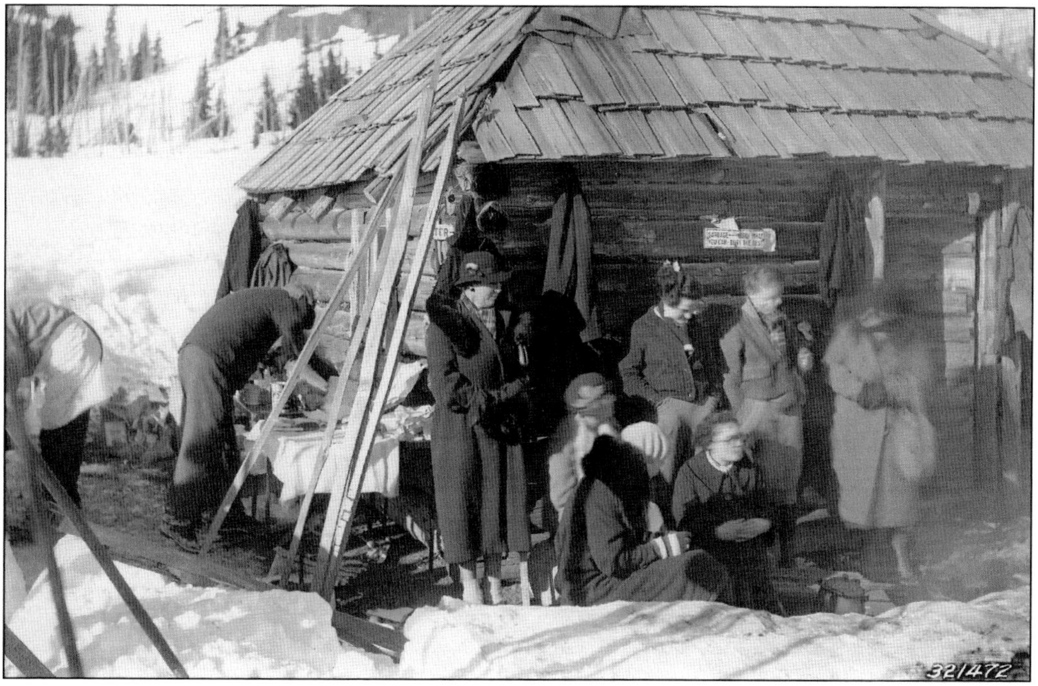

An elegantly dressed group enjoys an outdoor barbecue and picnic at the sheepherder's cabin in February 1936. Presumably, many in this crowd were not planning on skiing, but they did manage to navigate the challenging road. Within a very few years, the ski area became well known throughout the Northwest. (Both, photograph by USFS, courtesy of ONP.)

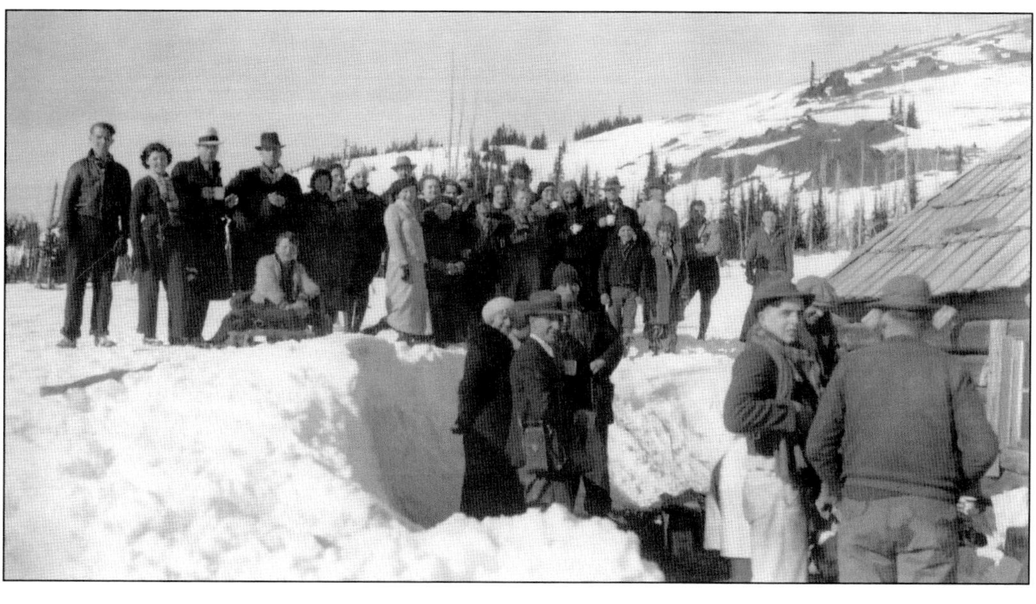

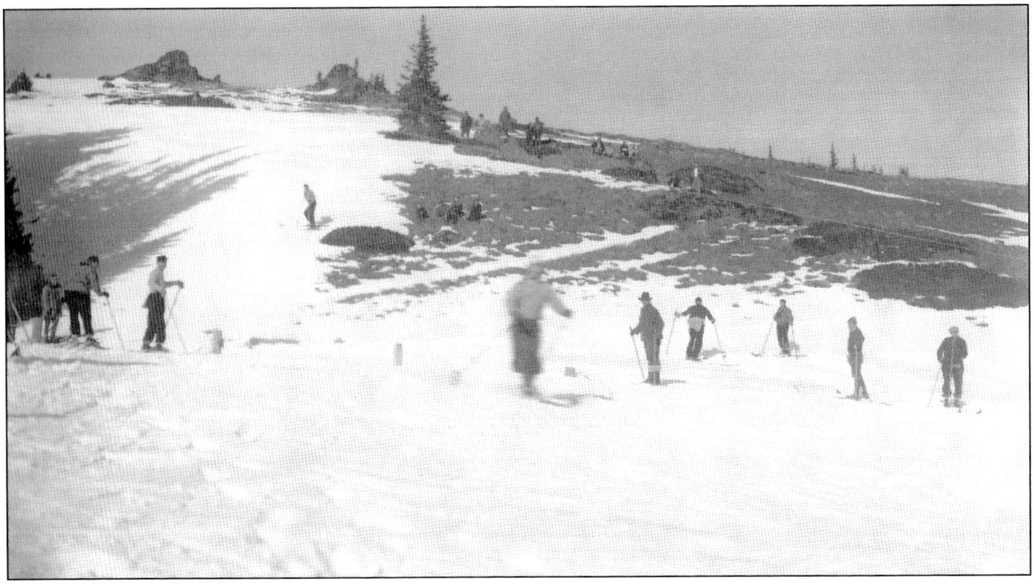

Opening weekend is pictured here in February 1936. These photographs show skiers, spectators, and the bare slopes, which were not uncommon at Deer Park. Snowfall is much lower in the northeast corner of the Olympics and increases substantially as one moves west. Deer Park lies in the well-known rain shadow of the Olympics. Crowds at Deer Park often numbered in the hundreds. In 1938, one event drew 800 people, a number hard to imagine given the road and limited parking. (Both, photograph by USFS, courtesy of ONP.)

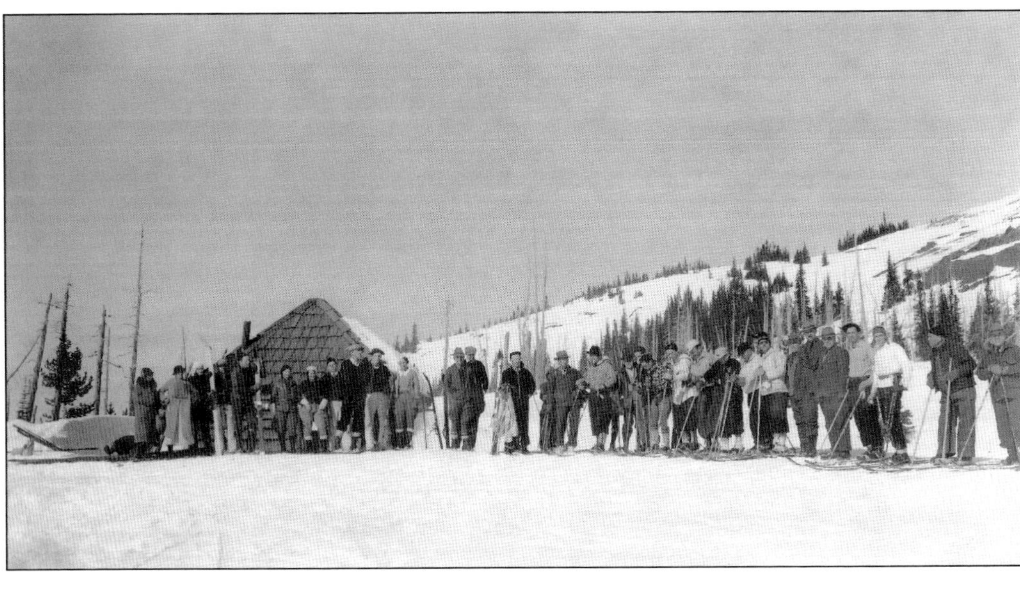

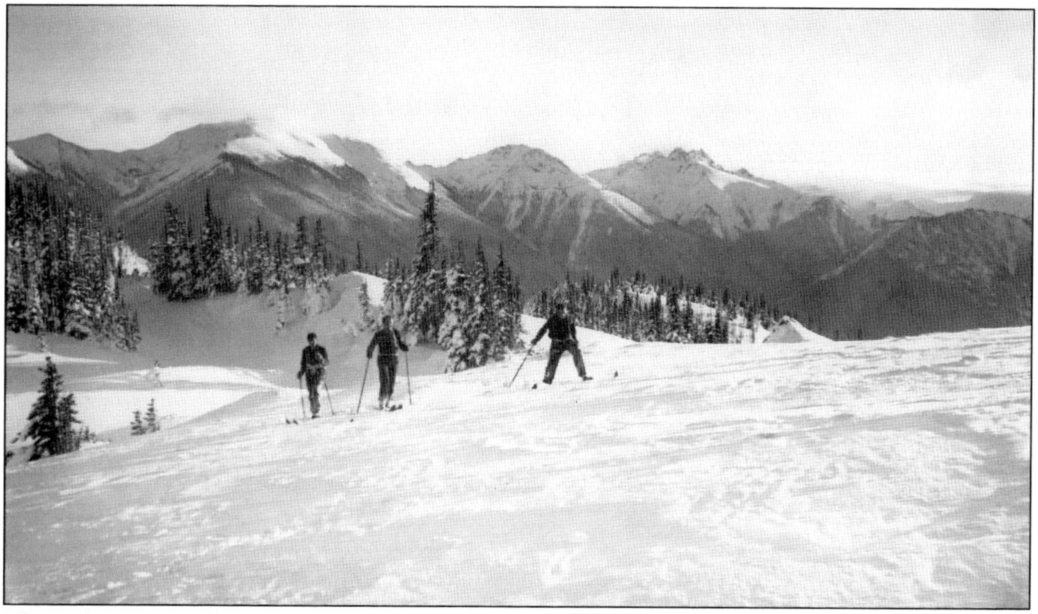

Three skiers ascend a ski slope without the benefit of a lift on January 10, 1937. Graywolf Ridge, the Needles, and Mount Deception are in the background. (Photograph by Richards, Elite Studio, Port Townsend, courtesy of ONP.)

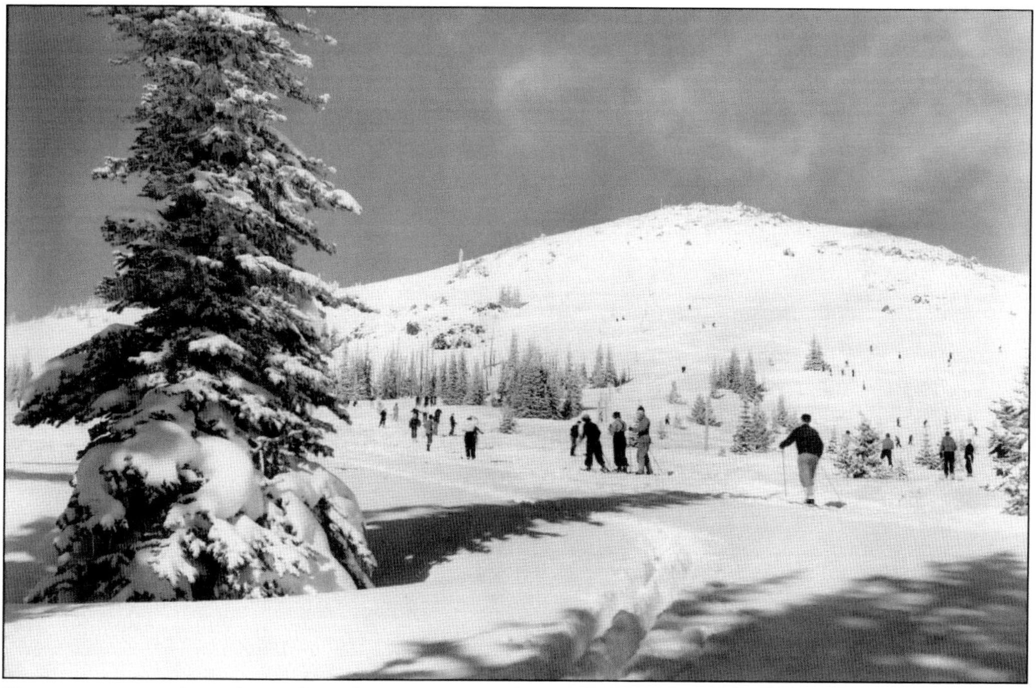

One can appreciate the rather deep snow tracks in the foreground of this photograph. Snow cover extends all the way to the summit, which is not always seen at Deer Park. There was no snow-grooming equipment available, so the racetrack was set by skiers sideslipping the course. Otherwise, one skied in the conditions available. (Photograph by USFS, courtesy of ONP.)

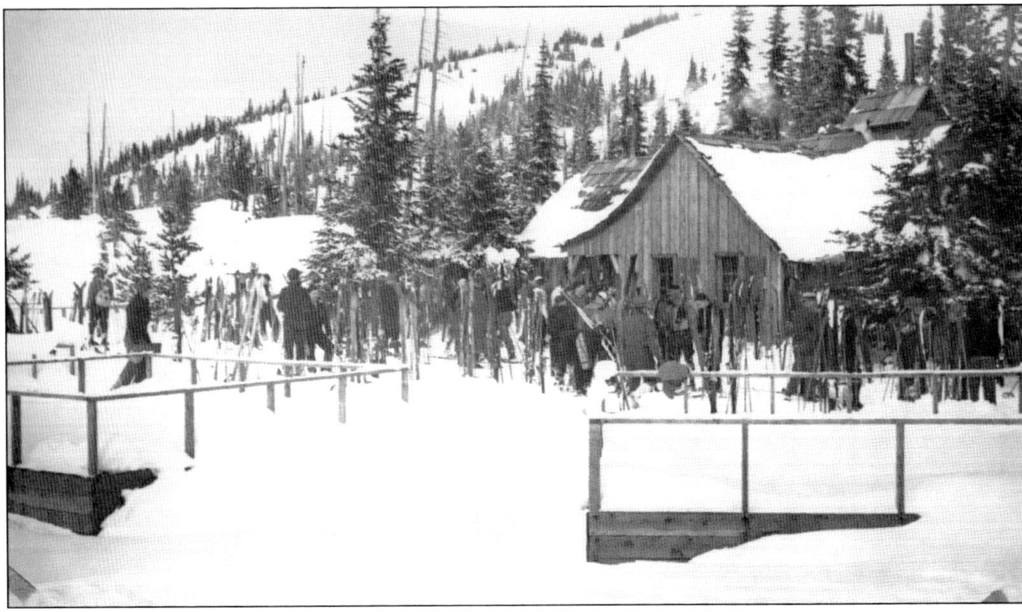

The January 1937 photograph above is labeled "Lunch time at the CCC mess hall." This CCC barracks was remodeled to accommodate overnight guests, and it was further remodeled in the late 1940s to include an upstairs dormitory for women. It was to become the place to be on winter Saturday nights, often featuring live music, ski movies, and dancing. Artist and local community leader Esther Webster was a regular visitor and could often be seen sitting in a corner with her sketchbook. (Both, photograph by USFS, courtesy of ONP.)

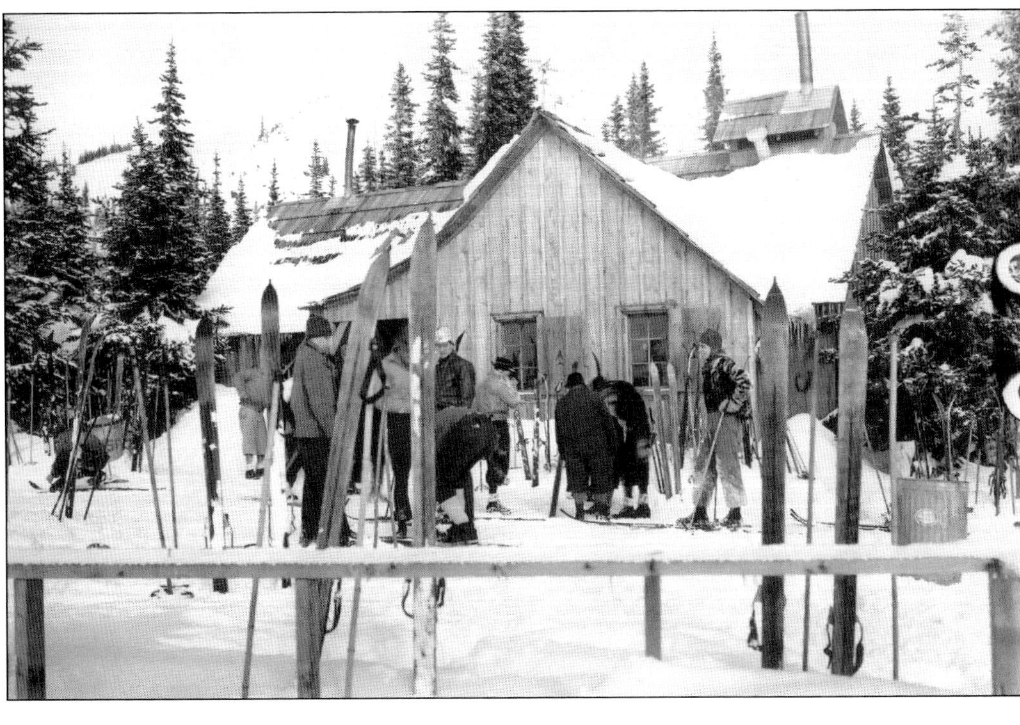

This Esther Webster painting called *Ski Spill* shows her characteristic style. Her friends report that she was not interested in skiing, although she did give it a try. She did enjoy the Olympics in all seasons and was particularly fond of Mount Angeles. She wrote several articles on Deer Park for family-owned newspaper the *Port Angeles Evening News* using her pen name, Jean Earl. (Courtesy of Jake Seniuk.)

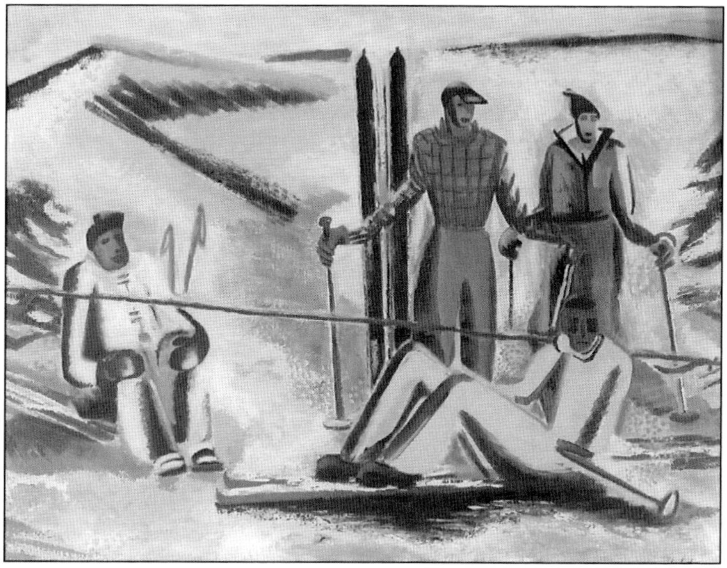

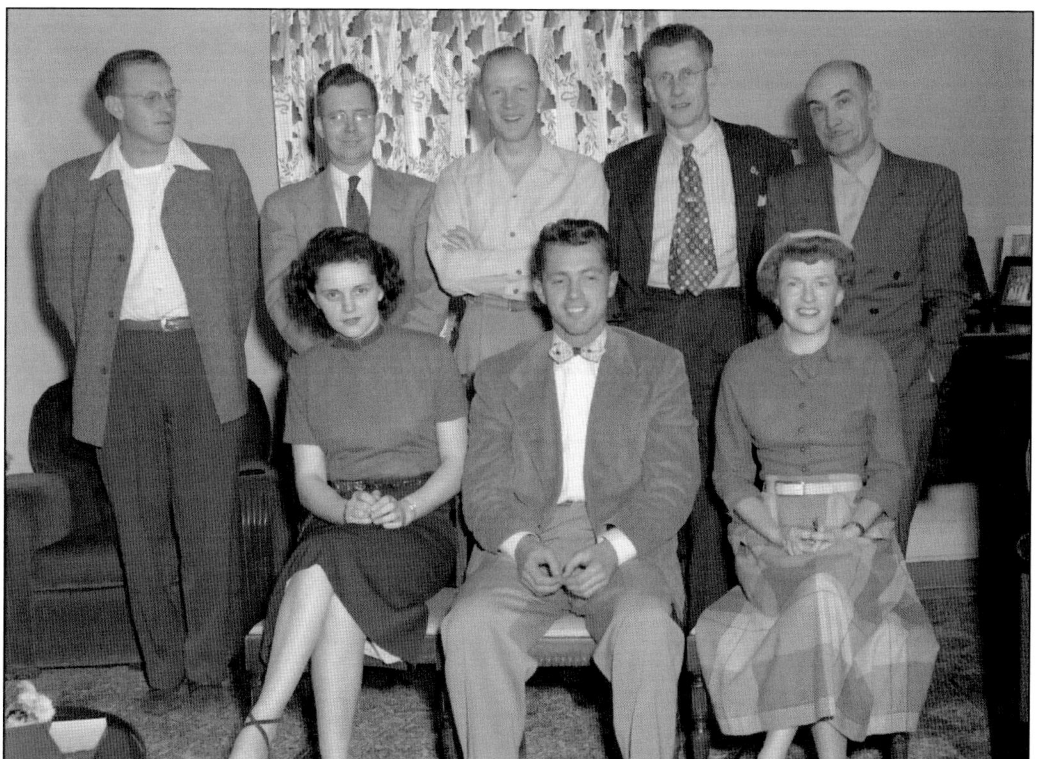

The board of the Olympic Ski Club is pictured in 1950. From left to right are (first row) Hattie Berglund, Richard Owens Jr. (president), and unidentified; (second row) Henry "Henie" Hollatz, John Driscoll, Everett Berglund, unidentified, and Carl Anderson. Although the club was not active during World War II, it was reorganized in March 1946. President Dick Owens was in Europe with the Counter-Intelligence Corps after the war and skied with the US Army ski team. (Photograph by Leo White, courtesy of the White family.)

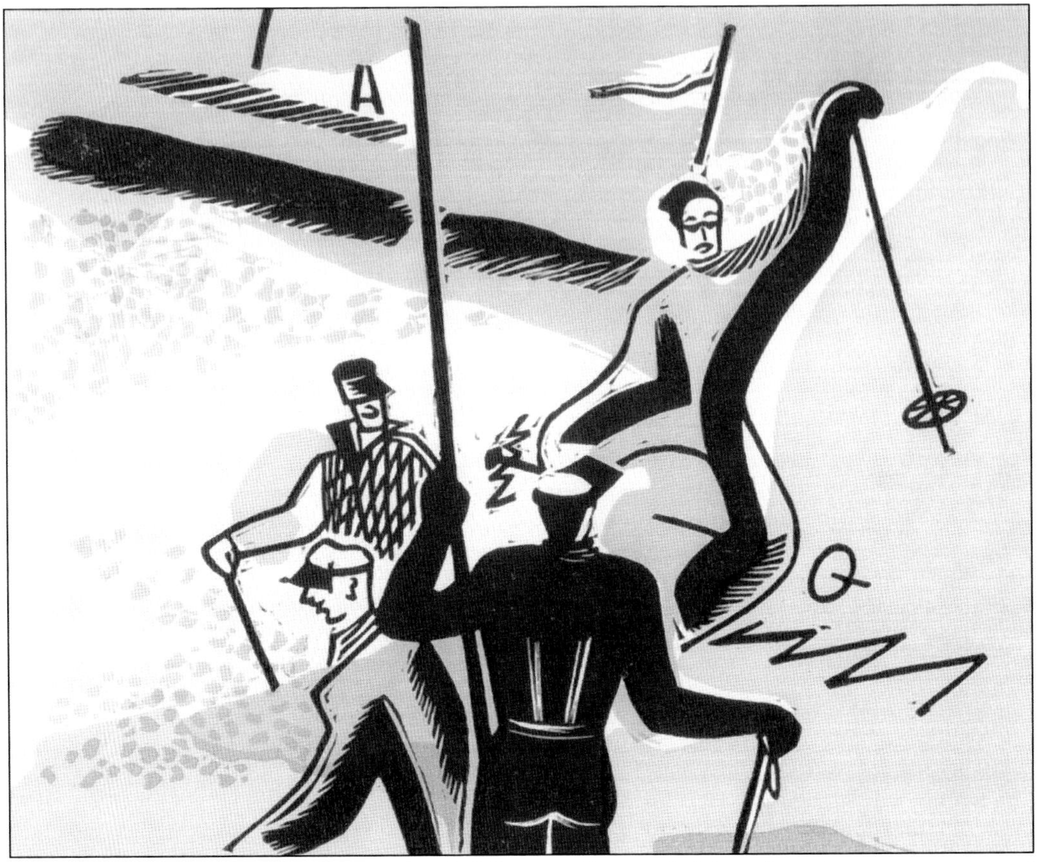

This 1938 work by Esther Webster is entitled *Skiing at Deer Park*. There have been many prints of this popular painting. Esther later gave her home and grounds on Beaver Hill in Port Angeles to the city, and it is currently the Port Angeles Fine Arts Center. (Courtesy of the author.)

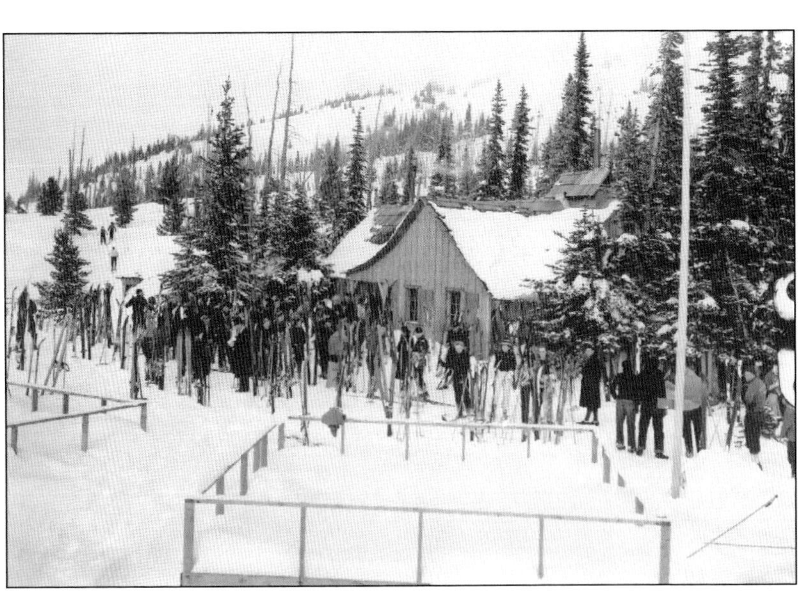

These are the crowds that Esther enjoyed and loved to sketch. While most visitors were local, there were often large groups from Victoria, Bremerton, and Seattle. The small, cozy lodge added a special dimension to the area. Note the tent frames in the foreground. (Photograph by USFS, courtesy of ONP.)

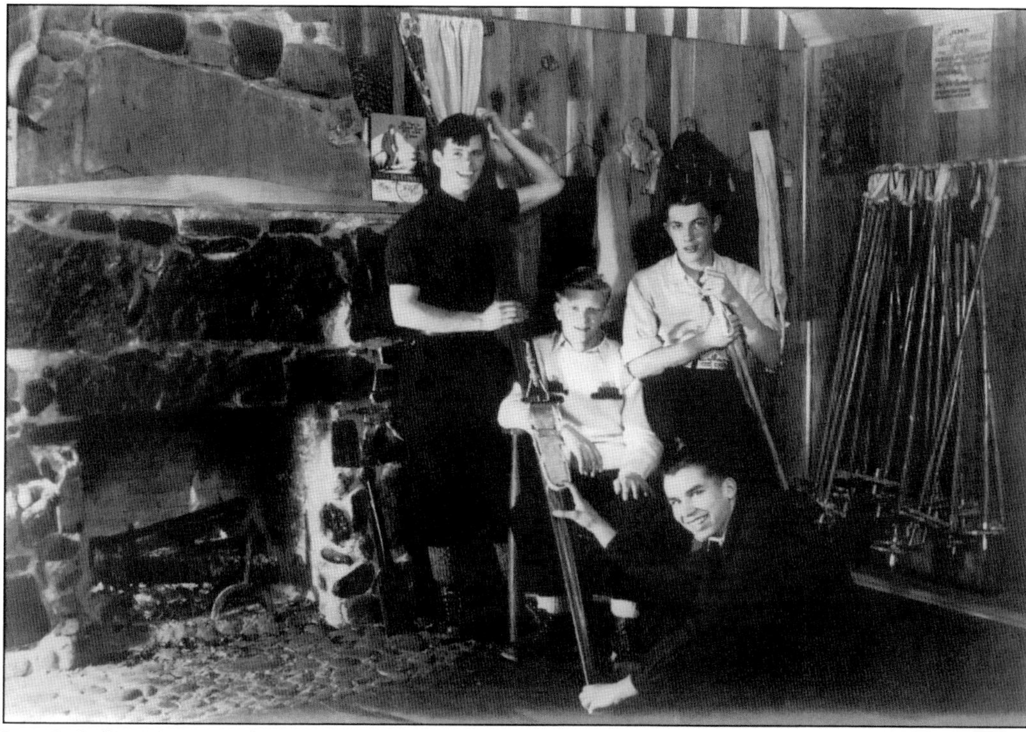

Jim Cahill's Olympic Ski Lodge on East Tenth Street in Port Angeles is shown in 1940. Pictured above are, from left to right, Jim Cahill, Guy Johnson, and Richard Owens Jr., with Ray Lane in front. High school carpentry instructor Roy Chapman built the "lodge" (there was no lodging) for Cahill, who provided new and used ski equipment, rentals, and repairs, organized carpooling to Deer Park, and provided a small van service. The chimney is still standing. (Both, courtesy of Jim Cahill and ONP.)

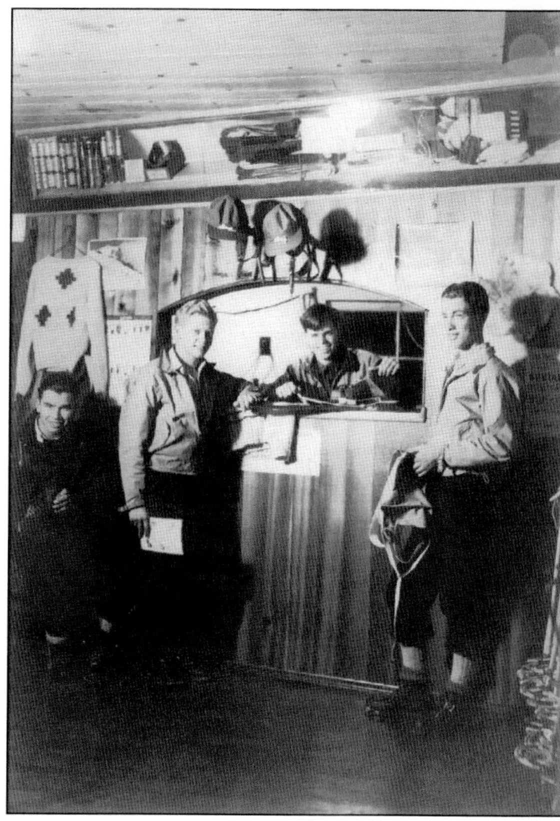

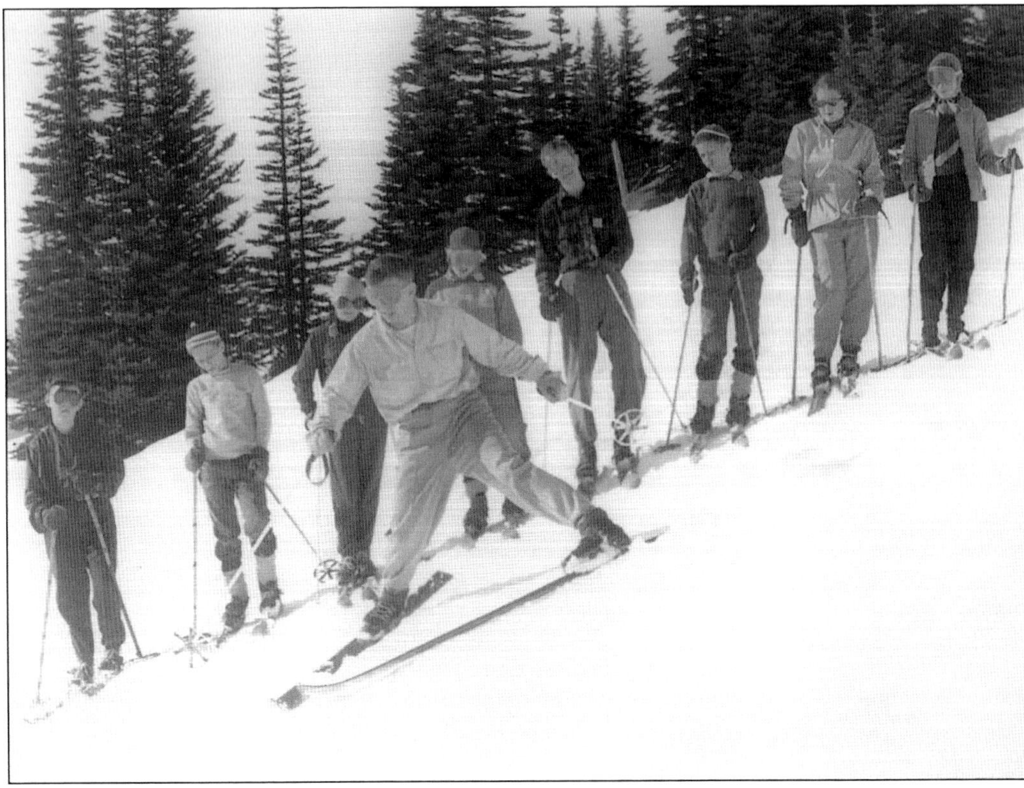

Most of the early skiers at Deer Park were novices, so ski lessons were a necessity. Here, an instructor is about to demonstrate a snowplow. Instructors initially came from Seattle, including Jim and Joy Lucas, who also ran the lodge in 1940. Joy reported that they netted $90 that year for three months work. (Photograph by Art Jackson, courtesy of ONP.)

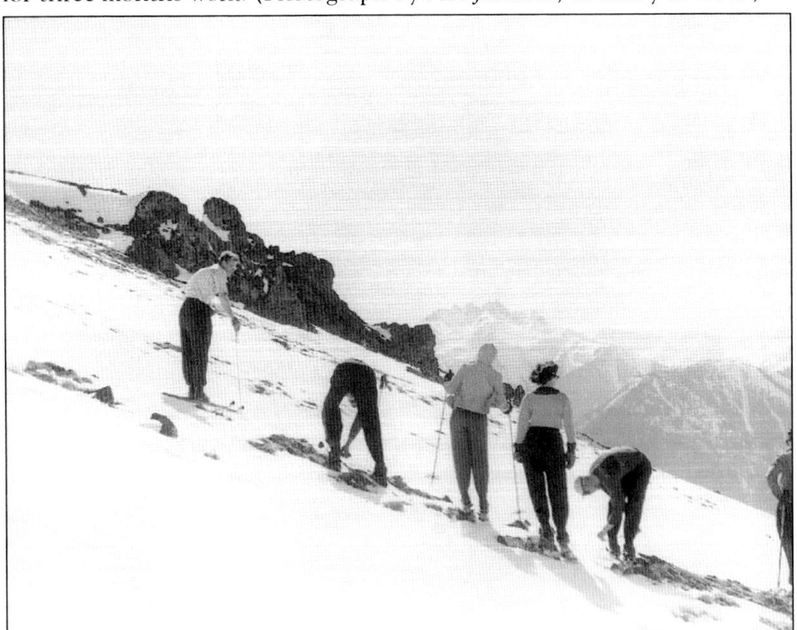

One hopes these skiers brought their rock skis. They are on the north slopes of Blue Mountain, which were steeper than the slopes on the Deer Park side of the mountain. Races were occasionally held on this north side, and a lift was installed for a brief period. (Photograph by Art Jackson, courtesy of ONP.)

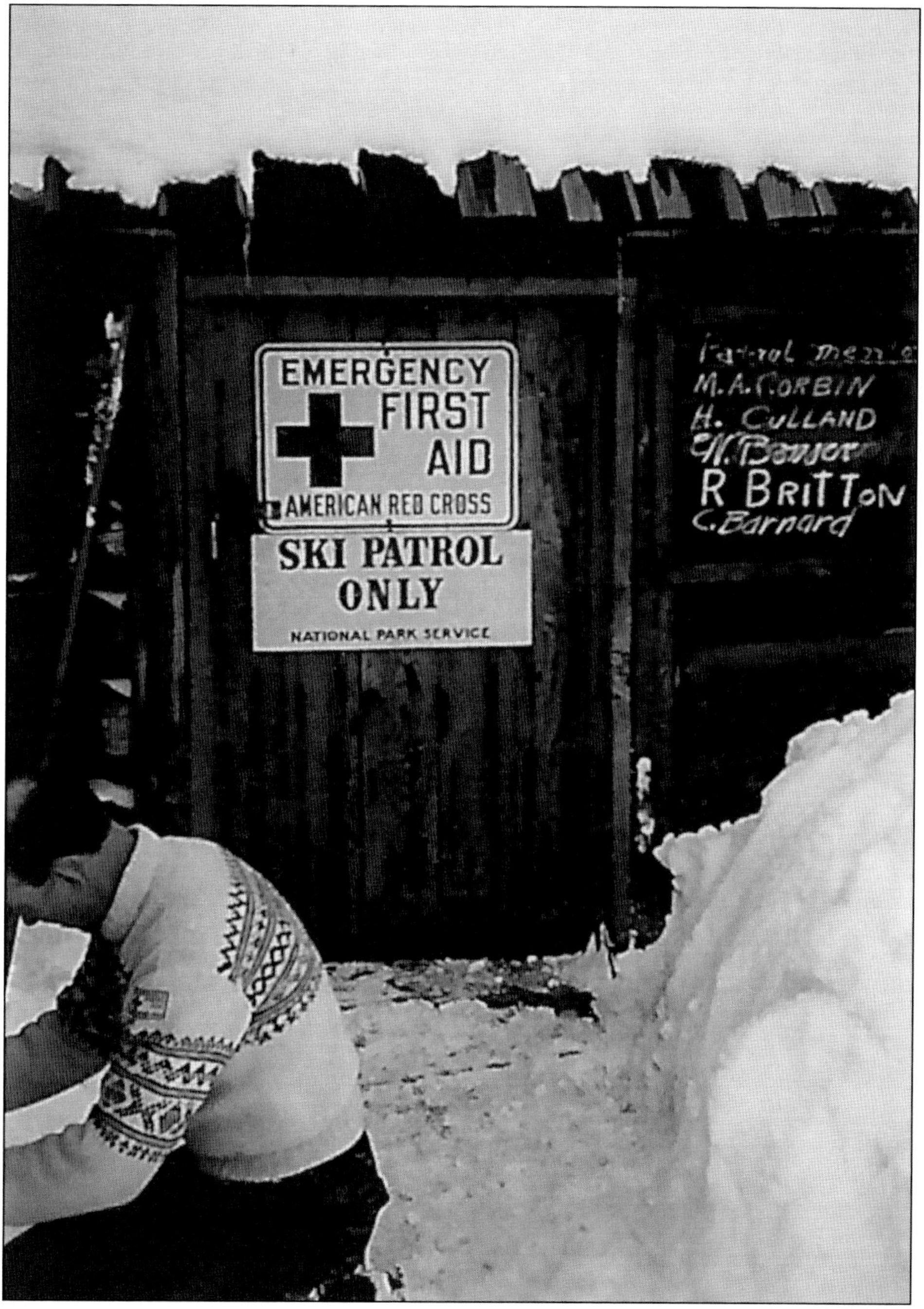

This 1938 photograph shows the entrance to the first-aid station at Deer Park, which was housed in the sheepherder's cabin. The ski patrol was formed in the fall of 1938 with the leadership of Hans Culland. Culland explained that the National Ski Patrol was dedicated to training volunteers for prevention of winter sports accidents. The Red Cross was also active in training US Forest Service and National Park Service personnel. Early ski-patrol members' names are visible on the cabin. When the Ski Patrol was re-formed in 1947, Culland, Barnard, and Britton were still involved. (Photograph by Jim Byrne, courtesy of Bernice Byrne.)

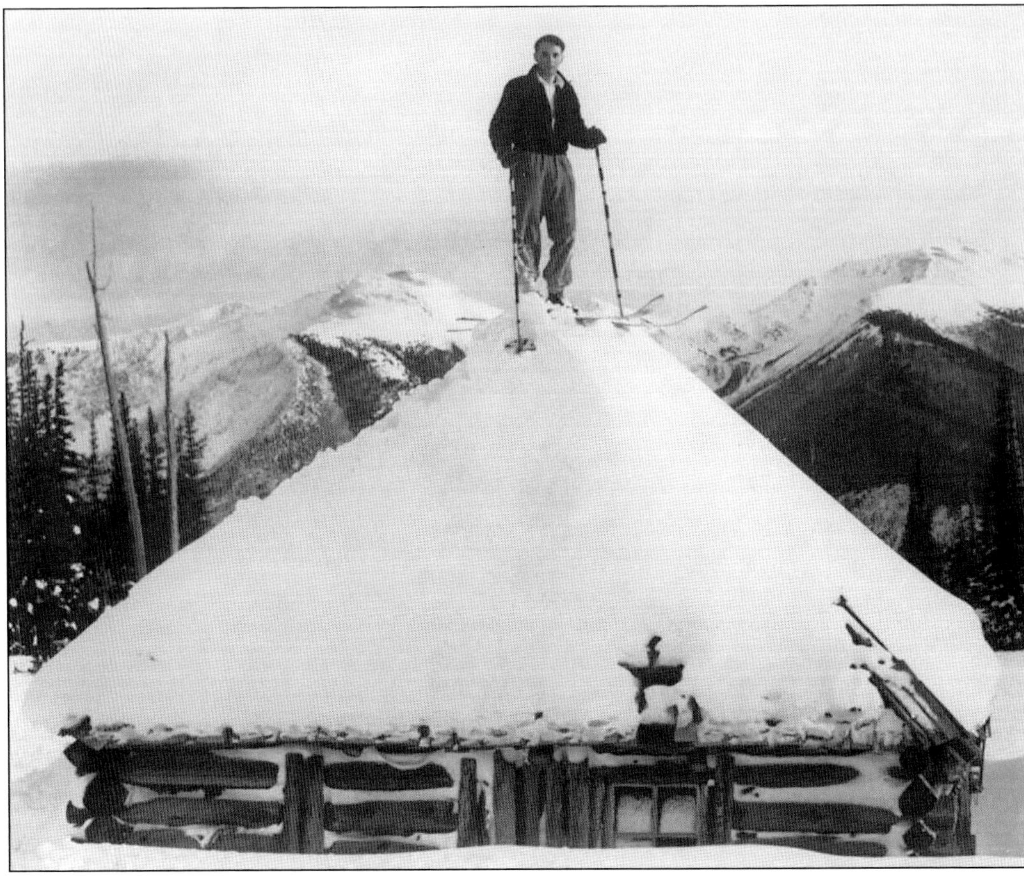

In the above photograph, Joe Faires of Port Angeles stands on top of the Deer Park first-aid station, originally built as a sheepherder's cabin. One might wonder how he was able to gain this perch. Below, skier Clive McCloud stands near the cabin in the winter of 1938. This cabin was demolished in the early 1960s, but the idea of ski huts in Olympic National Park still holds interest for local skiers. (Above, photograph by Jim Cahill, courtesy of ONP; below, photograph by Jim Byrne, courtesy of Bernice Byrne.)

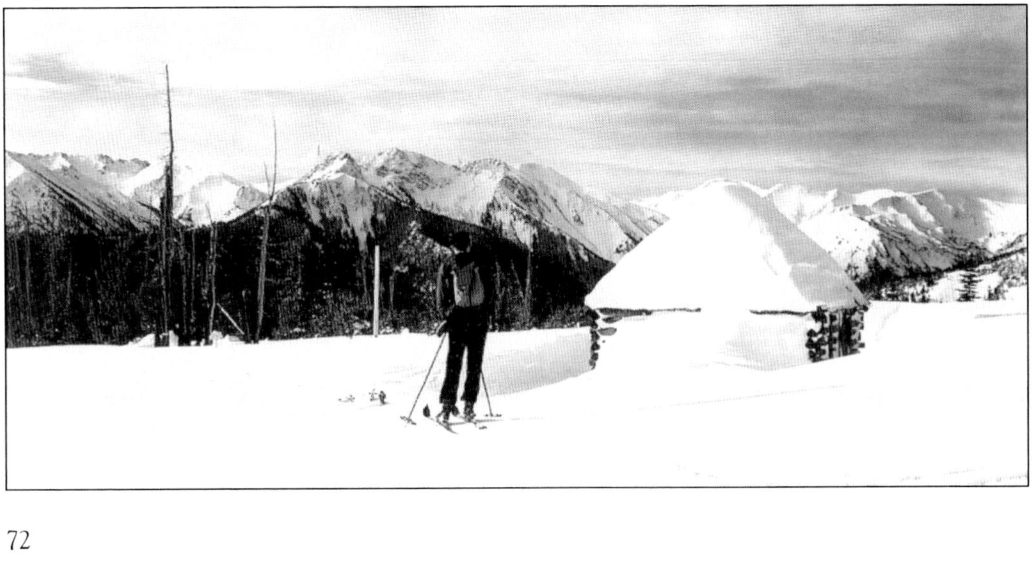

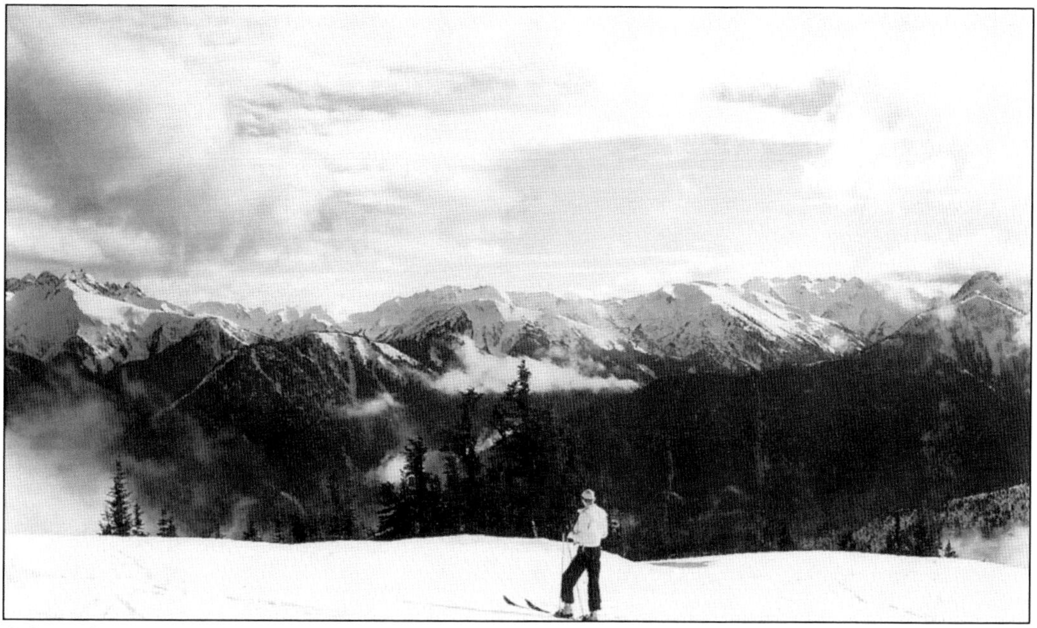

A lone skier enjoys the view out toward Mount Deception and the Cameron Basin in the winter of 1938. Mount Deception is on the left, and the valleys of the Graywolf and Cameron Rivers lie below. (Photograph by Jim Byrne, courtesy of Bernice Byrne.)

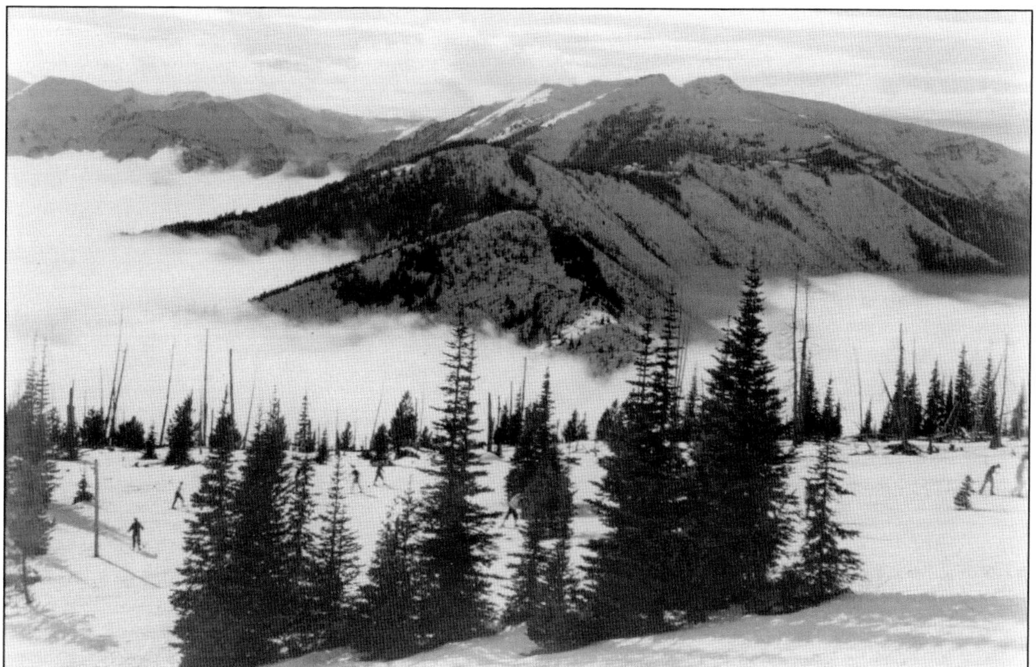

The view looking west toward Hurricane Ridge in this photograph of the Deer Park area could be called "the dance of the skiers," as one can see skiers scattered about the meadows and enjoying another sunny day. Getting to Deer Park was a challenge, but days like this made the trip worthwhile. In a 1958 newspaper article, Esther Webster writes, "For those who did not take the high ski runs, the road was the most exciting part of the trip." (Courtesy of ONP.)

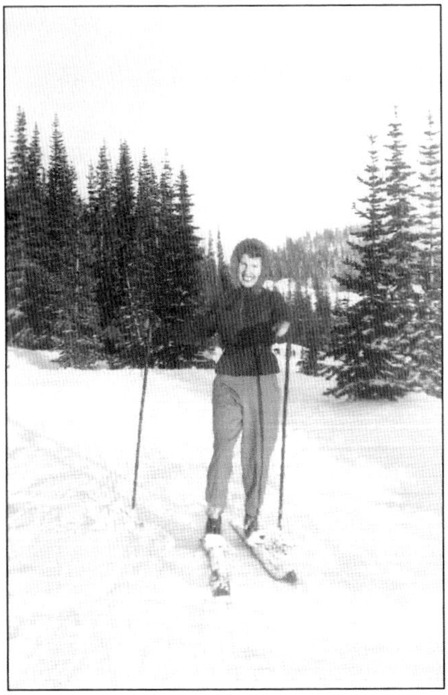

This attractive unidentified skier is wearing ski garb typical of the 1930s. Early on, skiers wore whatever they had that was warm. Fashion was not as important as comfort and cost. A newspaper article from January 1939 notes lots of new woolen shirts. It also notes that one of the smartest outfits on the trail was worn by Corrine Read, who had brown ski trousers topped by a gay yellow parka and matching gabardine ski cap. By the 1950s, fashion and "lodge skiers" had become more popular. An article by columnist Keith Patterson in the March 4, 1950, *Port Angeles Evening News* reads: "She was dressed to perfection as she stood at the crest of the hill and it seemed that once her skis began to move her passing would be poetry in motion. . . . Why, if that blonde beauty even so much as thought about starting down a ski slope she'd land flat on her beautifully costumed posterior (I. Magnin's $42.50)." Rumor has it that I. Magnin (and probably White Stag) caught the eye of some of Deer Park's best skiers. (Left, photograph by Jim Cahill, courtesy of ONP; below, courtesy of Bernice Byrne.)

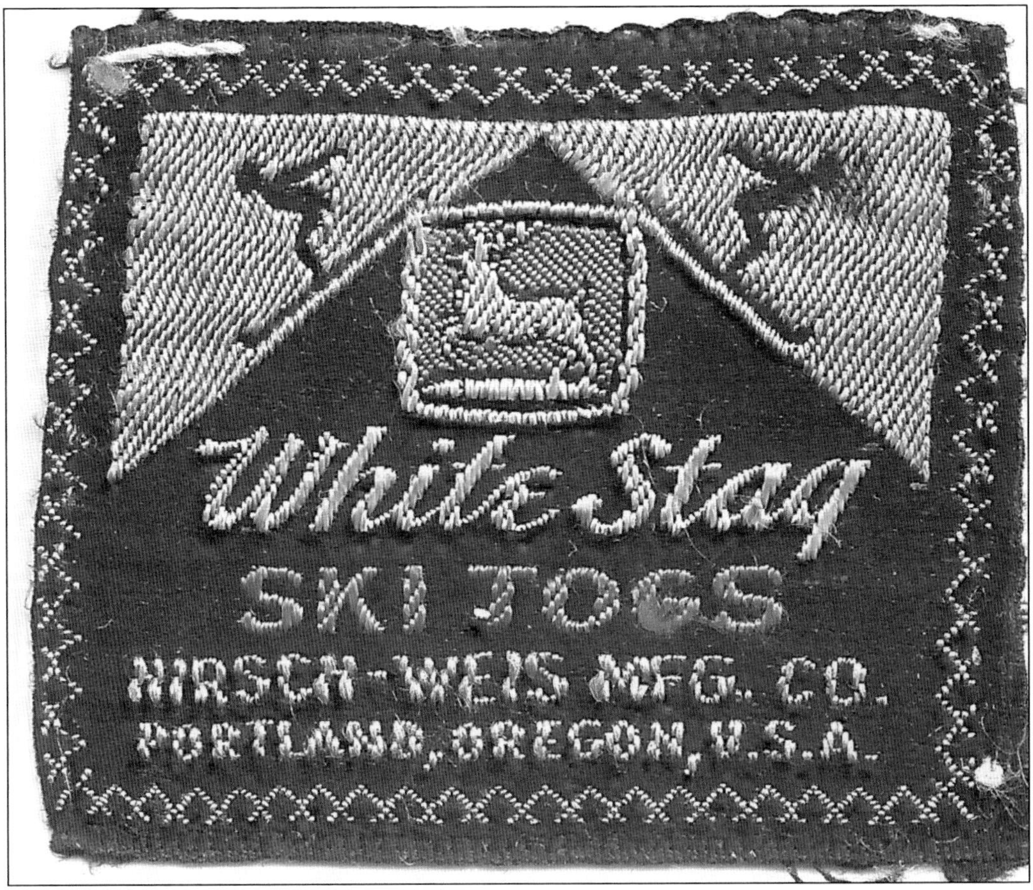

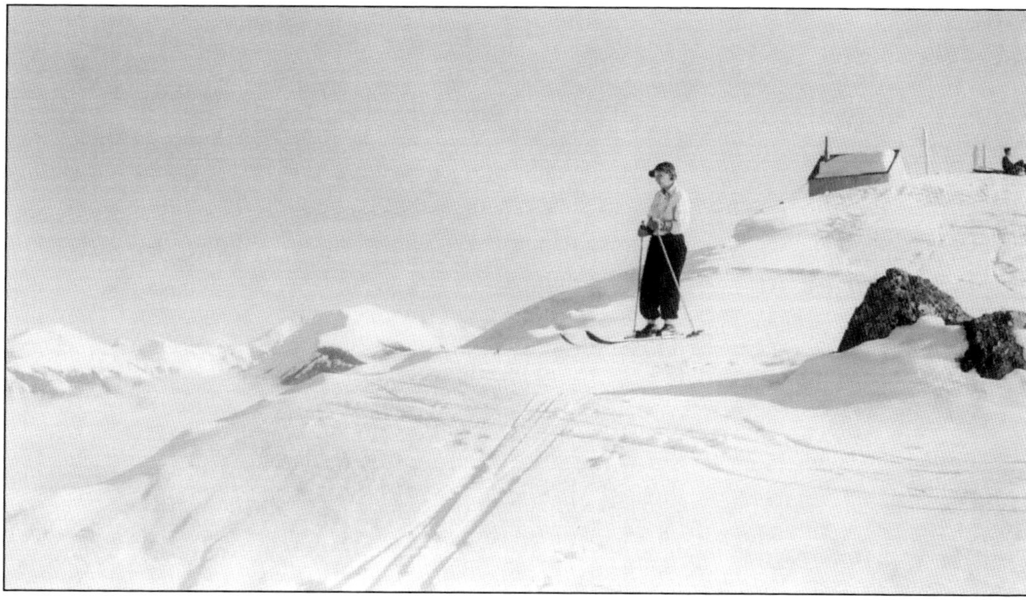

These two unidentified skiers are enjoying contrasting days at Deer Park. Above, a skier stands near the summit of Blue Mountain on a sunny, clear day, with the Deer Park lookout in the backdrop. Below, clouds so typical of the Olympics, often referred to as Olympic mist, are seen sweeping across peaks and ridges. Frequent visitors to these mountains are very familiar with these clouds and the mist that sweeps in and gives a feeling of calm and mystery. (Both, photograph by Jim Cahill, courtesy of ONP.)

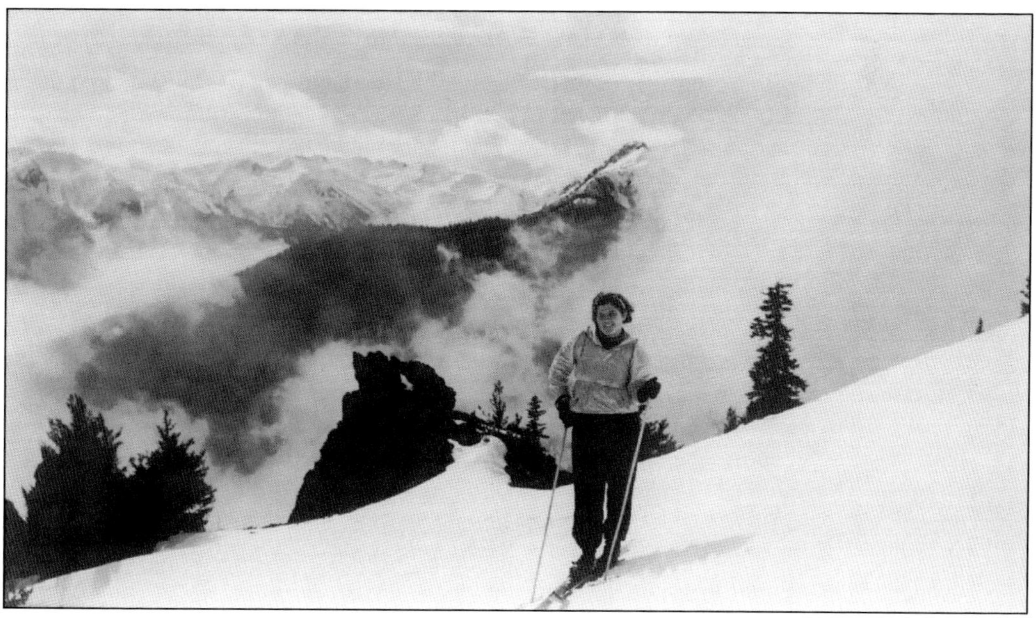

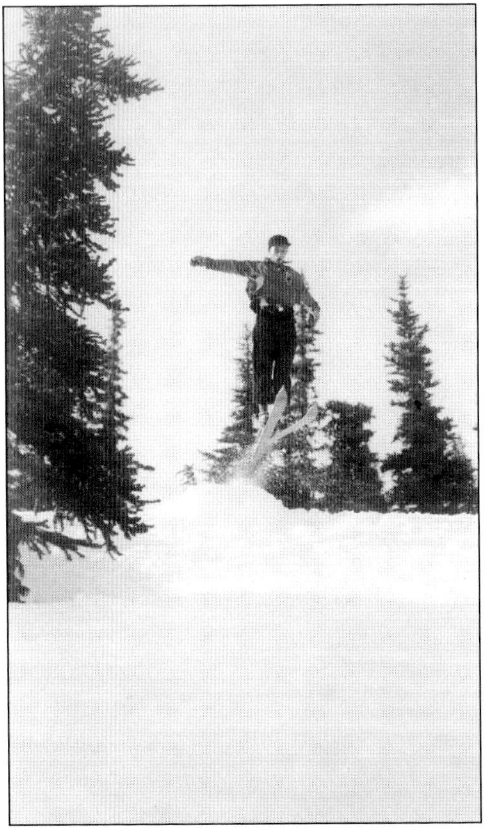

Preston Macy was Olympic National Park's first superintendent, arriving from Mount Rainier Park in 1938. He and his family enjoyed skiing at Deer Park and were frequently the first ones to the top. In the photograph on the left, his son Paul Macy, a frequent race winner, goes off a ski jump. Below, the entire family—from left to right, Ruth, Paul, Mary, Preston, Marshall, Emerson, and Esther—enjoys a family outing. (Both, courtesy of ONP.)

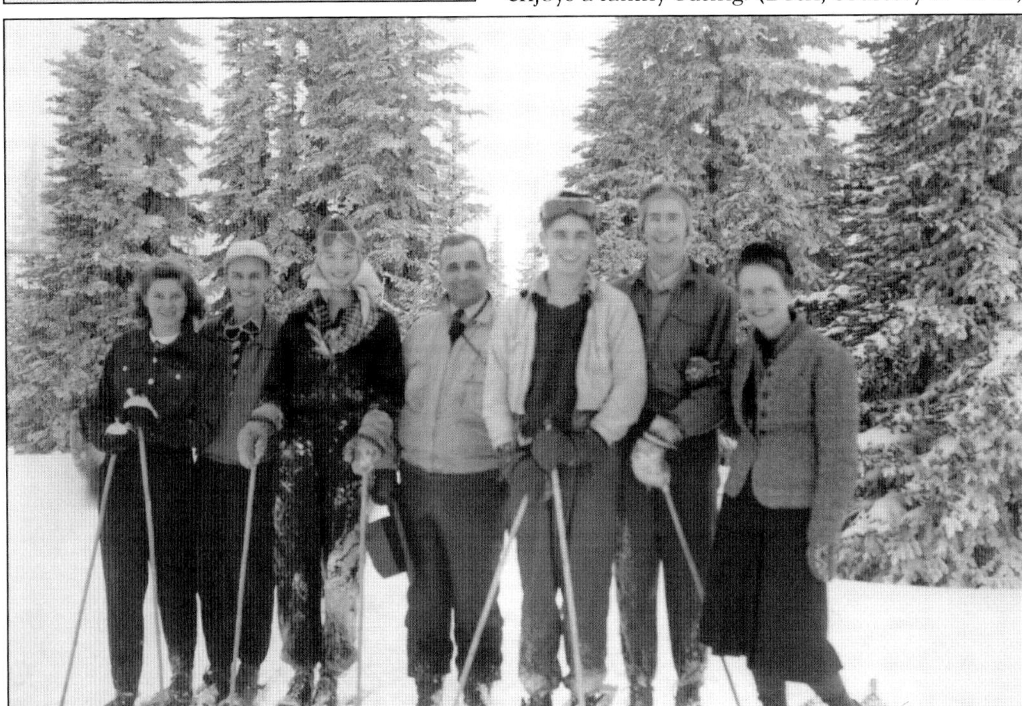

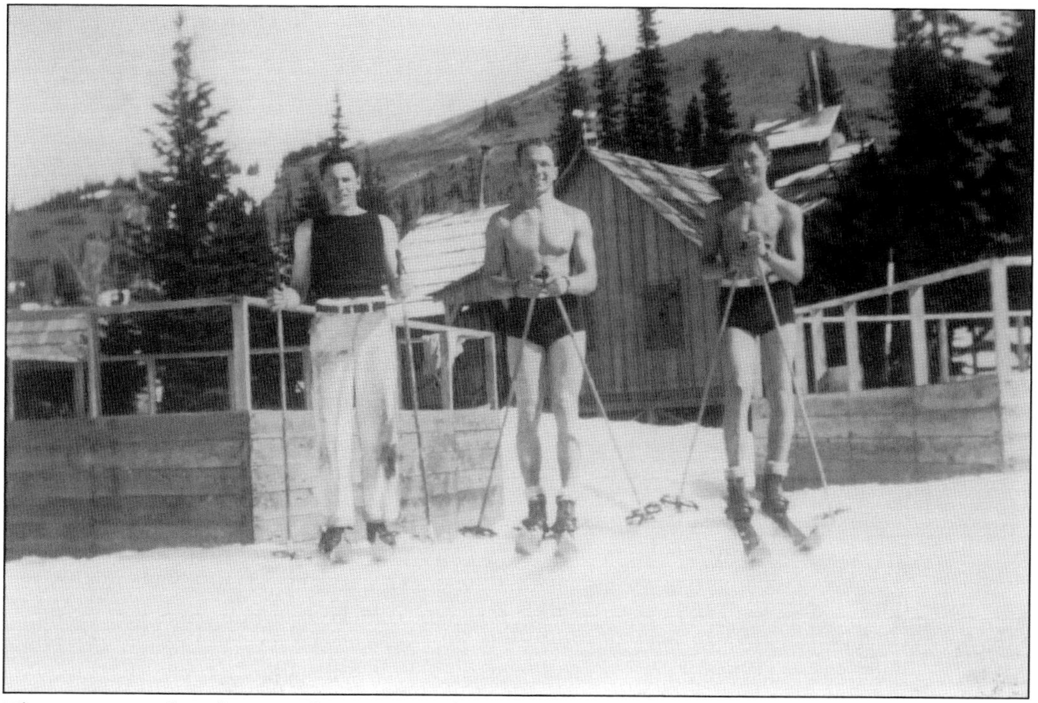

The caption to this photograph says, "Tent frames at Deer Park. Background buildings being erected by Forest Service and CCC," indicating it dates to about 1937. From left to right are unidentified, Cal Davidson, and Richard Owens Jr. Spring skiing at Deer Park often brought shirtless men and women in bandana tops. (Photograph by Jim Cahill, courtesy of ONP.)

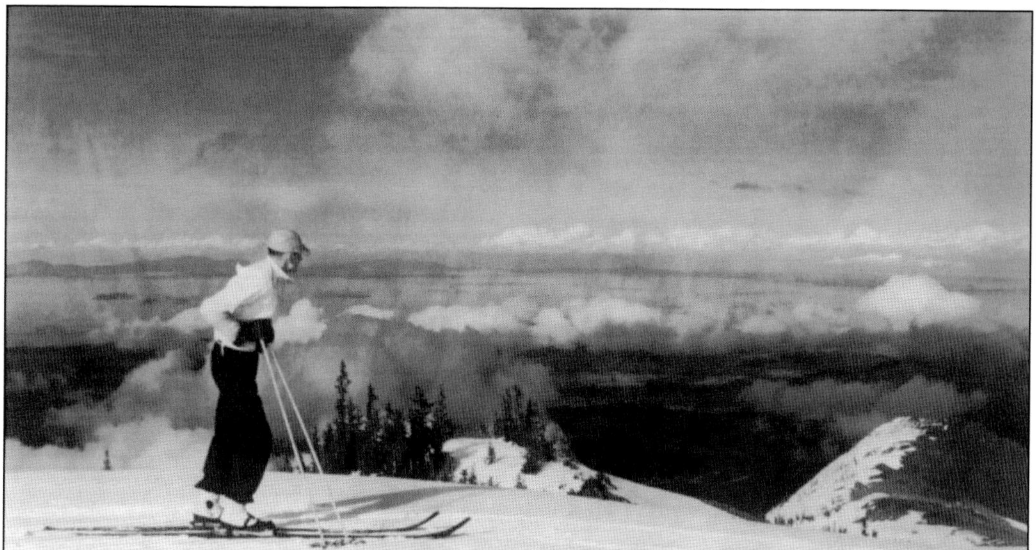

This lone unidentified skier is on the summit ridge looking out north toward the Strait of Juan de Fuca and British Columbia. On a clear day, he could see the San Juan Islands, Vancouver Island, the Canadian coastal range, and Mount Baker. At night, he could see the lights of Vancouver, British Columbia. (Photograph by Jim Cahill, courtesy of ONP.)

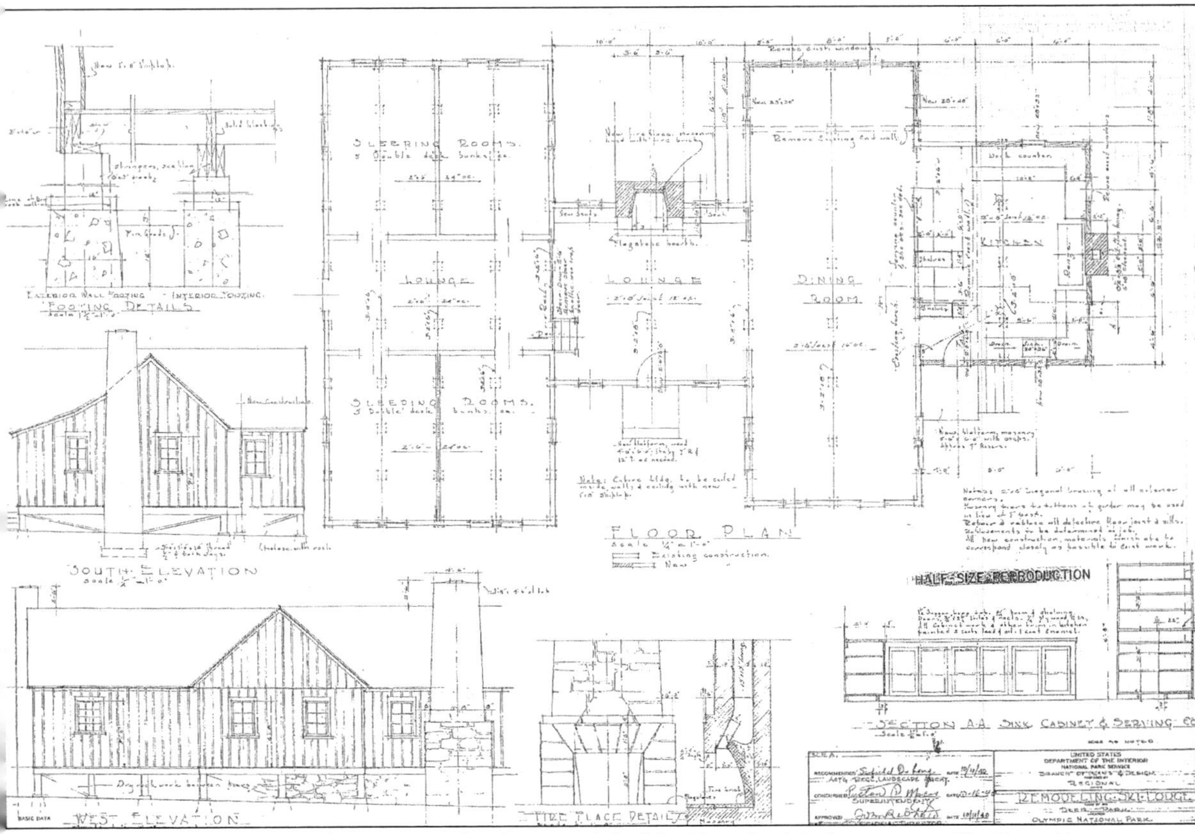

These architectural drawings are for the remodel of the Deer Park lodge approved by Supt. Preston Macy in October 1940. Only one season of construction was left before December 7, 1941, when members of the CCC were off to war. (Courtesy of ONP.)

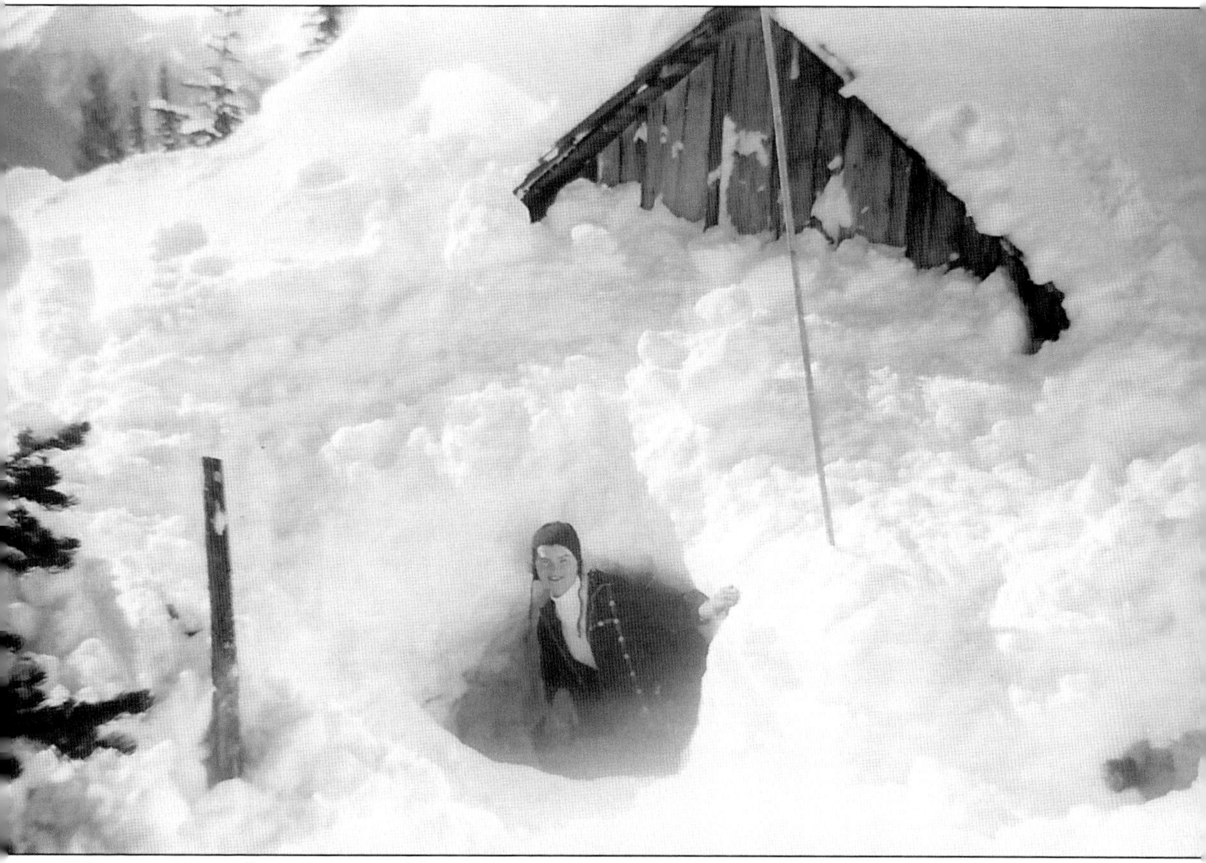

Winter visitors often mentioned having to pass through a snow-tunnel entrance into the lodge. While snowfall was not always as heavy as skiers wanted, it was certainly a frequent topic of discussion. One writer accused Ed Halterman, the lodge manager, of cutting four feet off his snow gauge to give higher readings. This unidentified girl gives perspective to the snow depth at that time. This photograph serves as a transition to some postwar skiing photographs at Deer Park from 1947 to 1957. (Courtesy of Kaye C. Winters.)

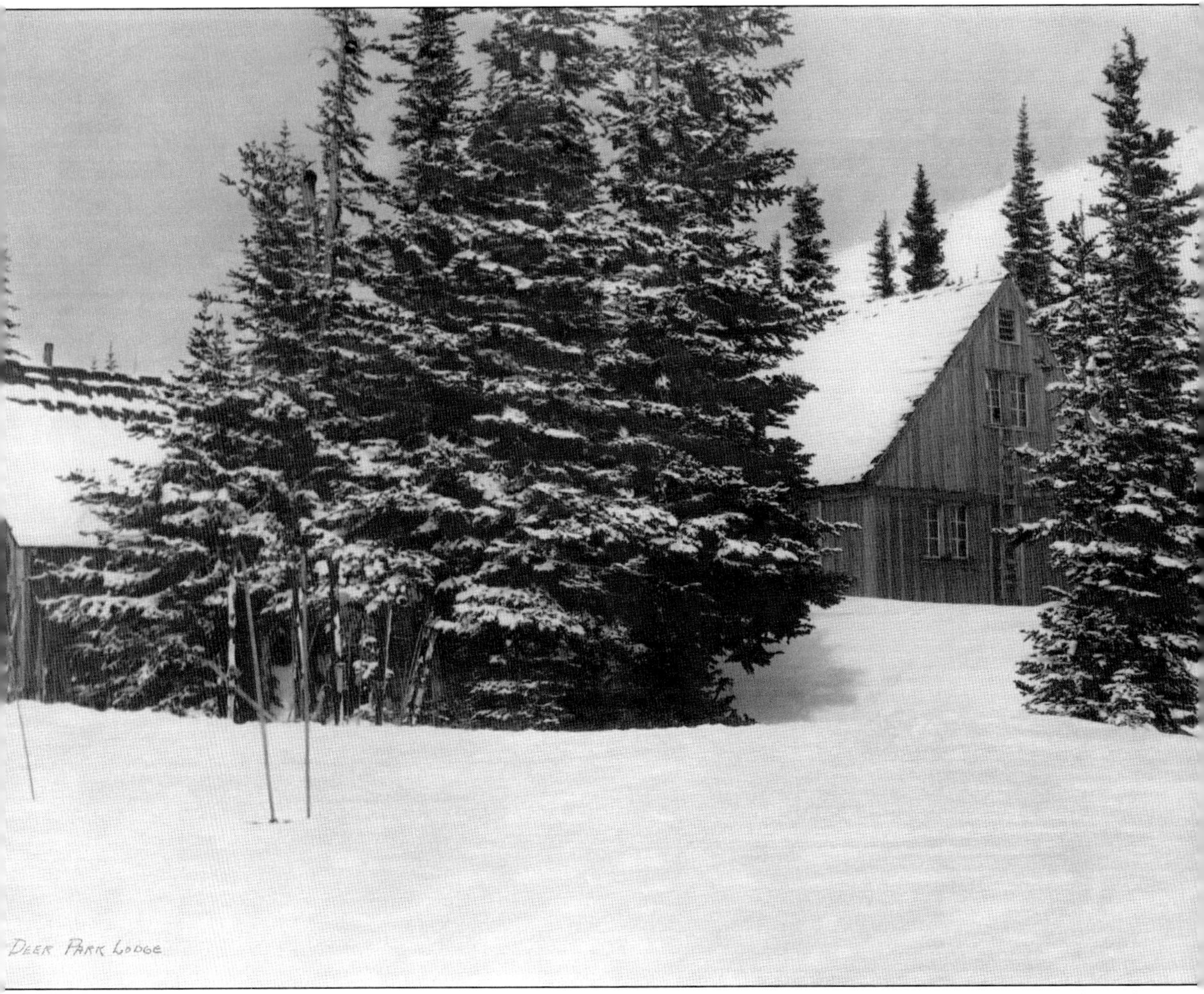

By the spring of 1946, the war was over and Olympic Ski Club was reorganized. Deer Park and the lodge were reopened for alpine skiing in January 1947. The remodeled lodge now had running water and electric lights. Bunks were $1 per night and had springs and mattresses, but visitors still brought their own bedding. By the following winter, new chimneys had been added, and the women's dormitory, which had been moved upstairs, had a new fire escape. The last winter for overnight facilities was in 1955–1956. (Courtesy of Claud Johnson.)

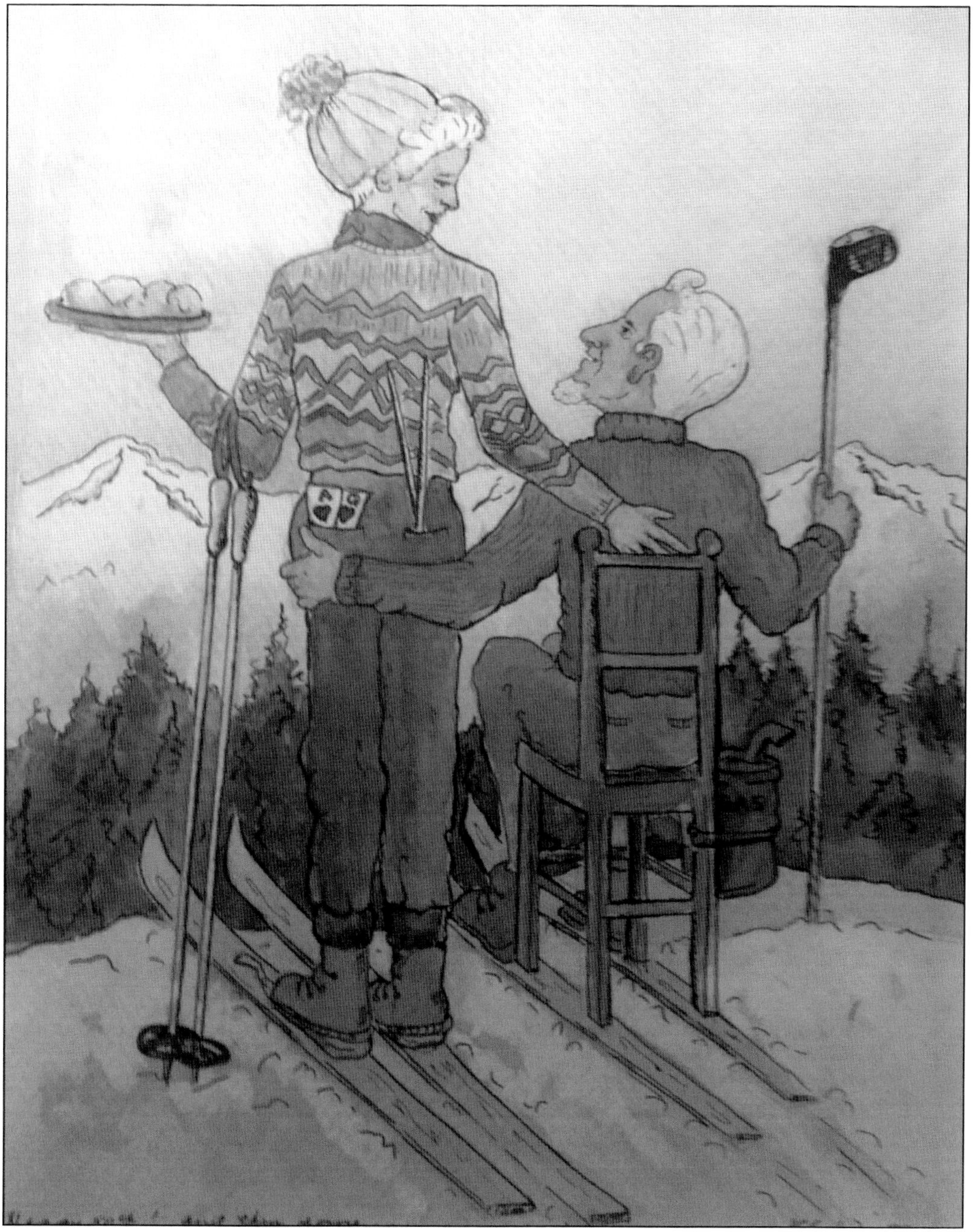

After the war, brothers Larry and Tom Winters took over the rope tows and lodge operations. They ran the lifts until they were moved to Hurricane Ridge, although they continued to operate them there, as well. Larry's wife, Dorace, was active in running the lodge. This painting by their daughter Kaye C. shows Dorace and Larry with their many interests. Larry is wearing one of Dorace's newly knitted sweaters and about to enjoy a freshly baked pie. He is on his "chairlift" skis and thinking about golf. (Painting by Kaye C. Winters.)

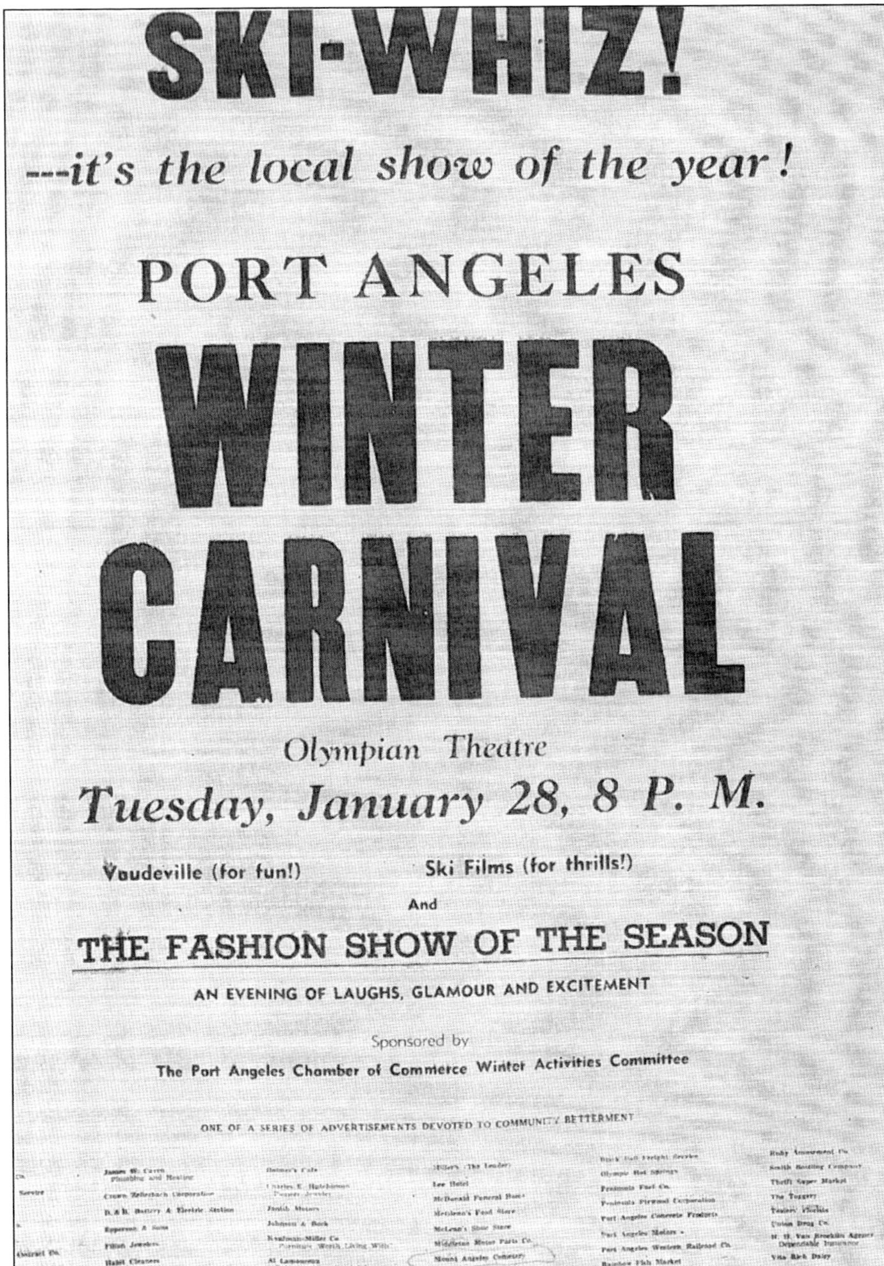

Writer Jack Henson, known as the "Wandering Scribe," wrote in January 1947, "There were no cash customers hanging from the chandeliers at the Olympian theatre last night for the winter carnival but they were lined up along the walls and in the back of the auditorium and many were turned back at the box office when the standing room only signal went out." There were at least 900 people present to applaud the vaudeville program, showing the popularity of skiing at the time. This advertisement in the *Port Angeles Evening News* promises "an evening of laughs, glamour, and excitement." There was music, dancing, and a fashion show with MC Jean Earl, the pen name of Esther Webster. This event was a predecessor of many skiing fundraisers to come. (Courtesy of the *Port Angeles Evening News*.)

Both of these photographs not only show the bare slopes common at Deer Park, but also the lifts of the 1950s. The lift operators were constantly changing the lifts. At times, there were lifts on the north side, the lower bowl, and toward the summit. Operators Tom and Larry Winters ran a tow on the north side of Blue Mountain for the 1951–1952 season. In 1953, they relocated a 600-foot rope on the lower practice slope for beginners to connect with the 300-foot upper tow at a relay and safety gate. The tow on the north side was relocated. (Right, photograph by Keith Thompson, courtesy of the author; below, courtesy of ONP.)

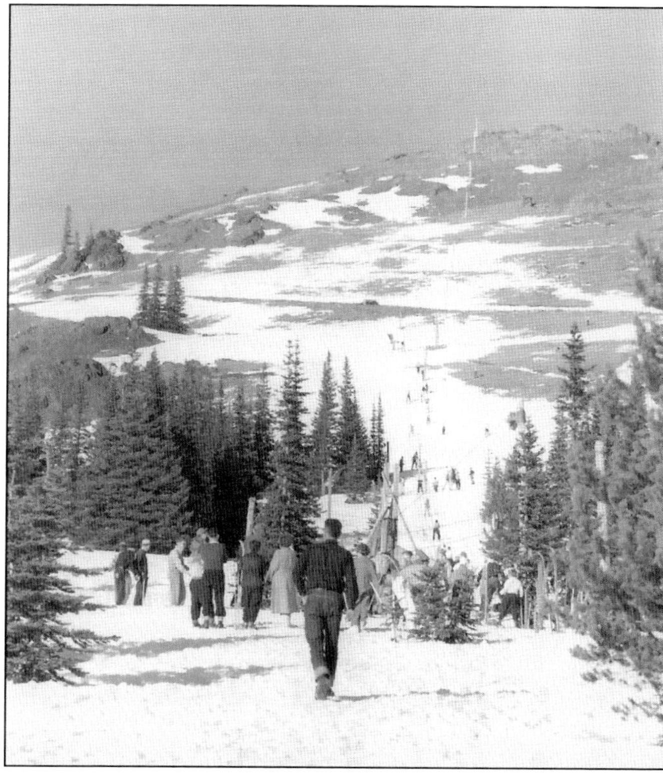

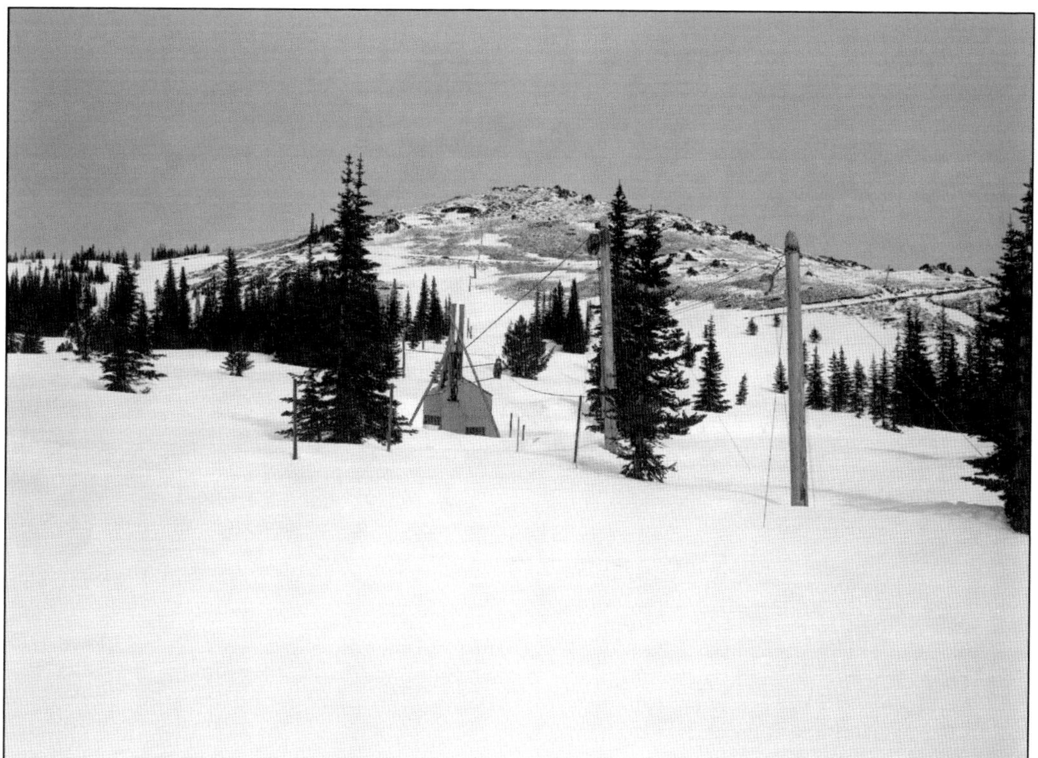

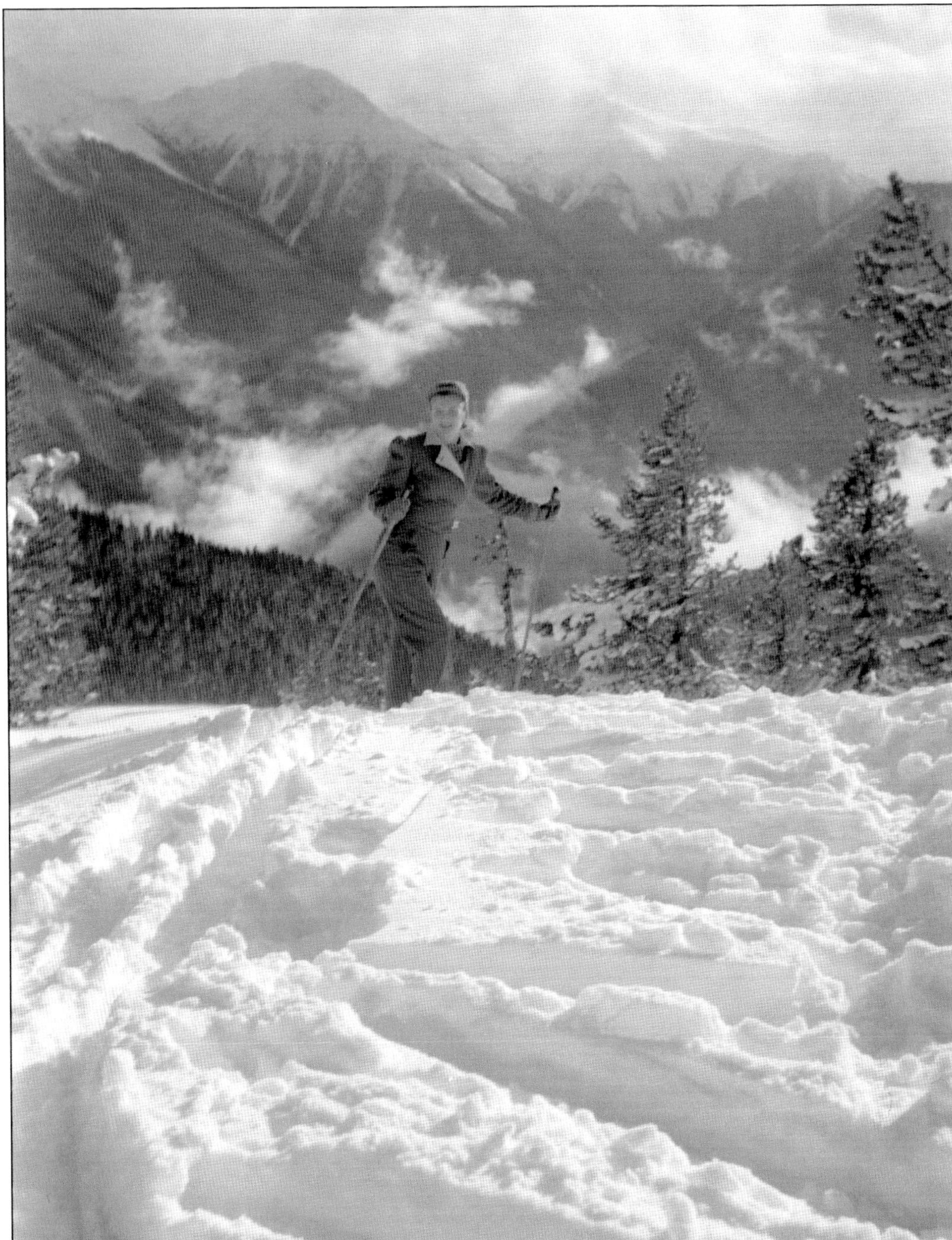

This 1949 photograph captures the beauty of Deer Park that was enjoyed by so many skiers from 1936 to 1957. It was a magical place, close to the sea yet, at 5,400 feet, heavenly in its feel. Besides the incredible natural beauty, there was a fellowship among those who experienced the one-way road, car chains, and warmth of the Deer Park lodge. Here, Margaret Powell enjoys the day, with the Graywolf and Cameron Valleys in the background. (Photograph by Leo White, courtesy of the Leo White family.)

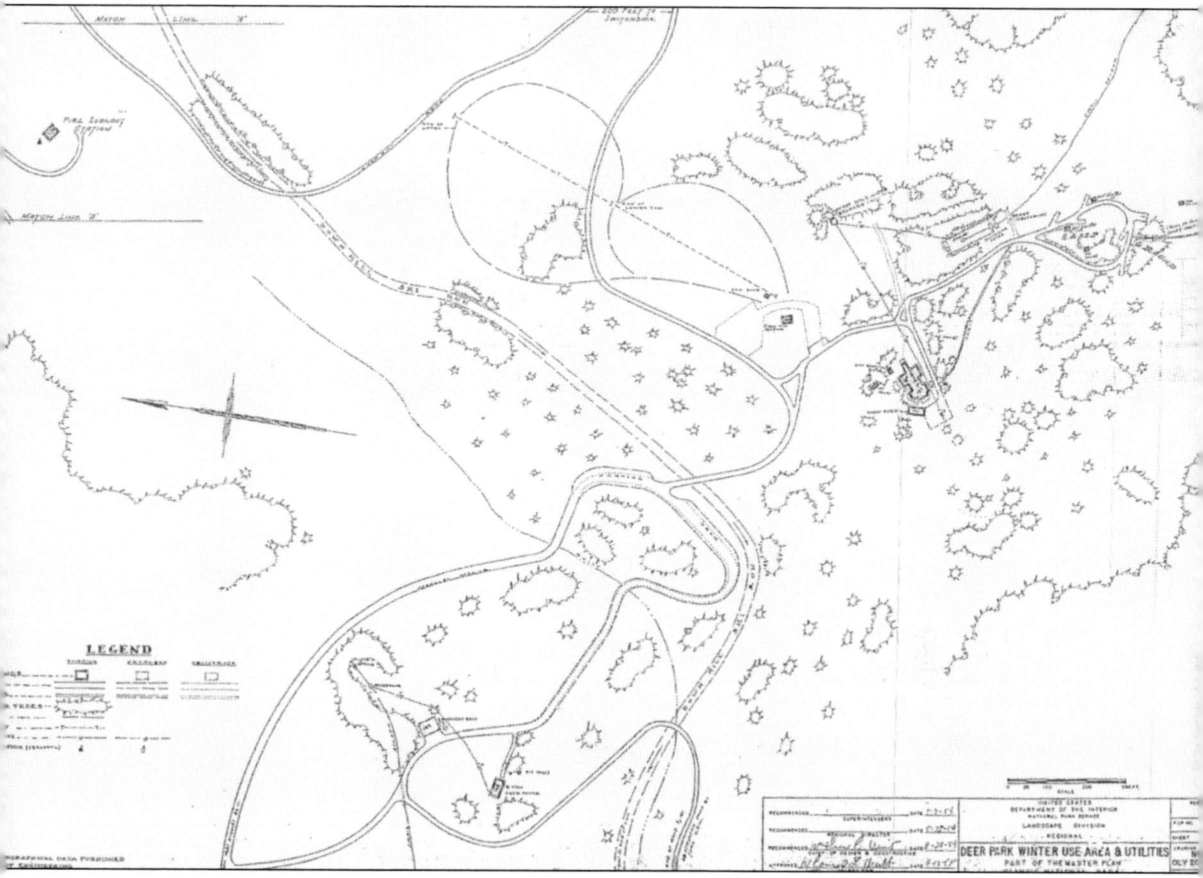

This 1954 National Park Service sketch of the Deer Park area shows both upper and lower lift locations, as well as the location of the lodge and the downhill ski run. Although the ranger station, two restored shelters, and campground remain, the other structures were razed in the early 1960s. Note the course of the downhill run, which was one mile long. (Courtesy of ONP.)

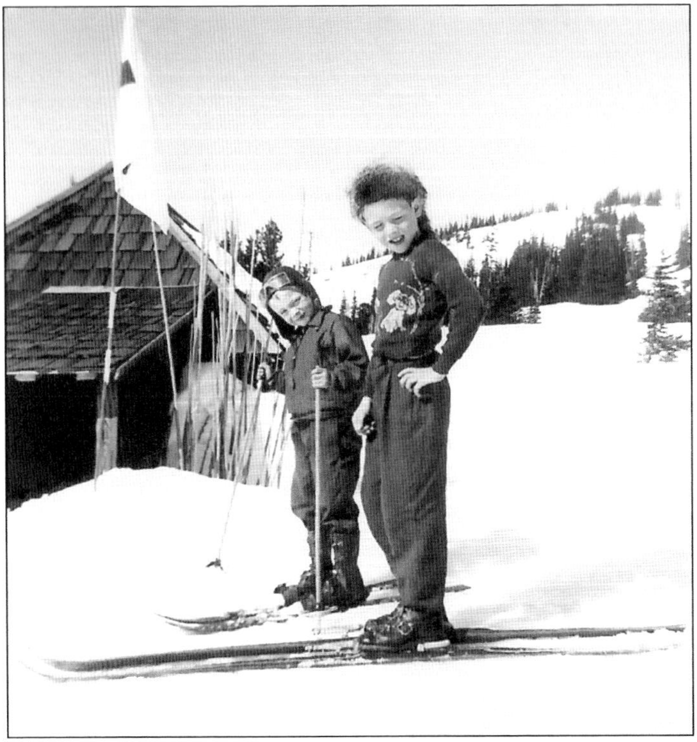

At left, Tom (left) and Jock Broadbent are seen near the first aid station at Deer Park. Their father, Jack, was the first permanent ranger in Olympic National Park. Jock recalls going to Deer Park every weekend during the winter after the war, starting when he was age four or five,. He also recalls being cold and hating it. Jack was in Alaska during the war and ran a ski area at Fort Richardson. Because he knew how to splice rope, he was always called on to perform that duty at Deer Park. Below, Ethlyn, known as "Lyn," and Jack Broadbent are at Deer Park in the 1950s. At the time, he was the district ranger. (Both, courtesy of Jock Broadbent.)

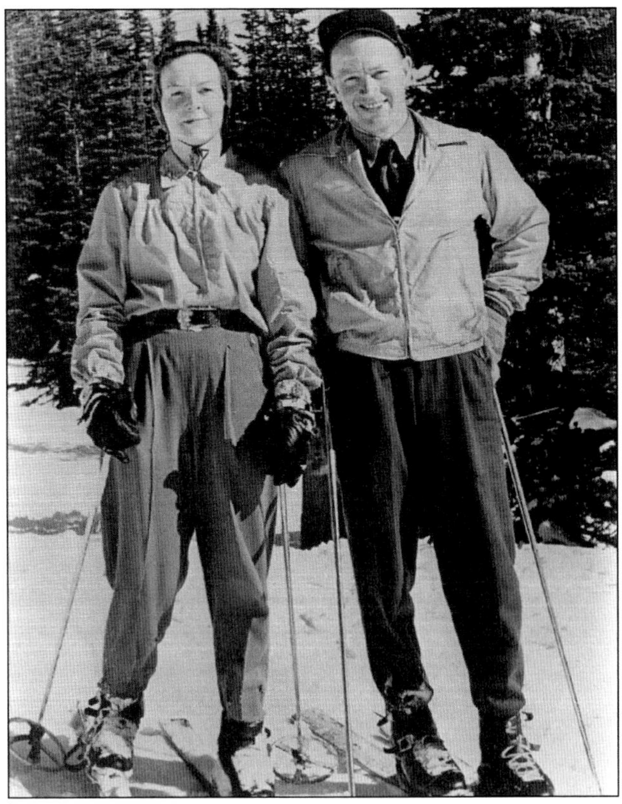

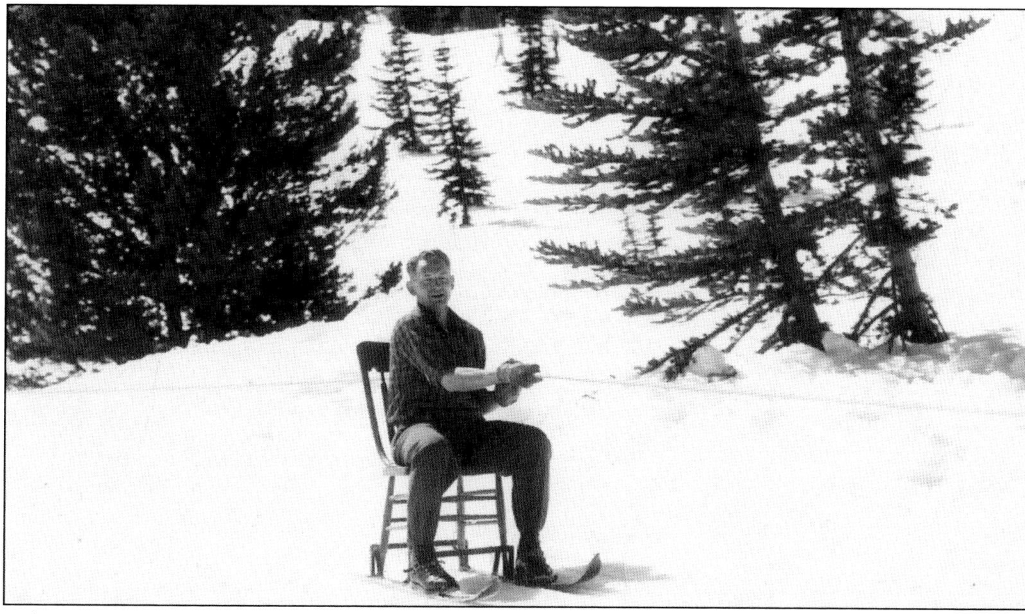

Lift owner Larry Winters rides Deer Park's new (and only) chairlift. Larry's antics were par for the course at Deer Park—people came to have fun. For many, skiing was only a sideshow. Camaraderie and good old-fashioned fun were much in evidence. (Courtesy of Kaye C. Winters).

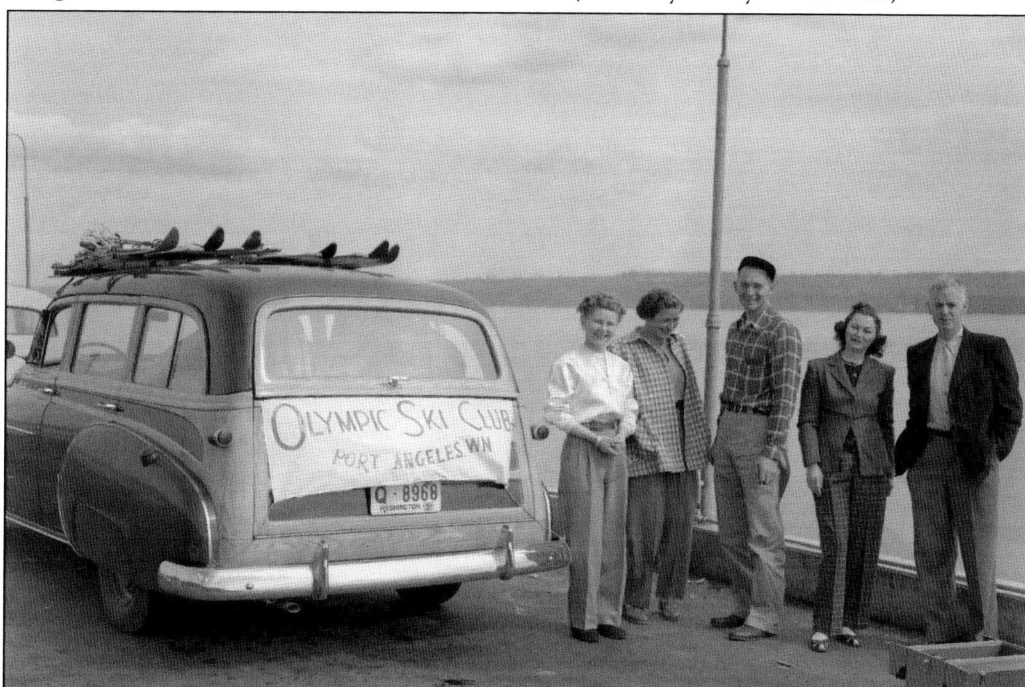

Sun Valley was a popular destination for Deer Park skiers. Here, from left to right, Clare Percival, Dorace and Larry Winters, and Margaret and Howard Doherty await the Hood Canal ferry on their way to Sun Valley in March 1951. They proudly display their Olympic Ski Club banner announcing they are from Port Angeles, Washington. (Photograph by Leo White, courtesy of the White family.)

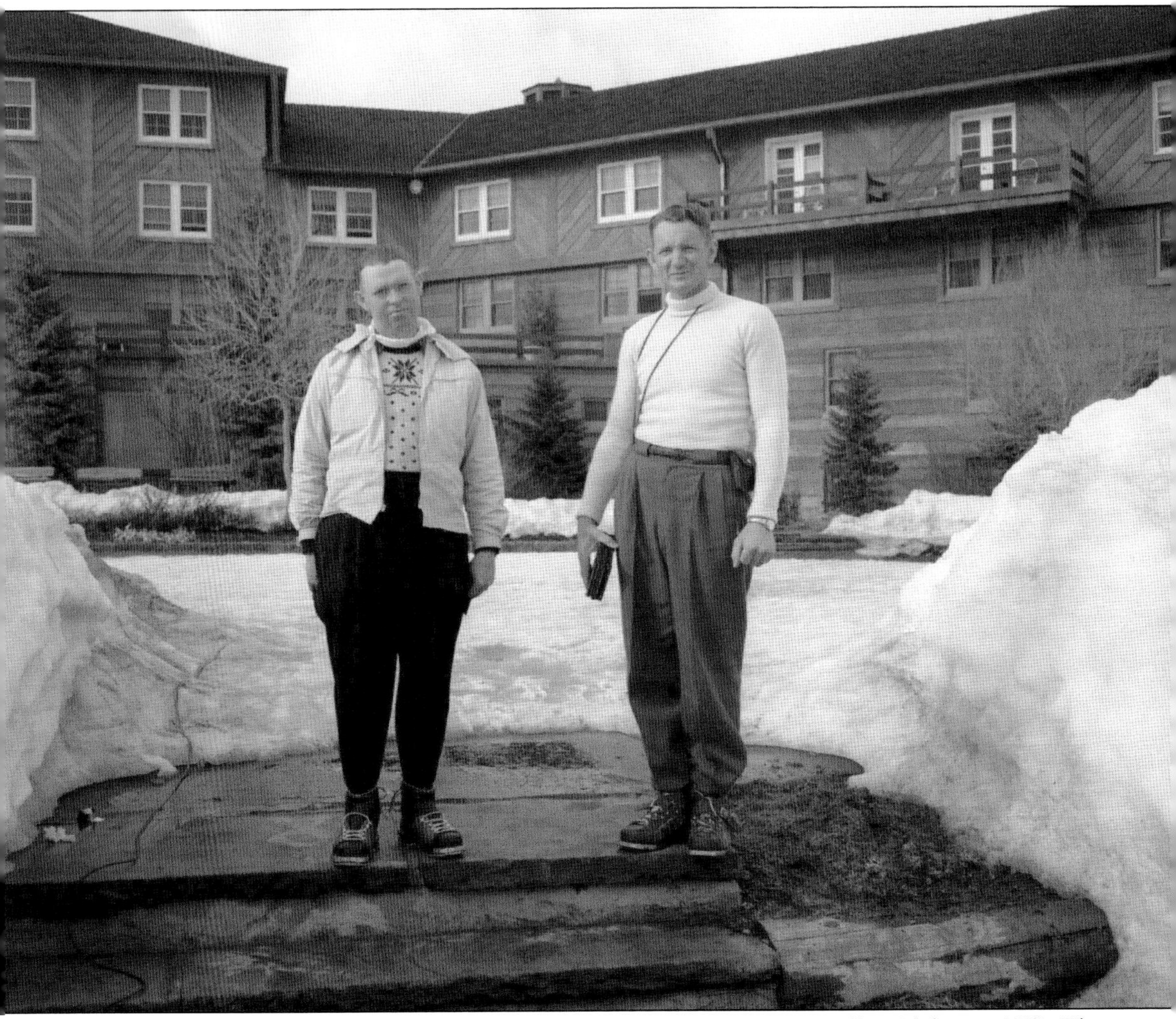

Leo White (left) and Larry Winters enjoy a spring vacation to Sun Valley, Idaho, in 1951. They were two of the most influential men during the Deer Park era of skiing in the Olympics, and they participated in all phases of the operation. Leo ran the Olympic Laundry in Port Angeles and was active in the community. He began his involvement with skiing at Deer Park in 1936. Both continued to be involved once the lifts moved over to Hurricane Ridge. Their involvement spanned a period of 30 years. (Courtesy of the Leo White family.)

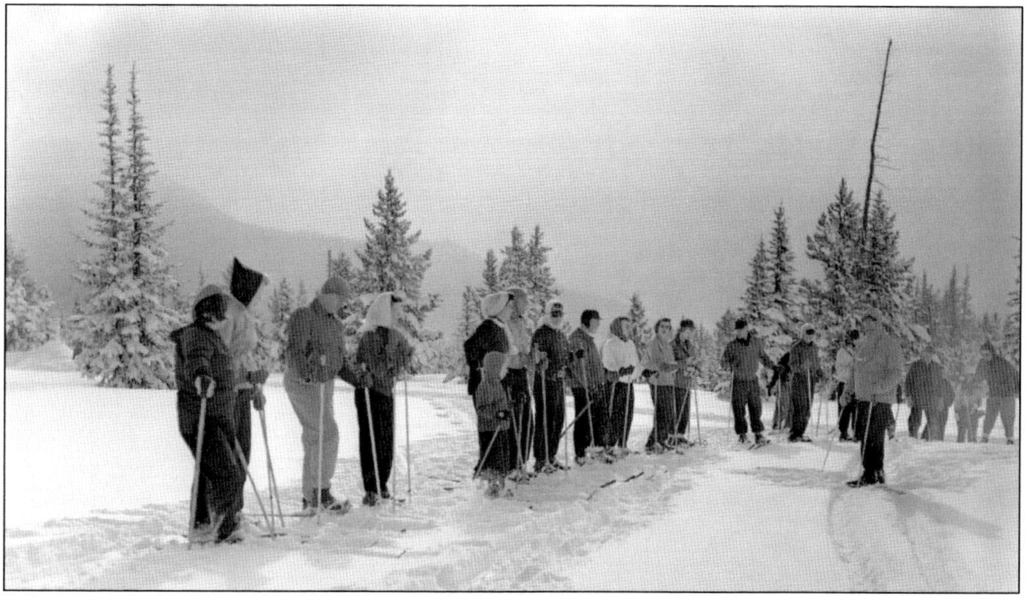

A large group of eager skiers takes lessons from instructor Leo White in March 1954. While most of those pictured here are adults, many children had their first skiing experiences at Deer Park, and junior races were frequently held. In 1950, the local newspaper editor, Ed Clark, said, "You don't have to be crazy to go skiing, but it helps." (Courtesy of the Leo White family.)

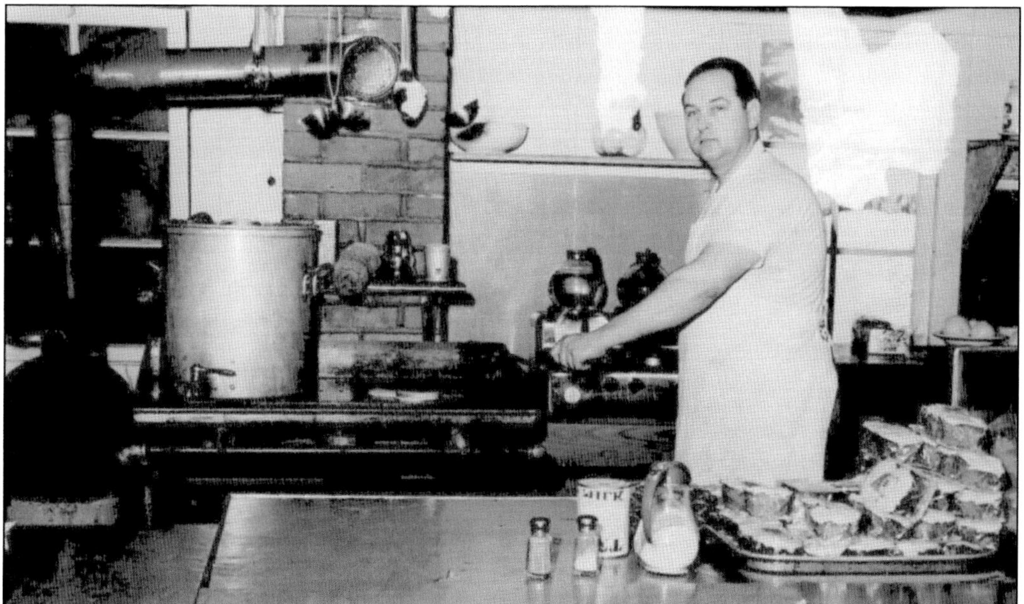

The small kitchen at the back of the lodge was able to turn out three meals a day for hundreds of hungry skiers. At first, local contractors ran the lodge, but park concessionaires later had the contract for services. In 1949, Mr. and Mrs. John Savage and Ed Halterman became the new caretakers. It was demanding work, especially around the holidays. Esther Webster, writing under her pen name, Jean Earl, in the January 3, 1949, *Port Angeles Evening News*, notes, "Mrs. Savage is blond with the kind of beauty that holds up through sleepless nights." (Courtesy of the Leo White family.)

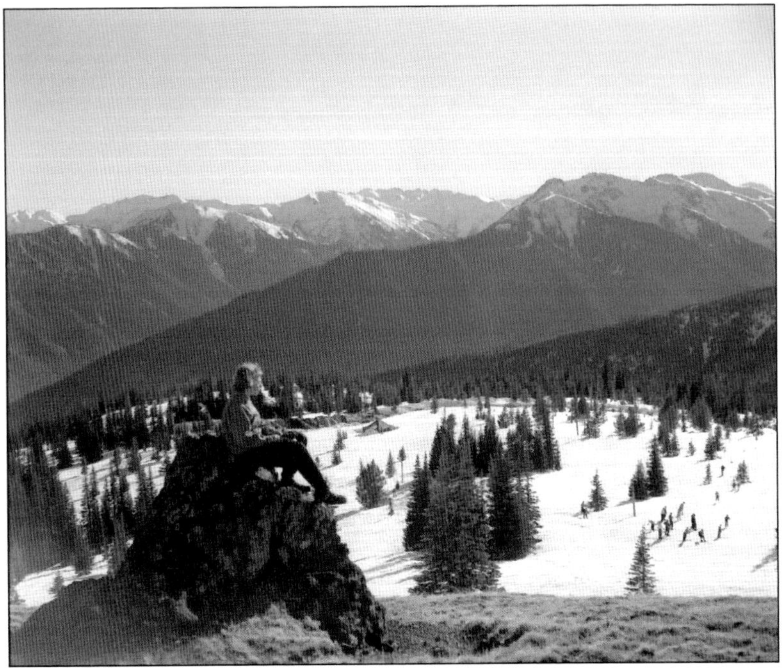

Kris White enjoys Deer Park's superb vistas as she looks out over the Deer Park ski area and beyond to the Olympic Range. The bench that is Deer Park, which is formed by a ridge of basalt that traps the erosion from above, is much in evidence here. The first-aid station is visible as well. (Photograph by Leo White, courtesy of the Leo White family.)

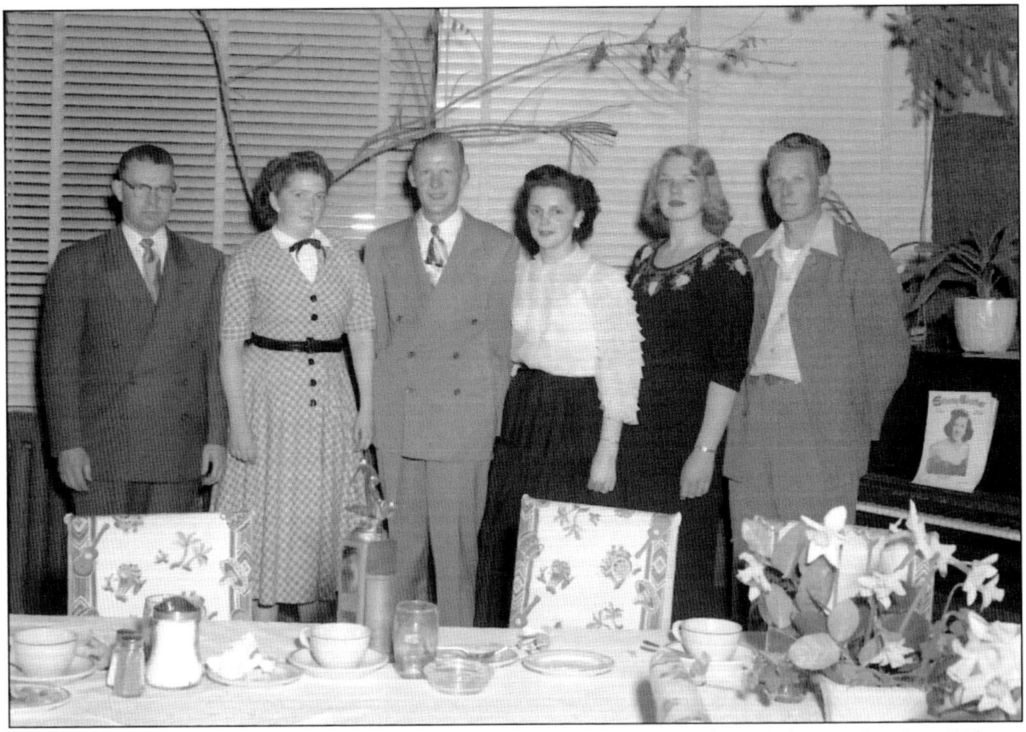

Pictured at an Olympic Ski Club banquet on April 15, 1953, are, from left to right, Leo White, Betty Hollatz, Everett Berglund, Hattie Berglund, unidentified, and Henry "Henie" Hollatz. These names are all strongly identified with the skiing history of Deer Park and Hurricane Ridge. Like many local skiers, Berglund and Hollatz worked at PenPly, a local plywood mill cooperative. Note the music piece on the piano, "Stormy Weather." (Courtesy of the White family.)

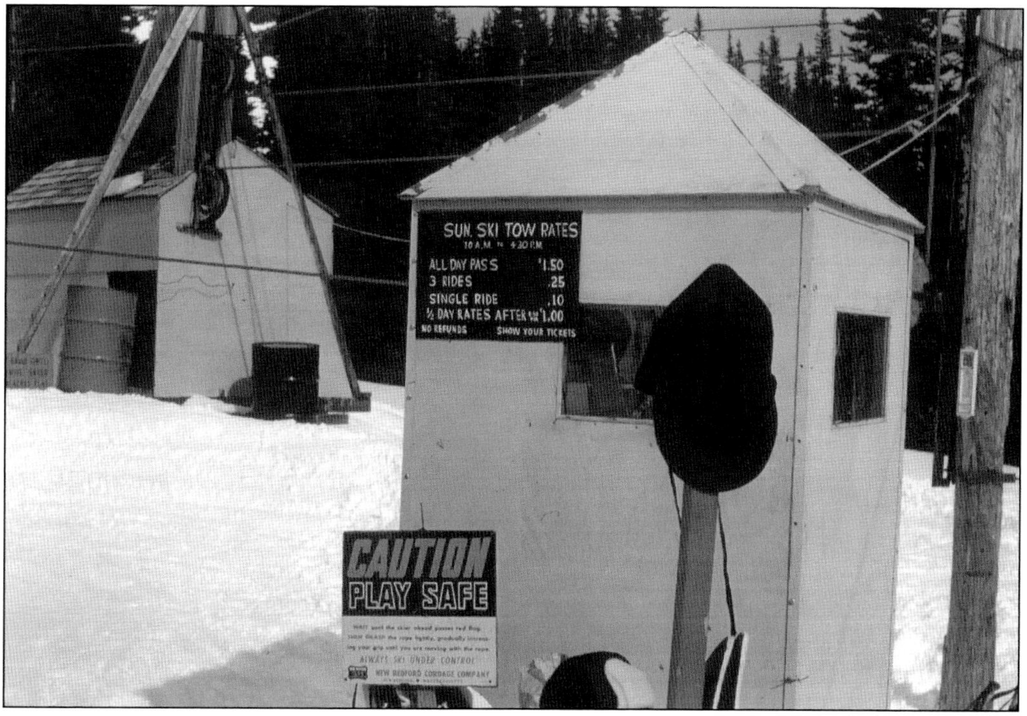

Ski rates were reasonable, especially compared with today's chairlift prices at large resorts. The four unidentified gentlemen below are described as "the first aid guys." They certainly look capable. (Above, courtesy of Rick Yates; below, courtesy of ONP.)

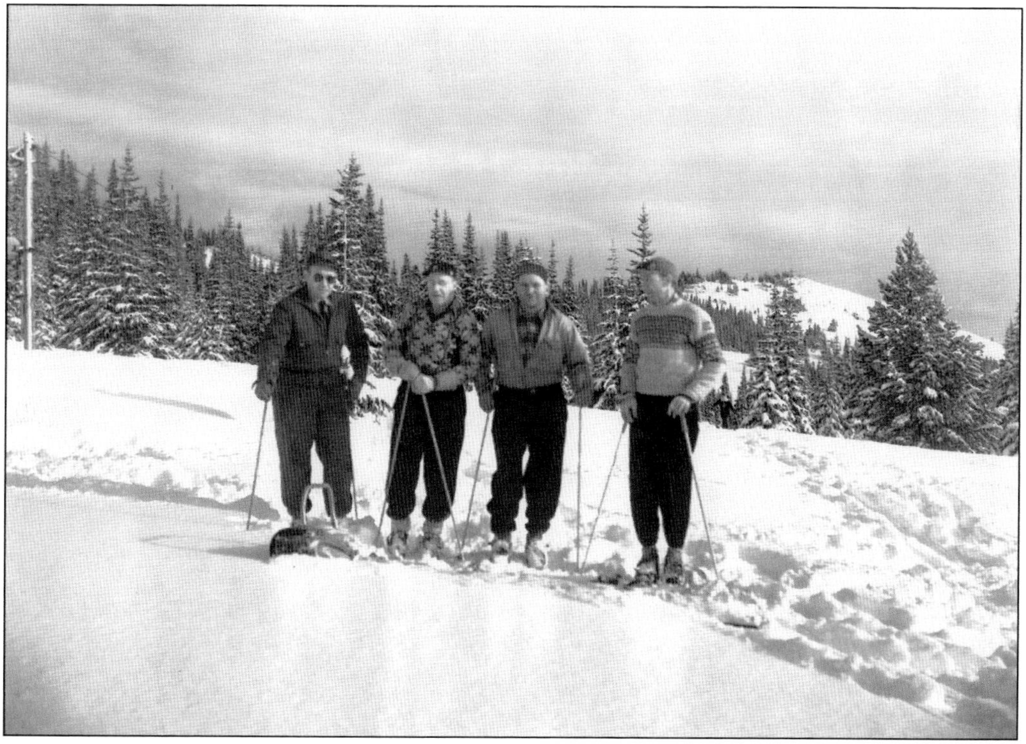

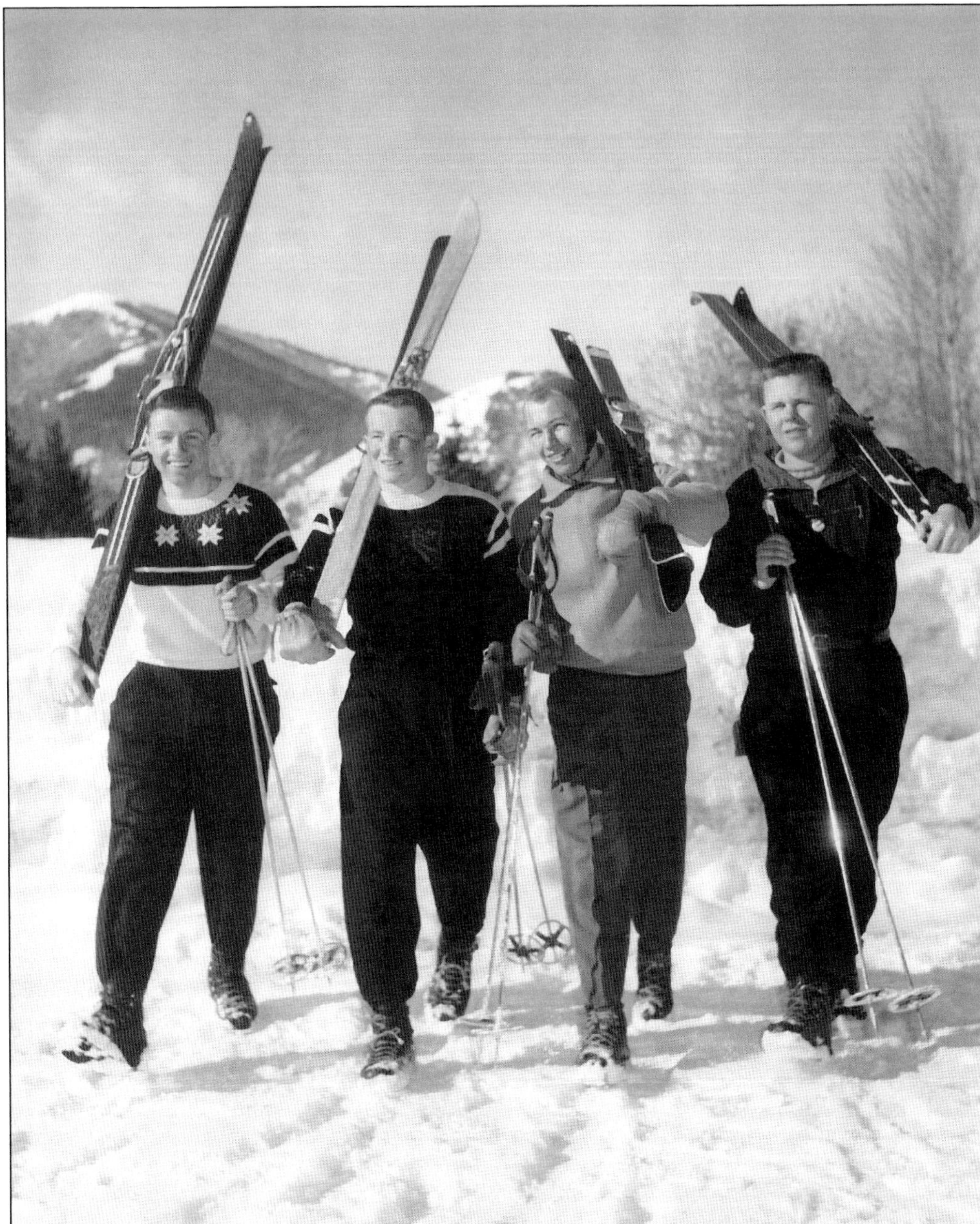

Four Deer Park skiers enjoy a vacation to Sun Valley, Idaho, in 1955. From left to right, Colin Saari, Anthony "Butch" Hoare, and Fritjof Klepper are high school students, and Don Johnson is the young adult who provided transportation. Klepper was the first exchange student from Rosenheim, Germany, to study in Port Angeles. (Courtesy of Don Johnson.)

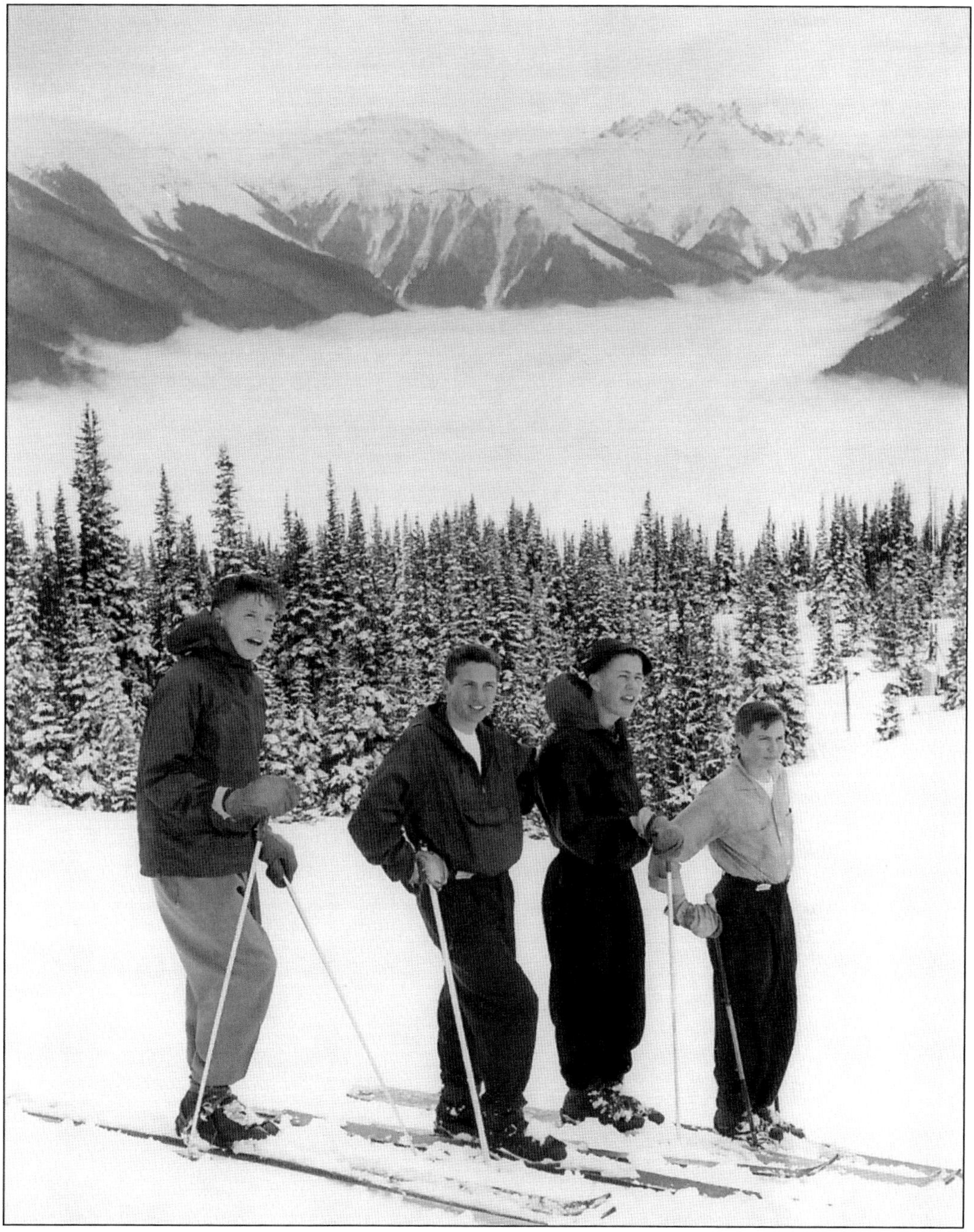

Port Angeles High School students, from left to right, Loren Stevens, Ed Jarvis, Noel Fagerlund, and Jerry Carr visit Deer Park in 1958. Students often worked on the road, in the lodge, or served on the ski patrol to pay for lift tickets and equipment. Jerry Fagerlund recalls bussing tables and washing dishes at the lodge in exchange for room and board and working on the ski patrol, which helped defray the cost of lift tickets. (Courtesy of Jerry Fagerlund.)

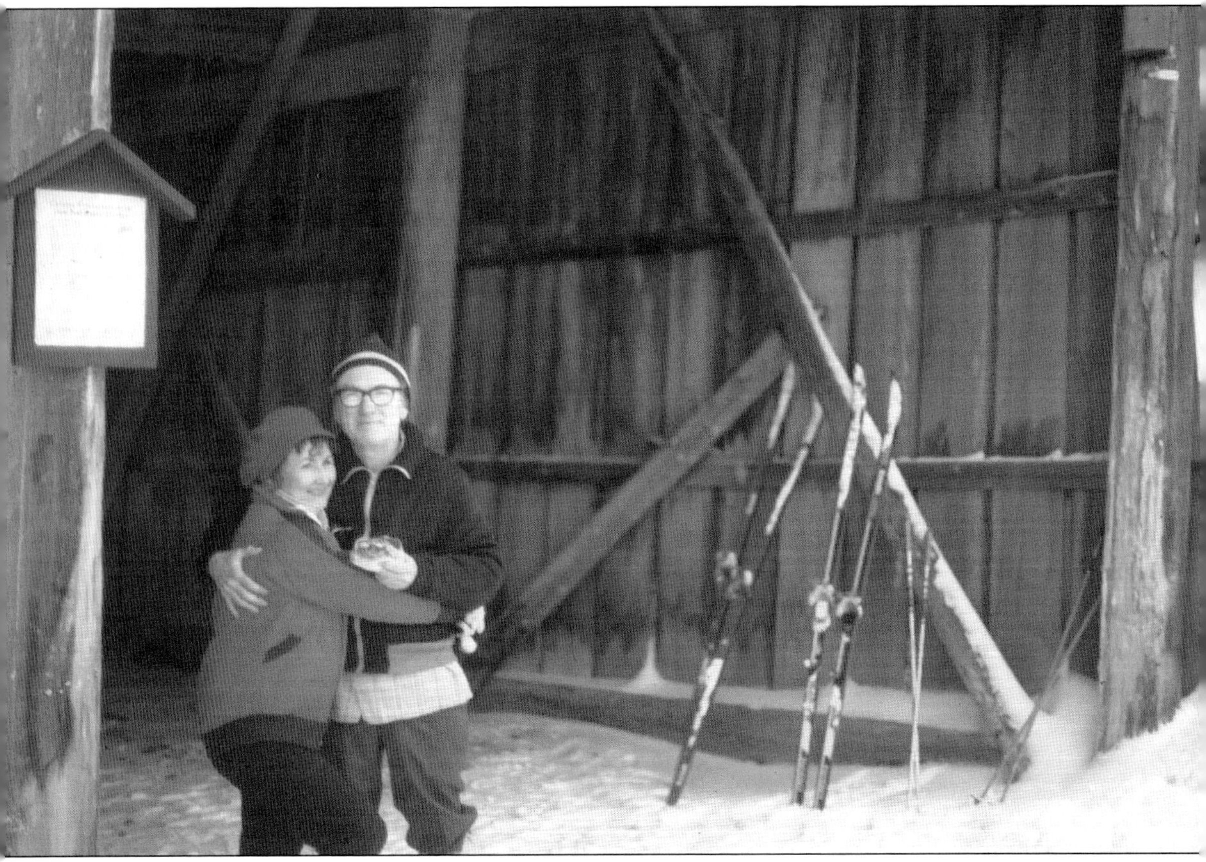

Years after the Deer Park ski area was closed, cross-country skiers could ski up the road, which was free of cars, and enjoy the meadows in relative solitude. Overnight camping, igloos, and moonlight skiing were enjoyed by the hardy few. Here, Joan and Bob Allman take a break in the equipment shed, which has since been razed. The Allmans became very active in supporting the new Hurricane Ridge ski area. (Photograph by the author.)

Four

Hurricane Ridge 1957–Present

In many ways, Hurricane Ridge was not the ideal choice for a new ski area in Olympic National Park. It was south facing and exposed to heavy weather patterns, as its name suggests. The old US Forest Service road up from the Elwha was tortuous and narrow.

The new road, most identified with the expansive mood of the Mission 66 era and influence of Sen. Henry Jackson, required construction of three tunnels and crossed 10 avalanche chutes.

There had long been an interest in developing a ski area farther west in the upper Soleduck (now Sol Duc) Park and Seven Lakes basin areas. The snowfall was heavier and stayed much longer on the north-facing slopes. A road up the valley already existed and could be advanced to the base of the basin without too much challenge. Interest in this area dates back to the early 1940s and continued into the mid-1950s. Forces opposing development in these pristine basins prevailed, and skiers were forced to look elsewhere.

Thus, Hurricane Ridge won out and became the new ski area in Olympic National Park. Larry and Tom Winters moved their lift operation from Deer Park to Hurricane Ridge once the new road was completed in 1957. They went about installing their Deer Park engines and rope tows in the area called the Big Meadow. Interestingly, two of those engines are still in use today.

Left behind were rustic but warm overnight accommodations and lots of memories. Gained were a better road, a newly constructed day lodge, heavier snowfall, more challenging slopes, and, eventually, a better ski lift.

Today, the Hurricane Ridge ski area remains a small, intimate facility, offering a family-oriented atmosphere, a ski and snowboard school, and a racing team. It is supported by an educational foundation that promotes winter recreation for the area's youth. Good winter access to the park's high country has also provided opportunity for sightseers, cross-country skiers, and snowshoers, as well as the expanding interest in backcountry skiing and snowboarding.

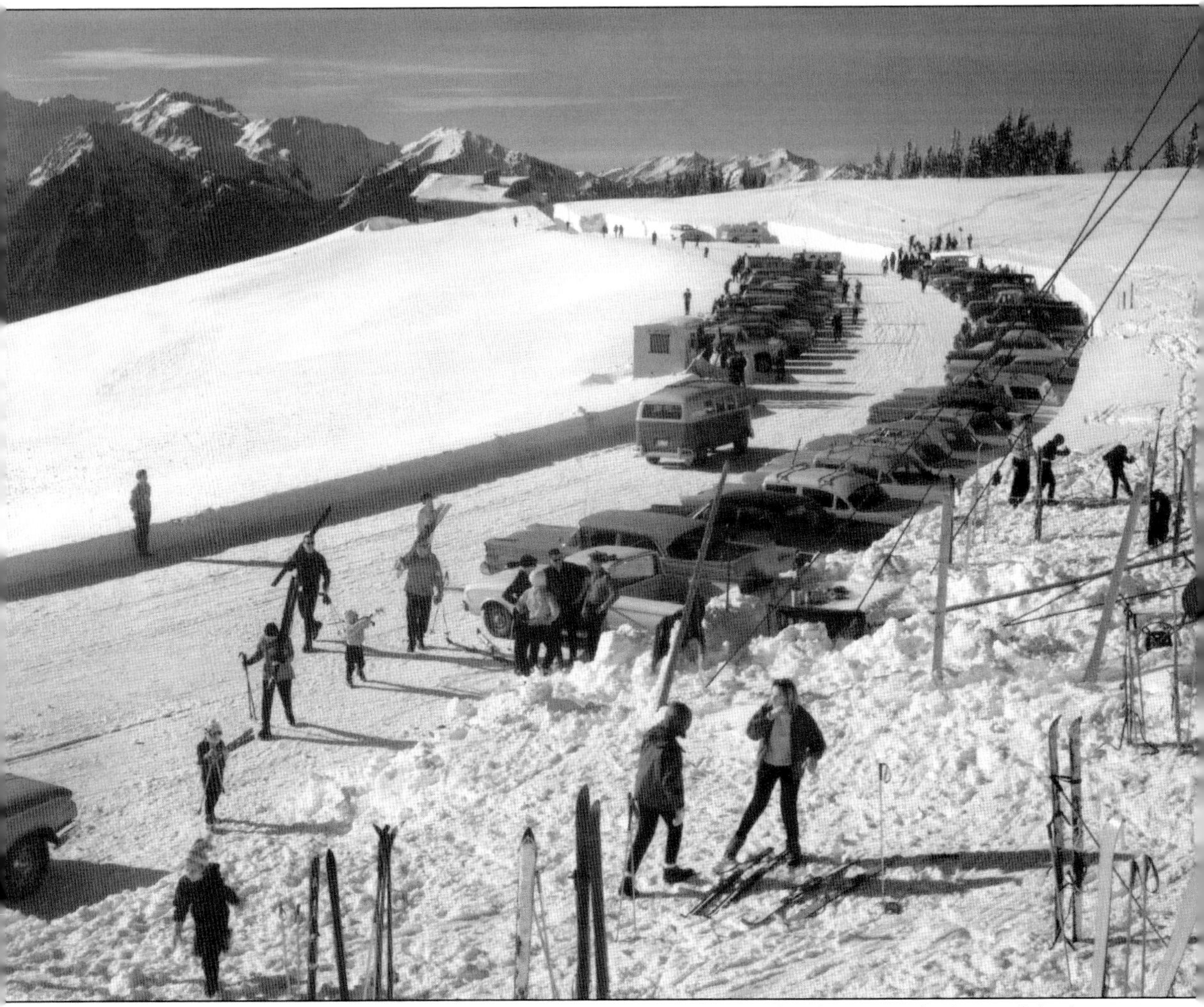

This typical 1950s scene gives an overview of the Hurricane Ridge ski area. The base of the bunny hill is in the foreground. The area looks much the same today. When Larry and Tom Winters moved their two tows over from Deer Park in the winter of 1957–1958, they set up a tow on the small slope in the foreground. It remains the beginner hill for the Hurricane Ridge Ski School. (Courtesy of ONP.)

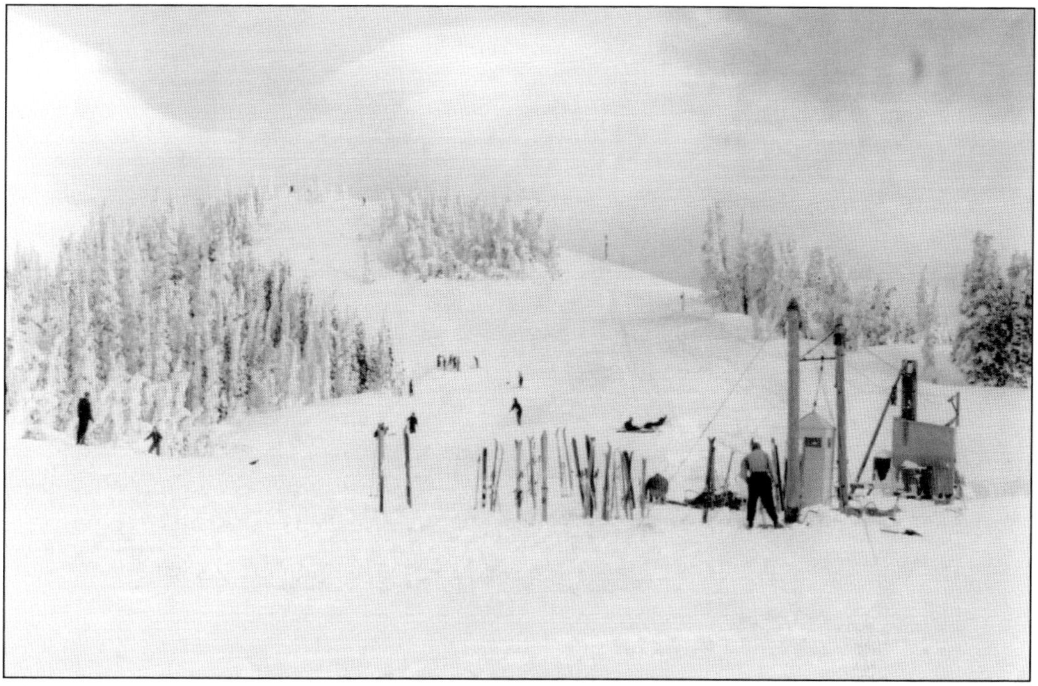

This is the intermediate rope tow as it was first aligned in about 1958, running diagonally up to the right side of the hill. Skiers often crossed under the rope on the way down. Later, an uphill track was cut through the trees on the left of the slope. (Courtesy of ONP.)

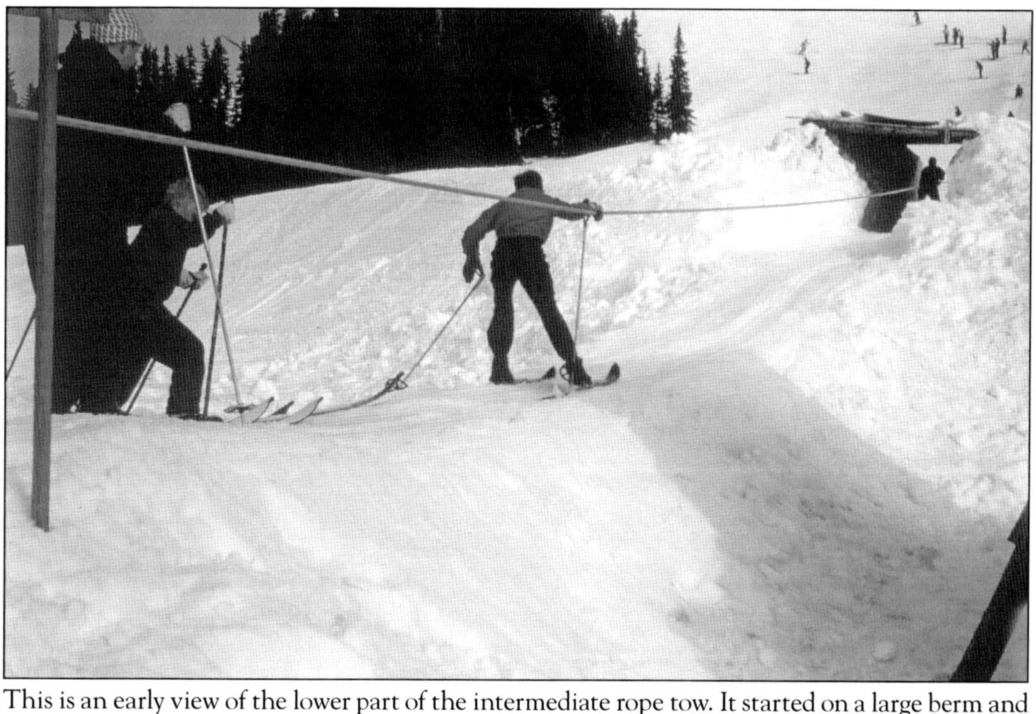

This is an early view of the lower part of the intermediate rope tow. It started on a large berm and ran through a tunnel on its way to the top. A large drift was forming at the base of the rope, so rather than move the rope, the drift was simply cut through. (Courtesy of Rick Yates.)

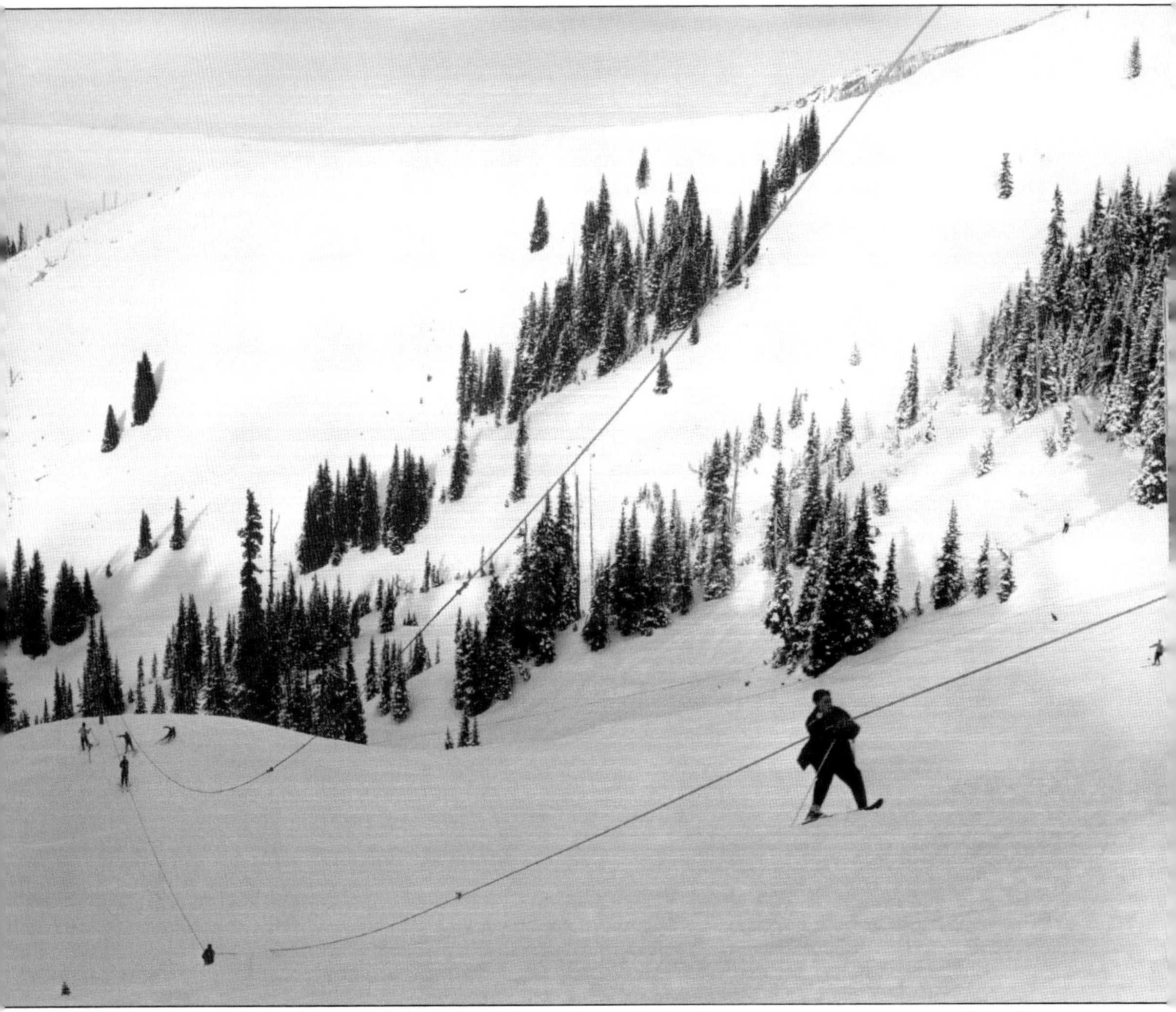

When the Winters moved their lifts from Deer Park, they were anxious to exploit the more protected north side of Hurricane Ridge on the Little River side. They constructed this bowl tow across the ridge from the bunny tow. It was a short, steep lift that was hard to ride, but it offered more terrain and a greater challenge for the better skiers. For a brief period, they ran a lower bowl tow as well. In later years, a Poma surface lift was installed in this area. The slopes in the background are known as "The Face," also called Sunnyside. (Courtesy of ONP.)

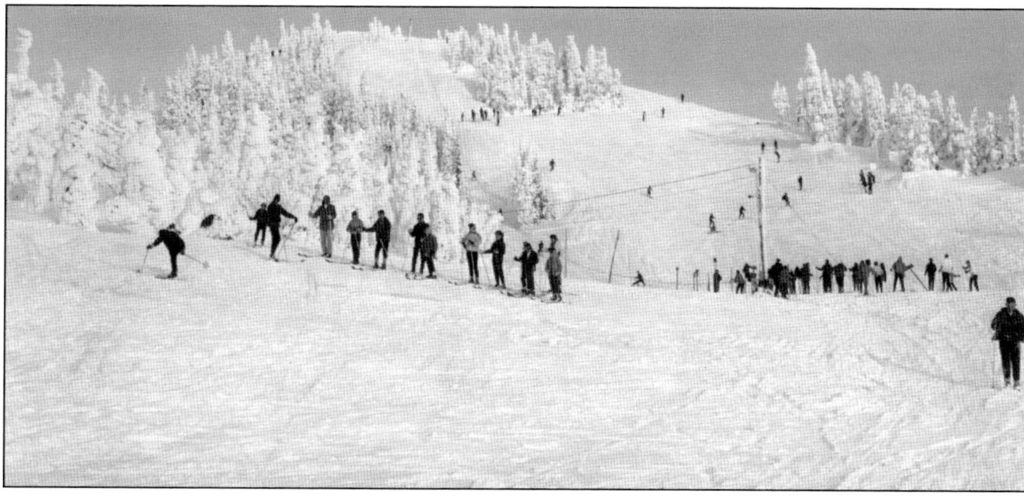

This is a view of the intermediate hill after the lift was moved to the left side of the slope. In the foreground is part of the bunny (or beginner) hill. The top pole of the intermediate rope tow is seen at the crest of the hill. Riding the top part of the lift was a challenge. Many got off below the top patch of trees, as seen in this photograph. (Courtesy of ONP.)

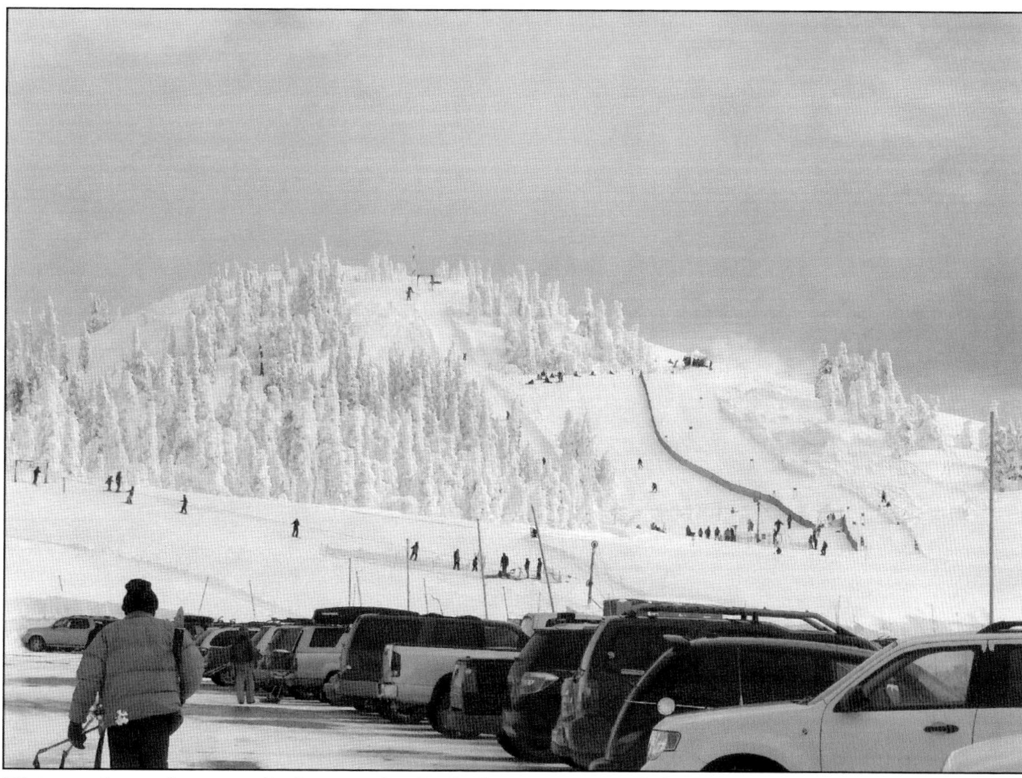

This is a later photograph showing both the bunny tow and the intermediate tow on a race day. One can see the racecourse set up on the upper slope and two portable tents that housed officials and cooking facilities. Carnivals and races are often held in March toward the end of the ski season, when days are longer and ski school is over. (Photograph by Bill Tiderman.)

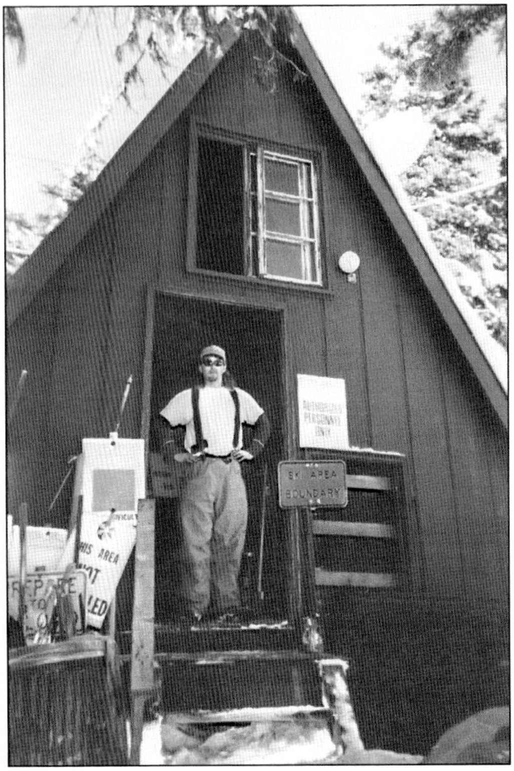

This A-frame structure is the intermediate motor house. It was constructed around 1970 by two local carpenters, Rich and Hughes, using two-inch-by-six-inch car decking. The motor is a 1946 Chrysler Flathead Industrial six-cylinder 298-horsepower gas engine. It has been rebuilt and is still in operation today. When it was moved over from Deer Park in 1957, it was mounted on two skid logs and housed in what amounted to a large plywood box. Its longevity is a credit to tender, loving care by mountain manager Craig Hofer and his crew. (Both, photograph by Craig Hofer.)

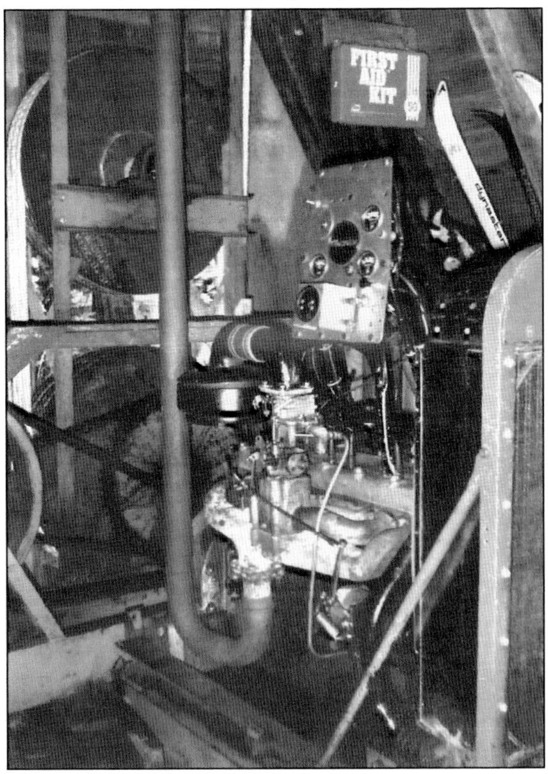

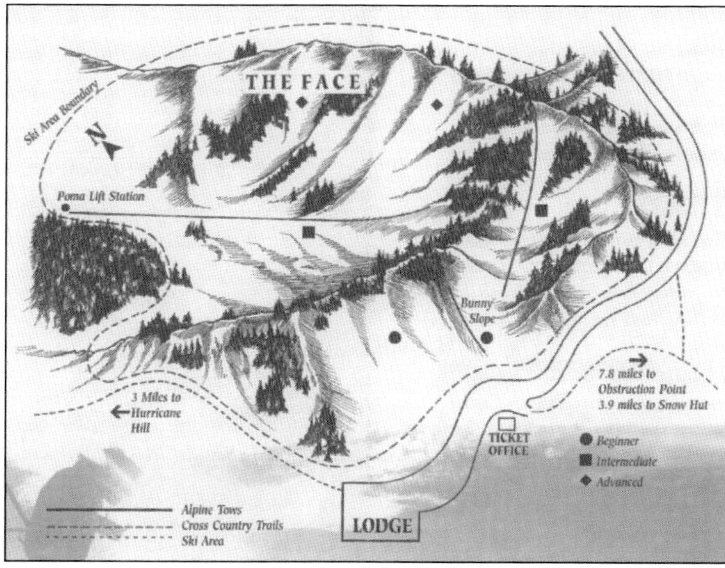

This drawing of the Hurricane Ridge ski area manages to beautifully capture the entire area with its northern and southern slopes. It shows the location of the Poma lift, which was installed in 1971. For a time, there was also a ski lift on the back side of the ridge, labeled here as "The Face." (Drawing by Laurel Black Design, courtesy of Hurricane Ridge Winter Sports Club.)

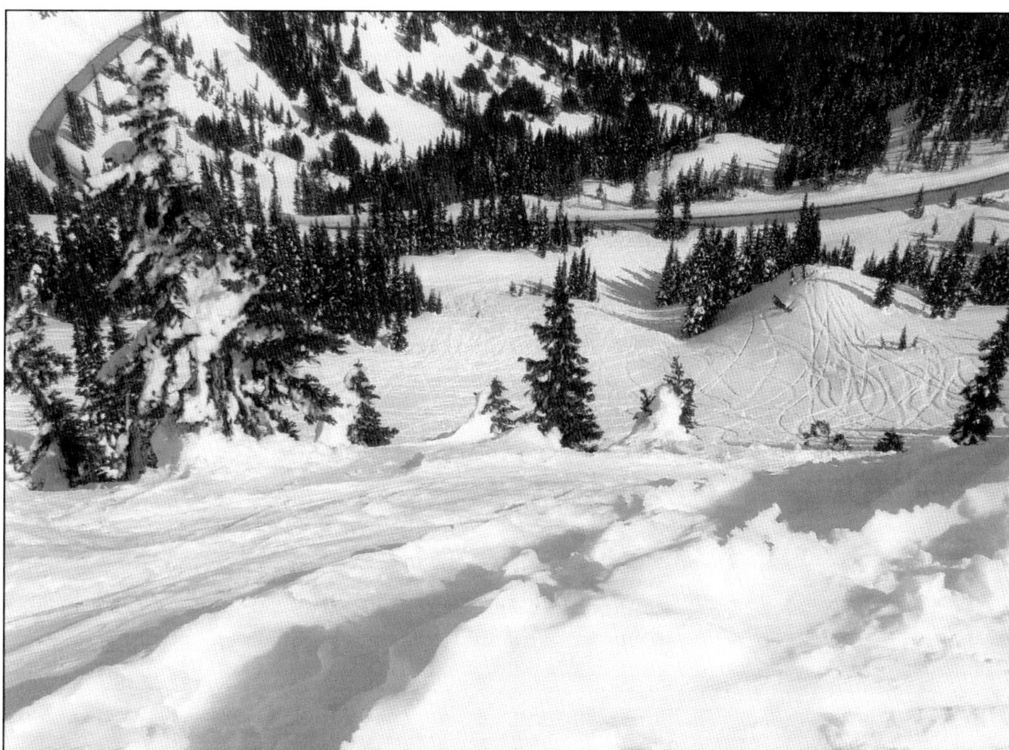

This is called the Sunrise area. It is located over the top of the ridge seen in the sketch at top and directly above the Hurricane Ridge road. In the 1960s, area operators Avon Miller and Ted Simpson briefly had a rope tow on this slope. It ran off of the motor of Miller's 1947 Reo flatbed truck, with gearing housed on the back of the truck. It could get a rider almost to the top of the ridge in 35 seconds. (Photograph by Bill Tiderman.)

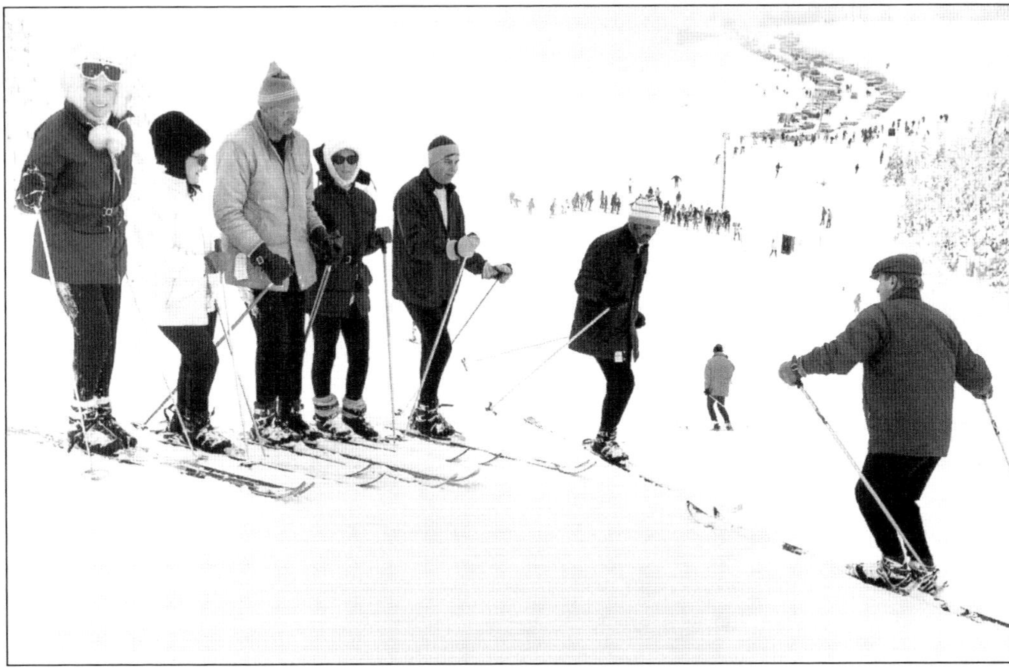

Hurricane Ridge has always had a ski school. In 1958, when the lifts moved over from Deer Park, instructors Henry "Hank" Brown, James Cahill, and Don Bailey came with them. In 1962, Hank took over as director of the ski school and ran it for many years. Above, he instructs a group of eager skiers. Below is a closer view of Brown with his students. From left to right are unidentified, Joan Allman, Rosalee Bingham, and Brown. (Both, courtesy of Carolyn Brown Mackey.)

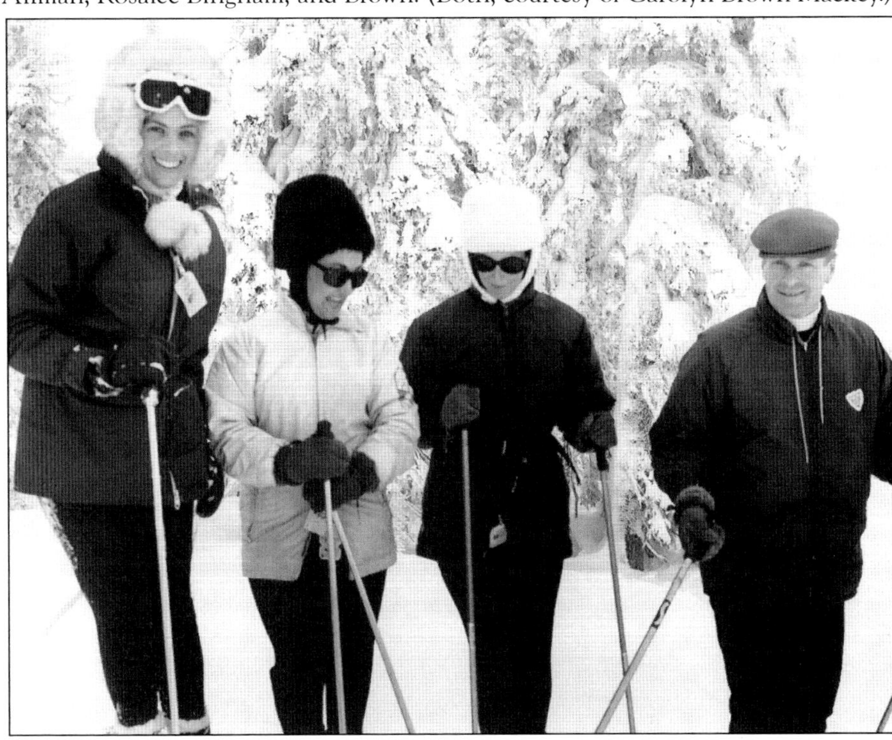

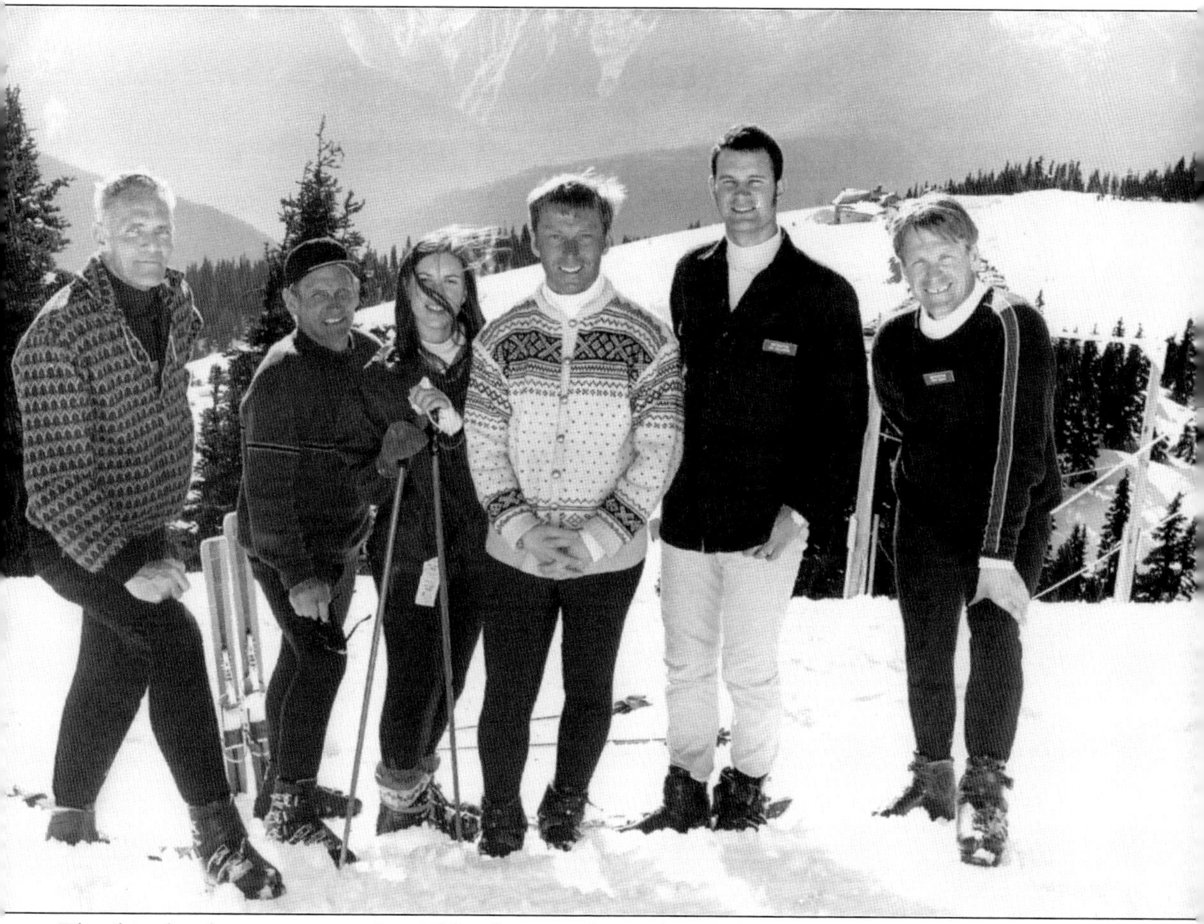

The ski-school instructors in this 1970s photograph are, from left to right, Bob Ross, Don Gerber, Carolyn Brown, Dave Hurd, Lee Callahan, and Hank Brown (director). In the early years at Deer Park and Hurricane Ridge, most skiers were novices. It was a top priority to offer good ski instruction. Local organizations—including the newspaper, radio station, and American Legion—sponsored ski instruction. In later years, the caliber of skiers improved. All instructors became certified, and skiers learning at Hurricane Ridge could ski anywhere. Hank Brown led this effort. Later, the ski school was run by Alexis Sorensen of Sorensen Sports and then the Hurricane Ridge Winter Sports Club. (Courtesy of Carolyn Brown Mackey.)

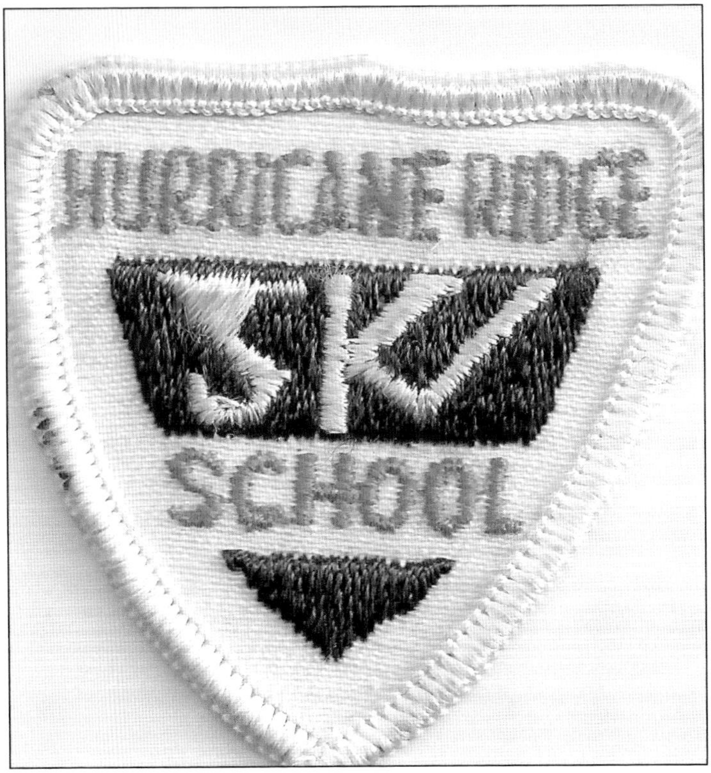

Pictured here is memorabilia from the early days of Hurricane Ridge. The patch was worn by ski-school instructors and available to students as well. The lift tickets have always carried the statement "I have skied in the Olympics" and the phrase "30 minutes Sea Level to Ski Level." (Left, courtesy of Carolyn Brown Mackey; below, courtesy of ONP.)

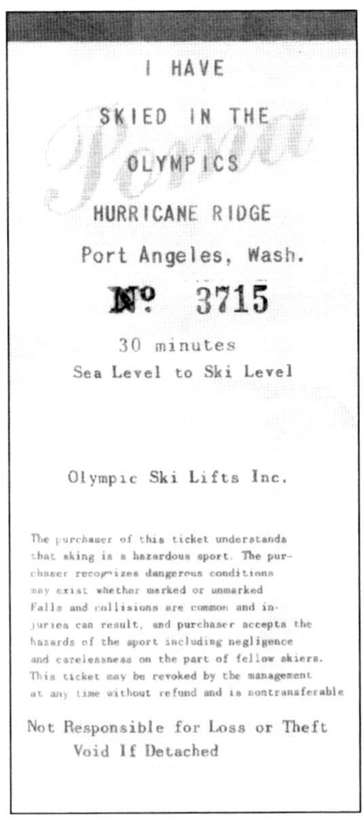

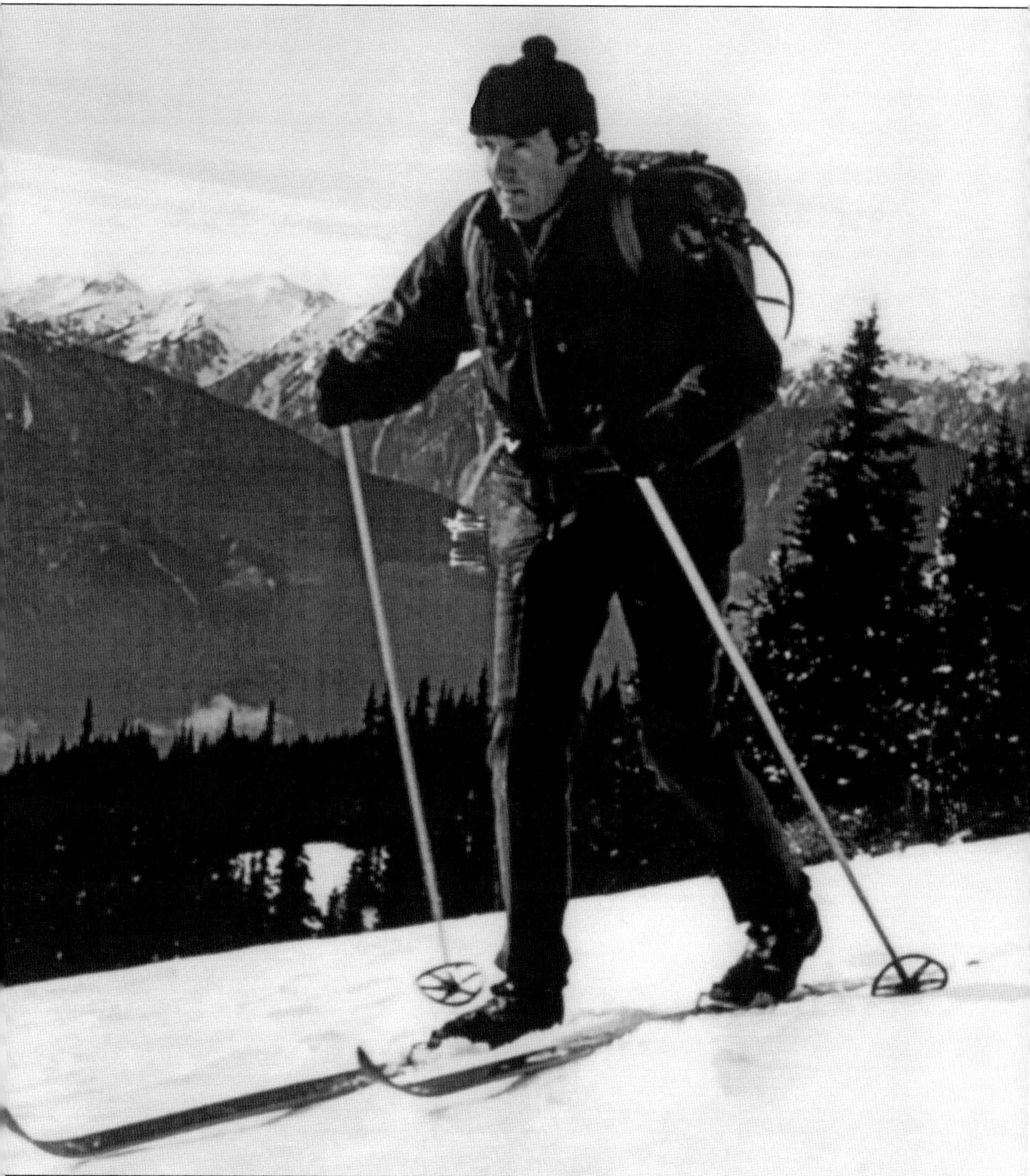

Jack Hughes arrived at Olympic National Park in 1965 and was assigned to Hurricane Ridge. He would spend the next 40-plus years in the Olympics as a skiing ranger and doing search and rescue. He was described by one colleague as "a ranger's ranger" and as "hickory hard" at six feet two and 175 pounds. Even in retirement, he was at times called out to help with search and rescue. He was said to have found more lost hikers during his career than any ranger in the park. He was also a leader in introducing Nordic skiing to the Olympics. (Courtesy of ONP.)

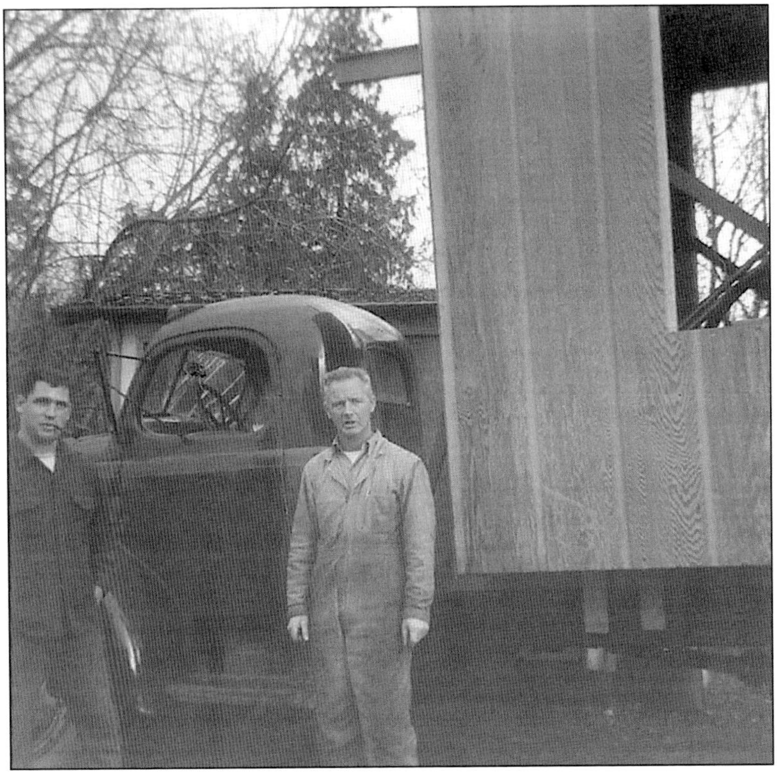

Here, Ted Simpson (left) and Avon Miller stand before Miller's 1947 Reo flatbed truck that served as the engine for the sunrise lift they installed in the 1960s. Simpson and Miller bought the ski-lift operation from Tom and Larry Winters in 1965. Miller offered the first ride on the new lift to Dr. Frank Skerbeck. Once launched on this steep, fast lift, Skerbeck got the ride of his life when Avon advanced the throttle. (Courtesy of Avon Miller.)

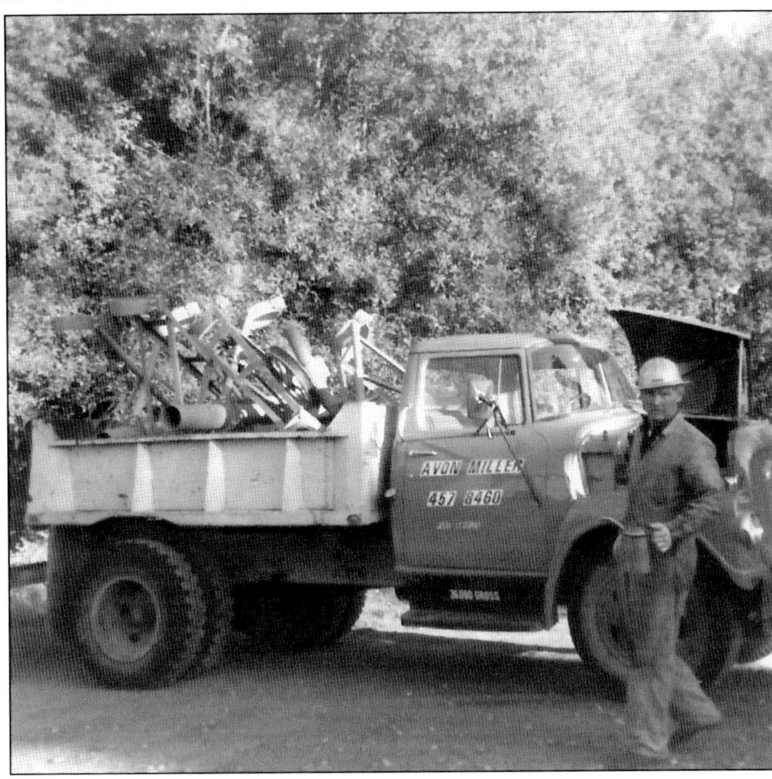

Avon Miller put his trucks to good use. Here, he hauls sheaves for the new Poma lift, which was being installed in 1971. Parts for the lift were hauled to Hurricane Ridge. The towers for the lift were then dragged over the snow and laid in place along the course of the new lift. (Courtesy of Avon Miller.)

Here is another view of the Poma lift being trucked up to Hurricane Ridge. The tower bases for the Poma were welded in Port Angeles by Lincoln Welding. Once they were hauled into place, they were raised by hand using a come-along. When inspection determined that new gussets were required, they were welded into place by Bill Possinger of Lincoln Welding after a welding machine was wrestled down the hill by hand. (Courtesy of Avon Miller.)

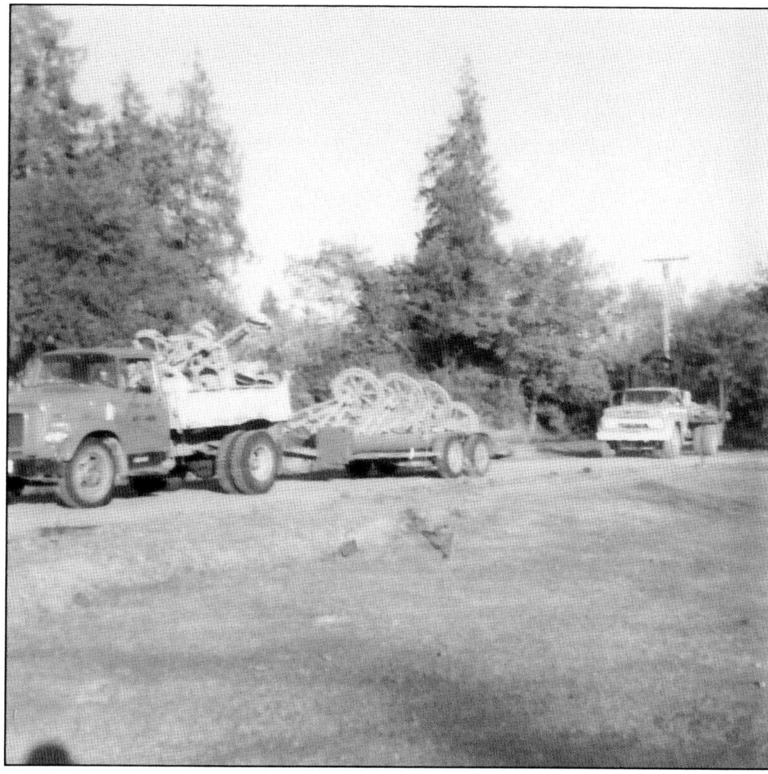

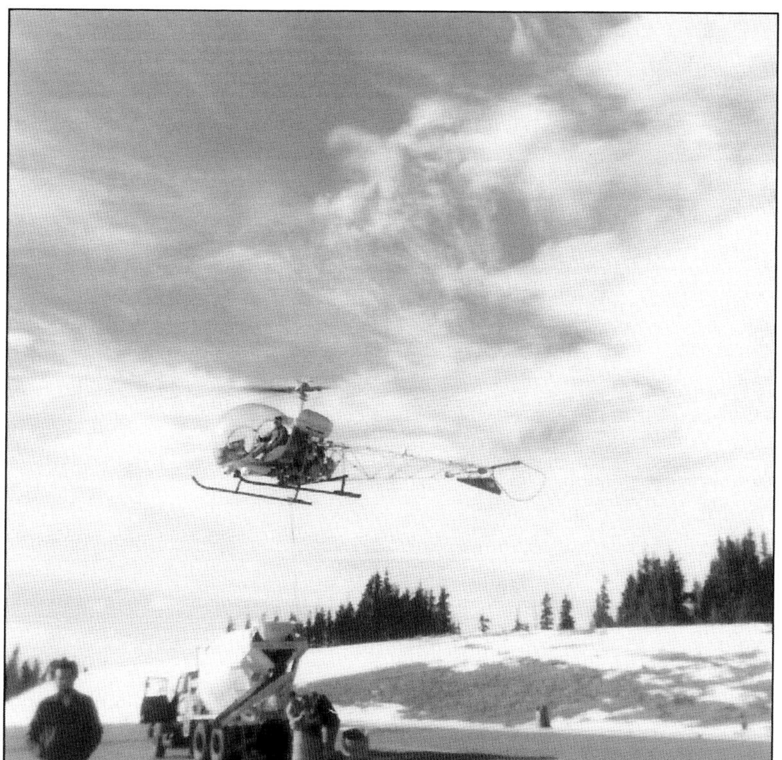

On three occasions, a helicopter was hired to move cement and parts into place. Here, a helicopter picks up cement in a 55-gallon barrel and delivers it to workers pouring the footings for the towers. Glenn Brown was in charge of the installation. Not including the base tower and the bull wheel at the top, 13 towers were installed. Extra towers were needed because of the terrain. (Courtesy of Avon Miller.)

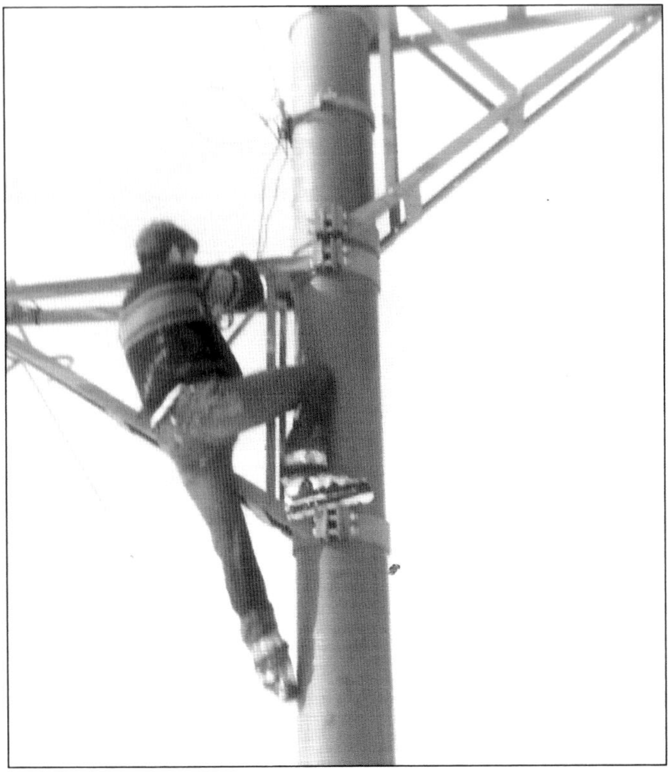

Both of these photographs show workers climbing on the towers, although the lower worker is hard to see. Tim Haley is in the left photograph. The Poma track was up a ravine and was initially pulling skiers off the ground at one point, so the next year an extra tower was installed. The towers had no ladders, so it was challenging to work on the wheels and cable. Skiers are handed a pole with a small basket at the end and must hold on as the pole ascends via a cable running through sheaves. This is the only installed Poma lift that makes a bend on the way up. It is about 1,500 feet long and it rises 400 feet. Glenn Wiggins, an active member of Olympic Ski Lifts, was the first rider. (Both, courtesy of Avon Miller.)

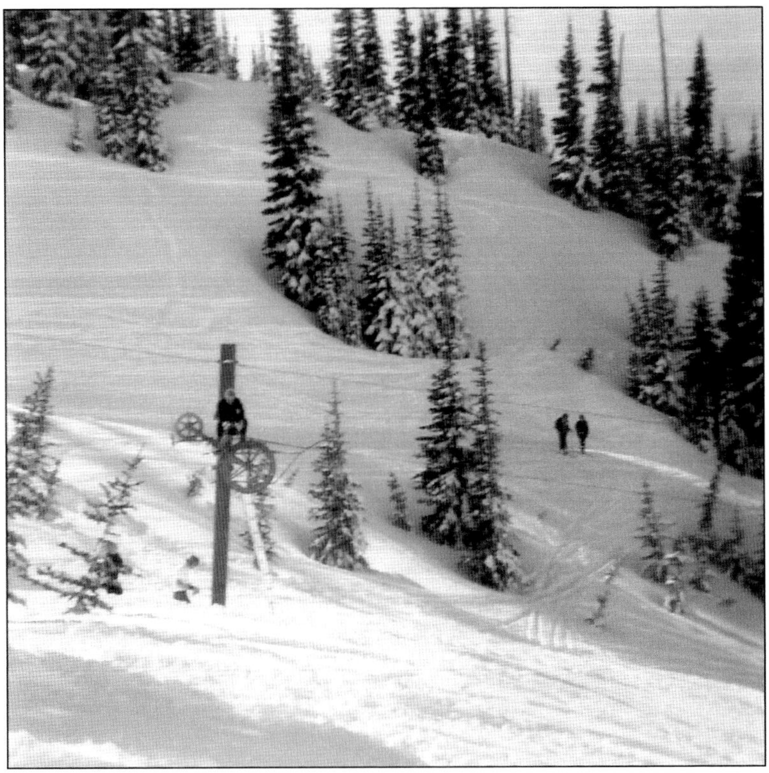

The Poma lift is powered from its lower terminus by a 1954 Chrysler Flathead Industrial motor that was originally used at Deer Park and later ran the lower bowl tow. Rich and Hughes built this Poma motor house around 1970, the same time that they built the intermediate motor house. (Photograph by Dan Hudgings.)

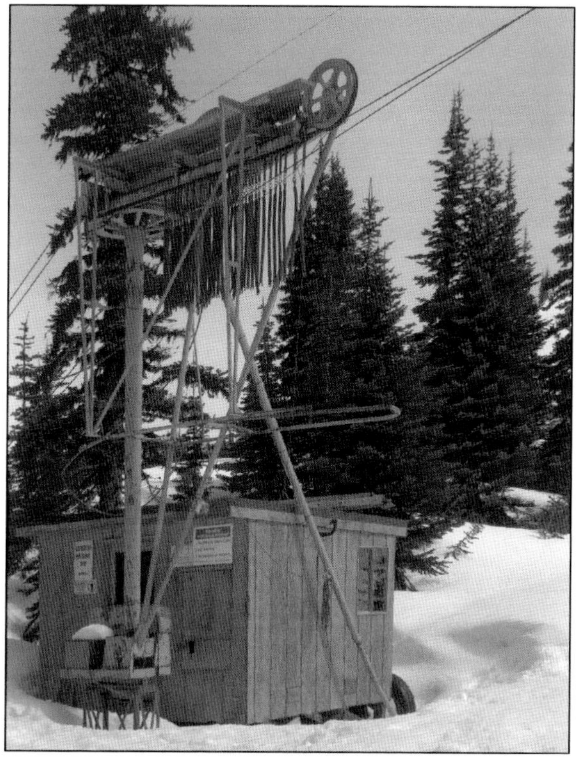

In 1972, Hurricane Ridge got its first snowcat, a 1965 model 1220 Sprite built by Thiokol. The men who operated it said it was a primitive model compared with those used now. Another (used) Thiokol was purchased in 1981, and the current snowcat was purchased in 1998. These machines were necessary to build the Poma track and offered groomed ski runs for the first time. (Courtesy of Carolyn Brown Mackey.)

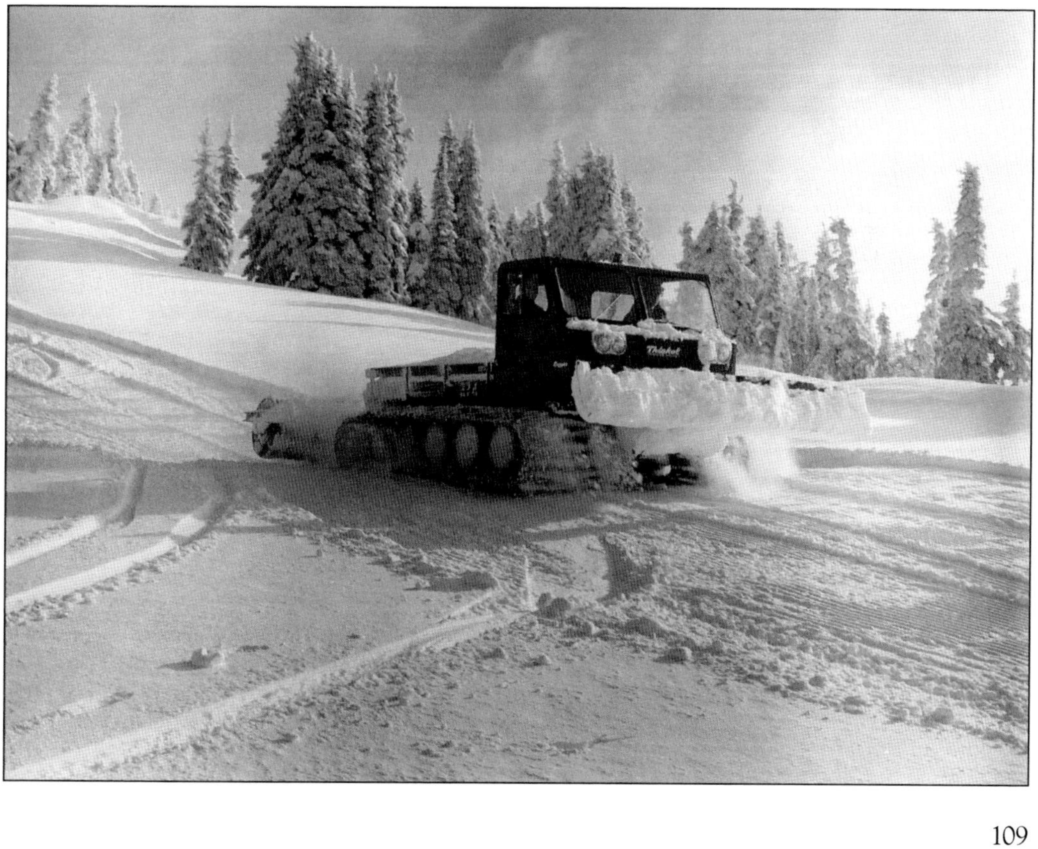

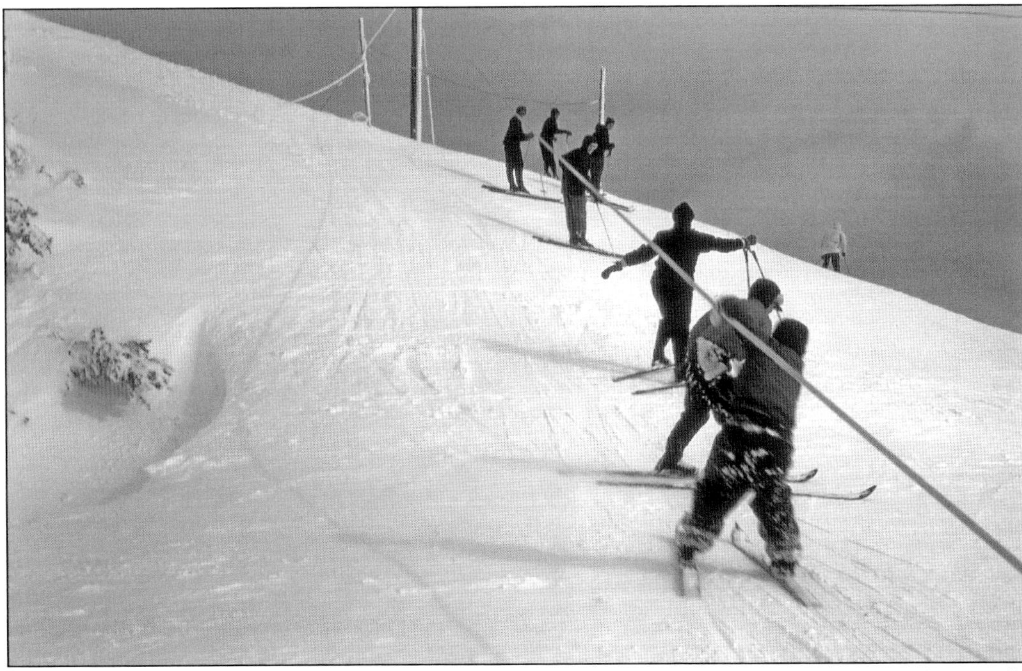

Pictured are two 1950s views of the intermediate rope tow. Early on, the tow ran diagonally across the ski slope and ended on the right side as one looked up the hill. The above photograph shows skiers getting off the tow in that location. Below, the tow has been moved more towards its present location. Eventually, a towline was cut through some trees to form the current route. The rope returns on a different route now through the trees to the left as one looks up the hill. Each year, the rope must be spliced together. A long splice is complicated but eliminates any knot in the rope. Young skiers used to wait for the knot so they could hold on better. (Both, courtesy of Rick Yates.)

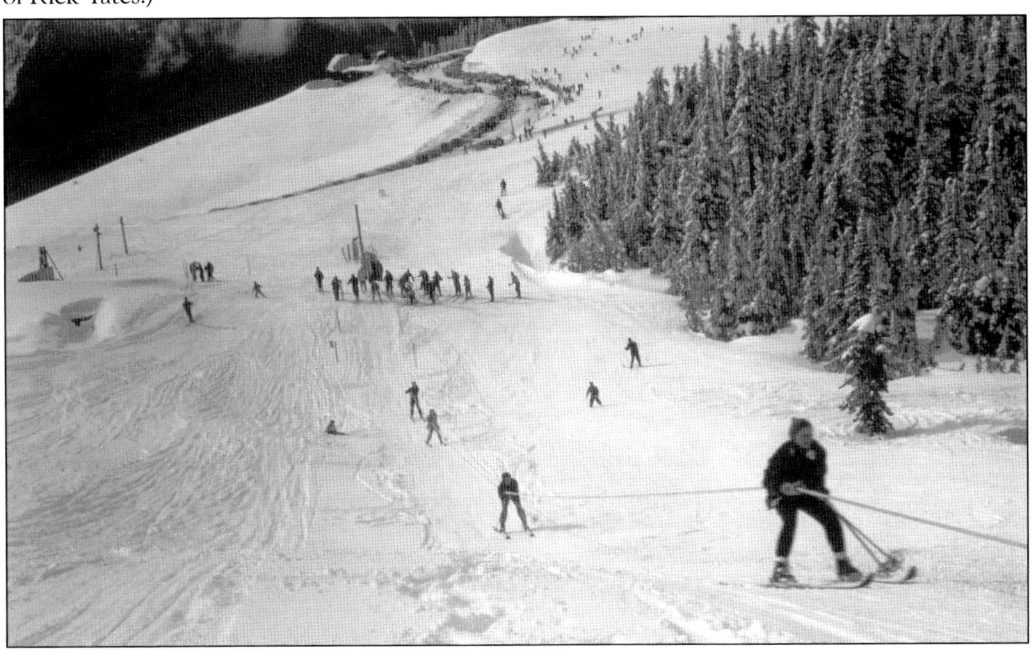

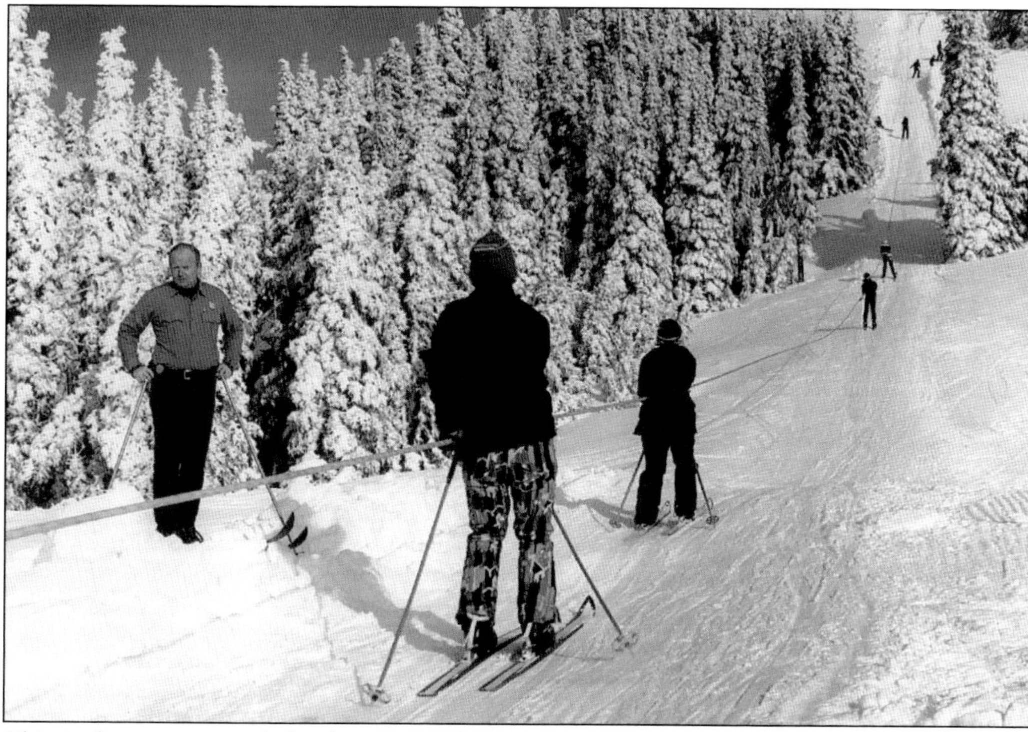

This is the current track for the intermediate rope tow. Skiers are spaced far enough apart to reduce strain on the lift. Upper skiers are getting off at the dogleg, which is the most popular point of egress. Ranger Al Cunningham is keeping a close watch. (Courtesy of ONP.)

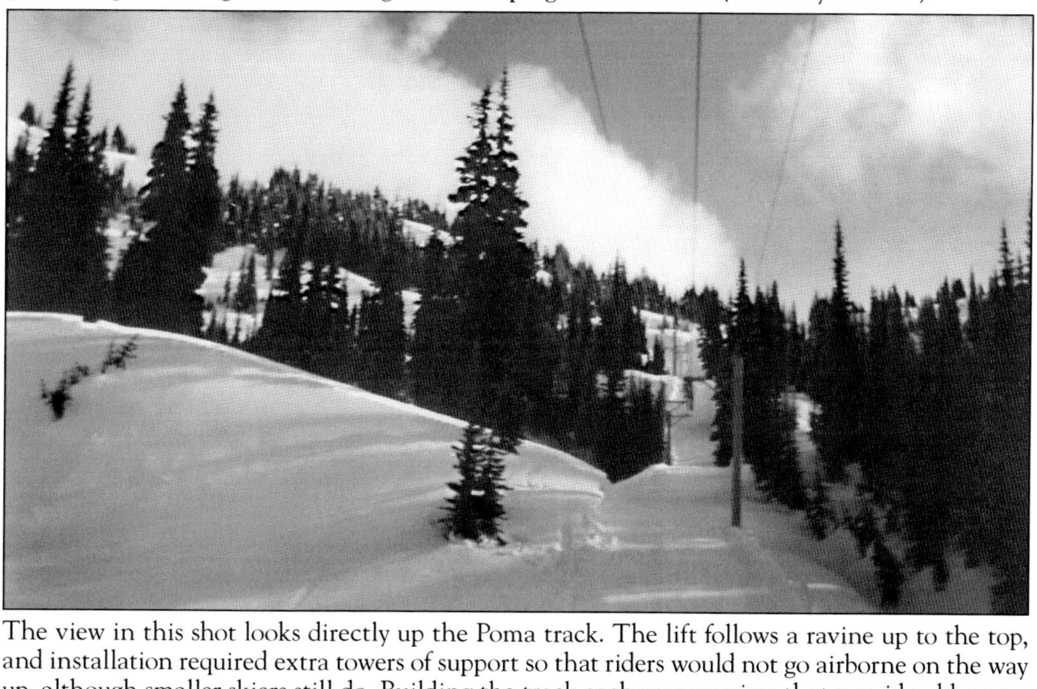

The view in this shot looks directly up the Poma track. The lift follows a ravine up to the top, and installation required extra towers of support so that riders would not go airborne on the way up, although smaller skiers still do. Building the track each year requires that considerable snow be pushed into the ravine, often delaying opening of this lift. (Photograph by Craig Hofer.)

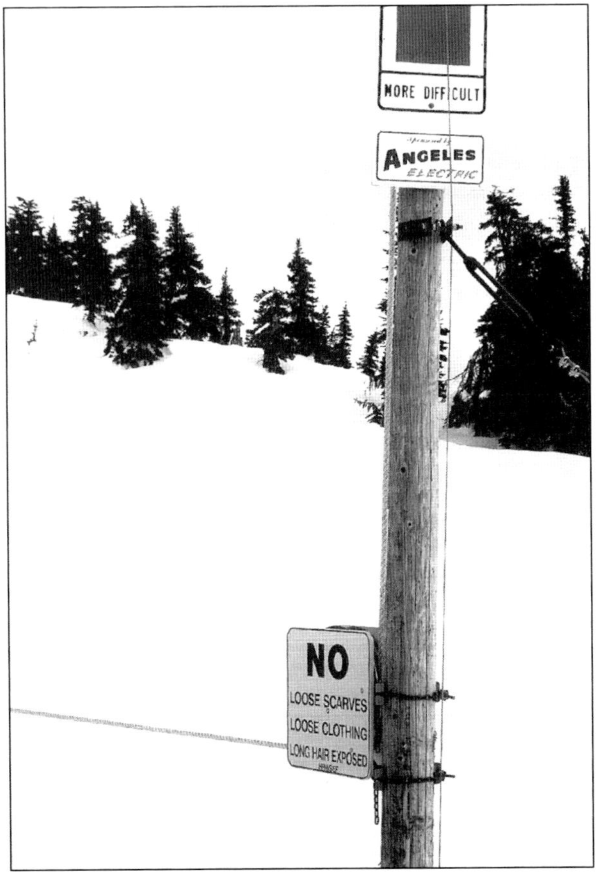

Safety is always stressed when skiing. Left, the base pole of the intermediate lift has a sign showing the degree of difficulty. The sheave for the rope is covered with a board that has a safety warning. Loose scarves and long hair can be hazardous on a rope tow. Area signage has often been provided by ski club supporters, as shown by the Angeles Electric sponsorship sign at left. One could consider the warning signs in the below photograph excessive. Since lines are always short at Hurricane Ridge, there really is not much time to read them. Safety has always been emphasized by all ski areas. Hurricane Ridge has also benefited from an all-volunteer ski patrol that maintains ongoing training both off and on hill. (Both, photograph by the author.)

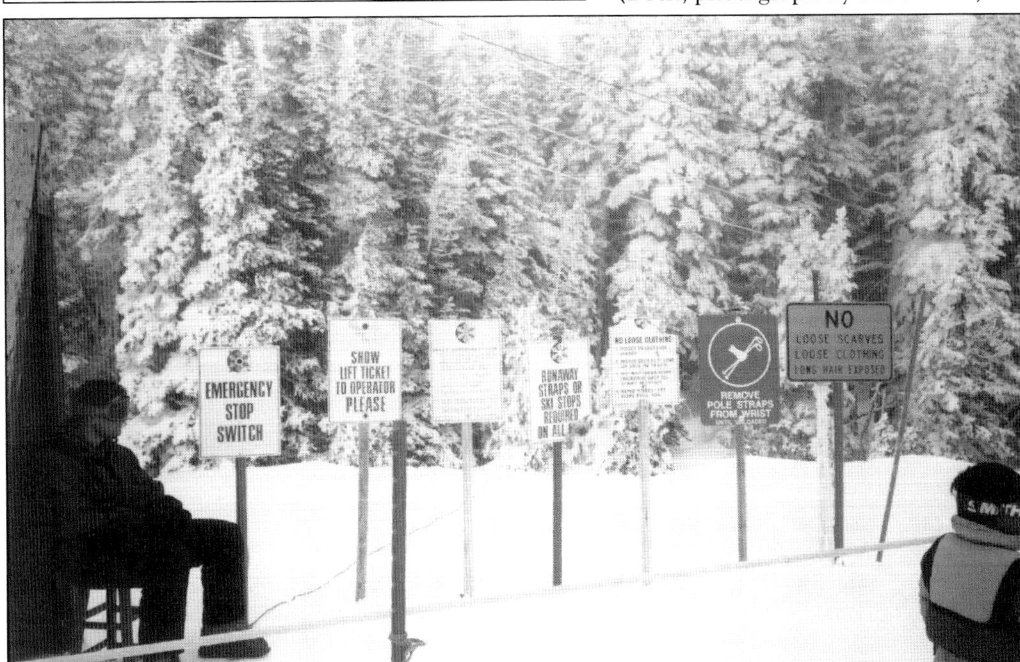

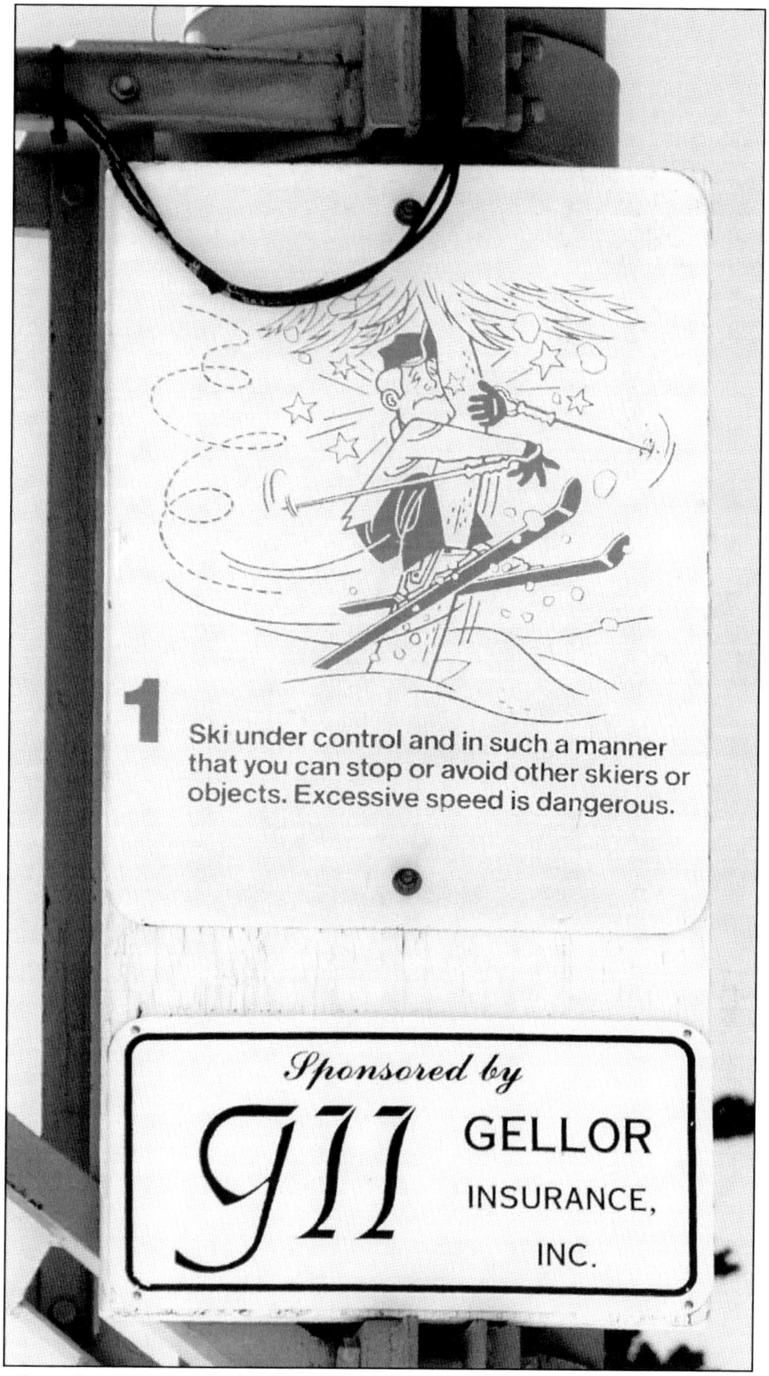

Speaking of safety, ski areas across the country have adopted a standard skier safety code, which is typically outlined numerically on lift towers, as seen here on the Hurricane Ridge Poma lift. Also seen here is rule number one: always ski under control. These Poma signs have been sponsored by local businesses as a fundraiser for the ski club. Concern about commercial advertising in the national park led to sponsor signs, which must always be linked to the safety rules of skiing, only being posted in areas away from the general public. (Photograph by Daniel Hudgings.)

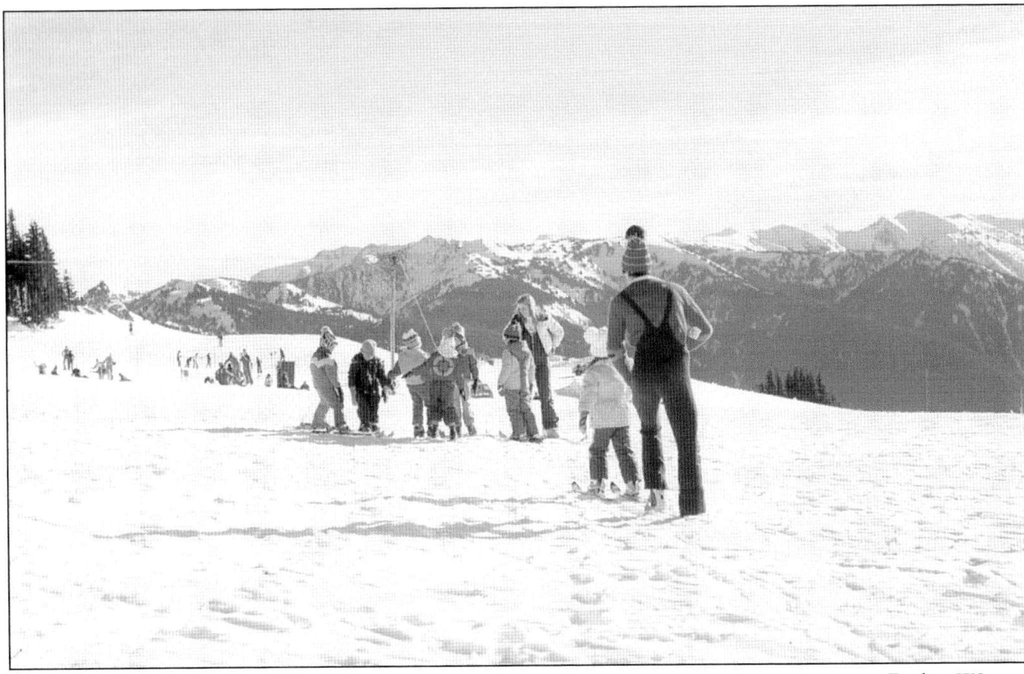

These two photographs show why the volunteers and employees of the Hurricane Ridge Winter Sports Club work so hard to keep this little area open: for all the little ones who learn to ski at the Ridge. Once Hank Brown retired from his duties as ski-school director, Rob and Alexis Sorensen took over the Hurricane Ridge Ski School, which was sponsored by their store, Sorensen Sports. They ran the school from the mid-1970s until just a few years ago, when the Hurricane Ridge Winter Sports Club took over the school. Instruction is now available for both snowboarding and skiing. (Both, courtesy of Rob and Alexis Sorenson and Steve Baxter.)

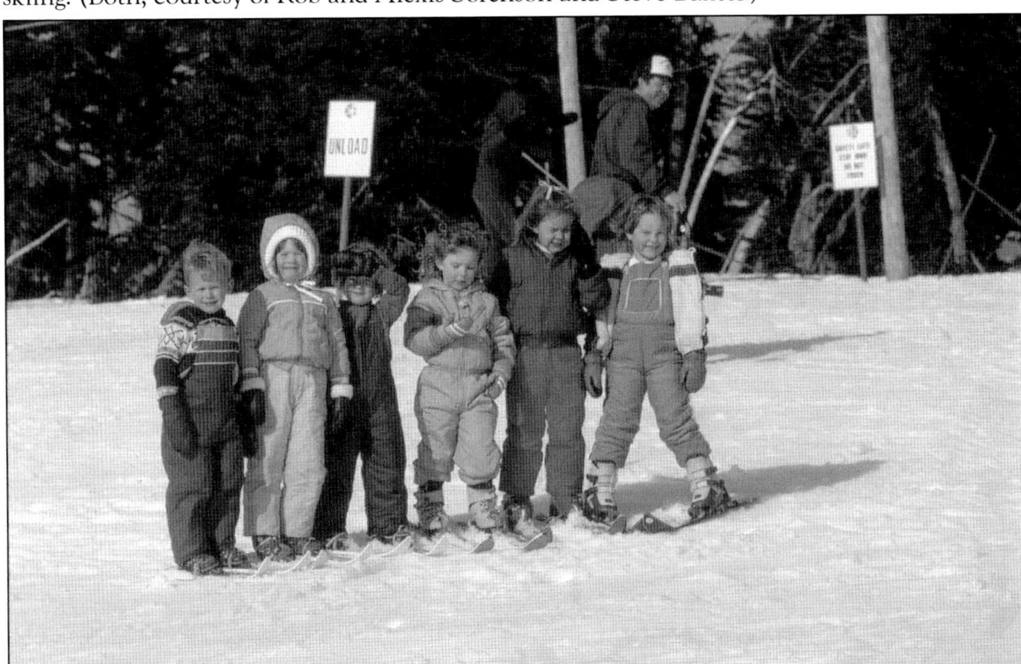

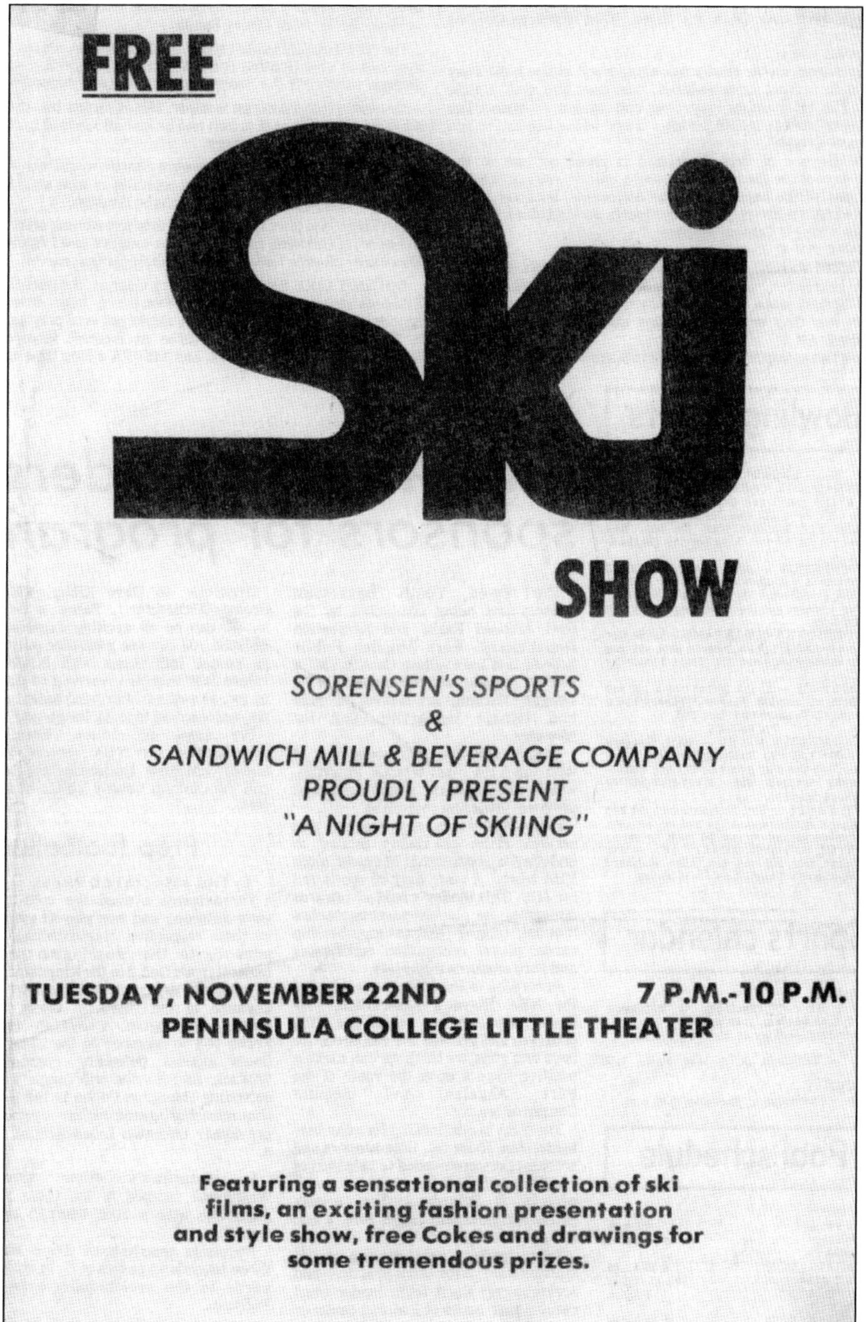

Proving that there is nothing new in this world of small ski areas, fundraisers have been a way of life dating back at least to the 1940s (see page 82). It was no secret that the best way to raise money among the skiing crowd was to have fun. From the vaudeville shows of the 1940s to the "SOS" (Save Our Ski Lifts) dinners of the 1970s to the Sorensen fashion shows of the 1980s, local skiers have had fun while supporting the ski area. Each fall as its major fundraiser, the club currently holds a Winterfest event featuring auctions, dinners, ski movies, and awards. (Courtesy of Rob and Alexis Sorenson and Steve Baxter.)

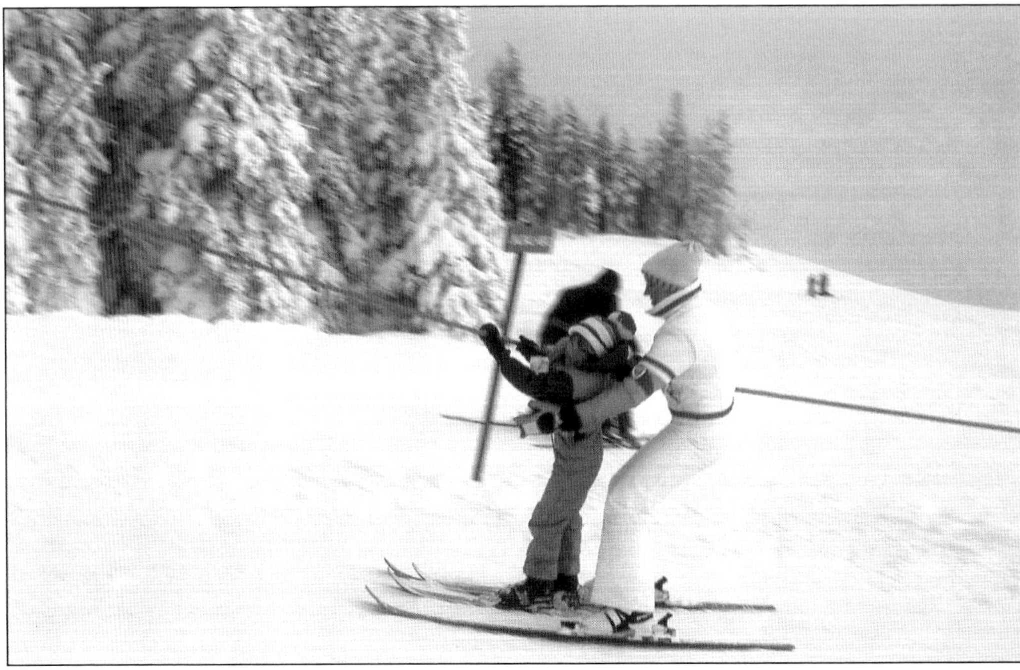

When recalling the era of the Sorensen-sponsored ski school, there are certain iconic visions, such as the above photograph that shows Alexis Sorensen shepherding a young skier up the bunny tow. Alexis's duties as ski-school director included organizing the school, recruiting instructors, certifying them, and doing lots of the on-hill instruction herself. She also organized the special events, particularly the season-ending carnival, which featured an obstacle course, Easter egg hunt, and races. Below, young skiers, from left to right, John Schiefelbein, Evan Oakes, and Stephanie Elmer proudly display their race trophies. Note the leather glove covers needed to ride the rope tows. (Both, courtesy of Rob and Alexis Sorenson and Steve Baxter.)

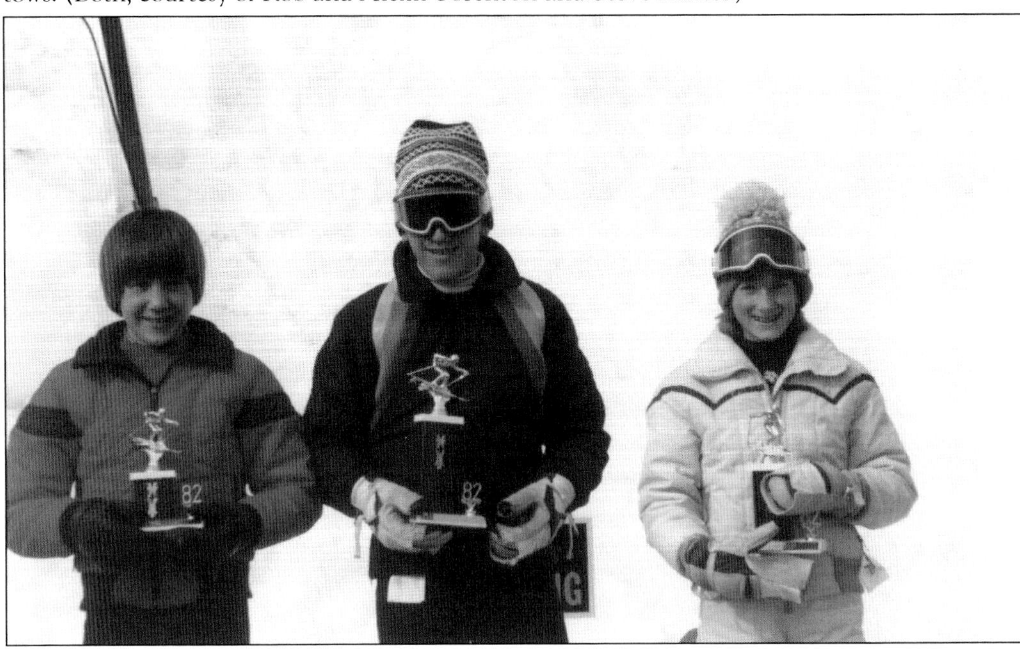

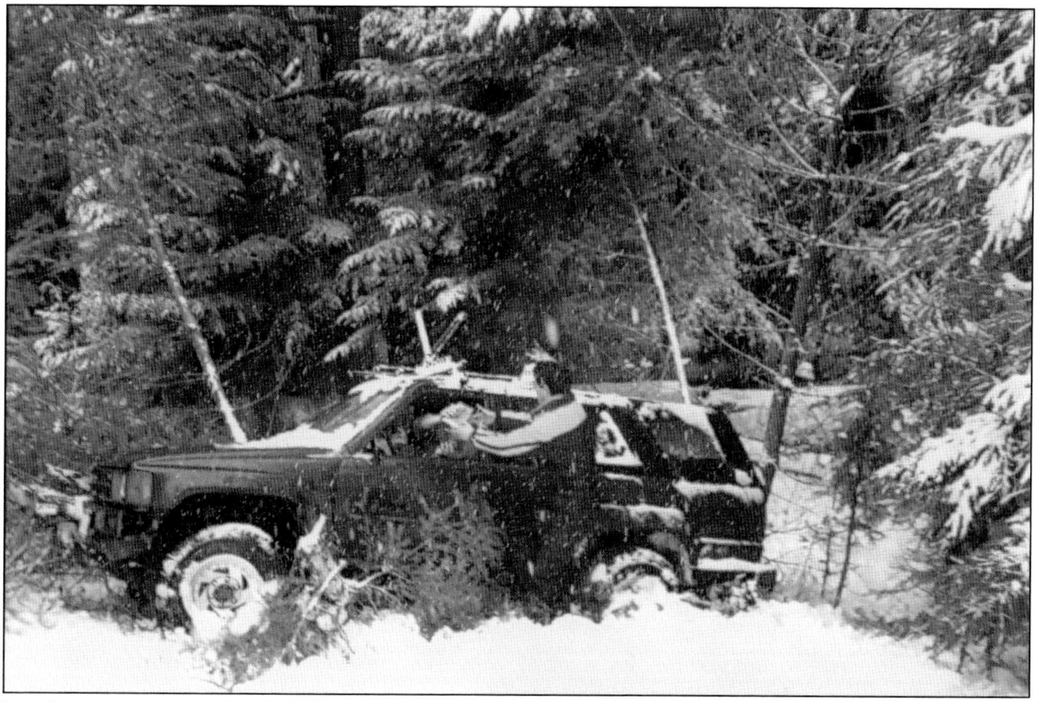

Just because it was March did not mean the snow had stopped falling or that the road was not slippery. Above, Rob Sorensen surveys the damage after his vehicle rolled off the Hurricane Ridge road on the way to the spring carnival in 1990. Fortunately, no one was hurt. The Sorensens were able to retrieve their supplies and proceeded to hold the carnival as planned. Right, they enjoy the end of a carnival day. (Both, courtesy of Rob and Alexis Sorenson and Steve Baxter.)

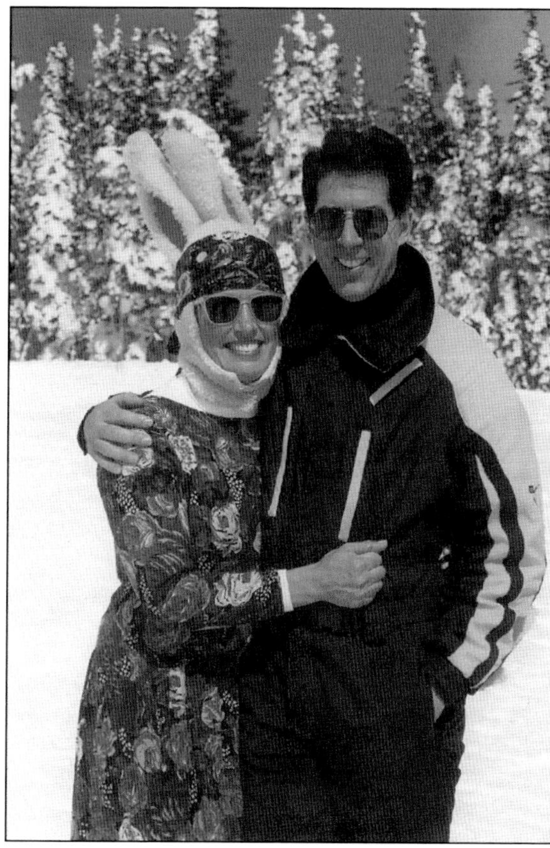

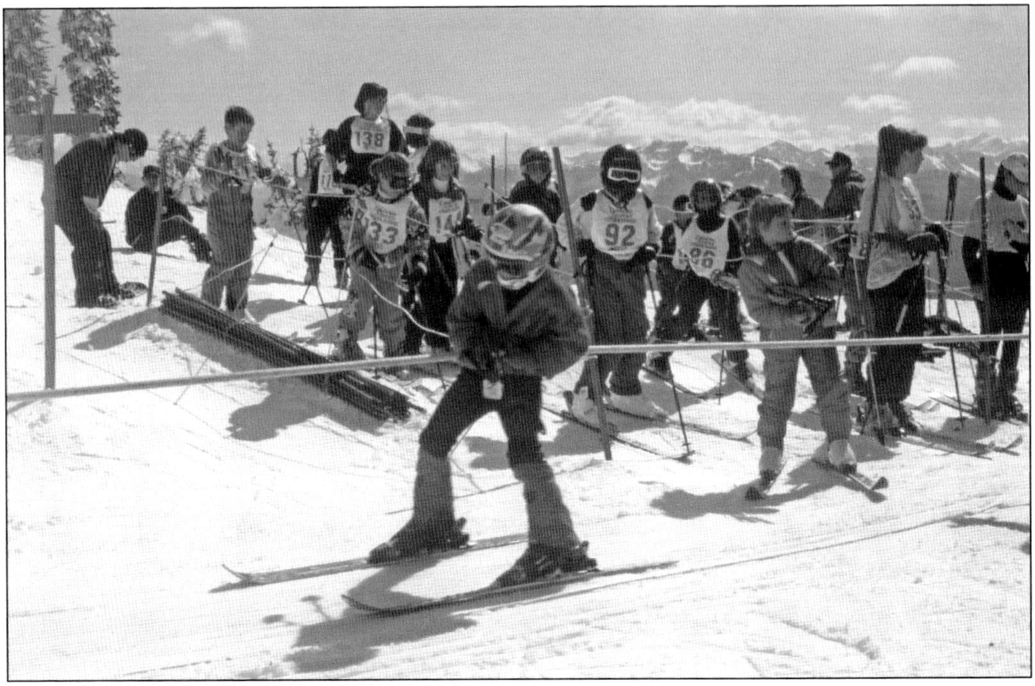

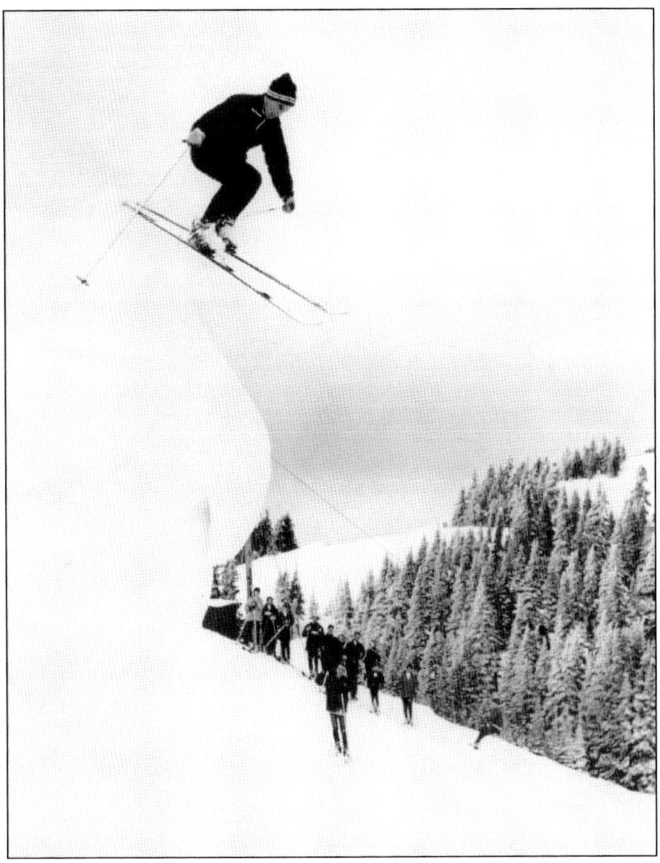

Junior racers wait to ride the rope tow to the top of the intermediate rope tow. A racing team has always been a part of the ski instruction at Hurricane Ridge, and the racing team has been a presence at many western Washington ski areas. The racing team has Don Huson, Curtis Shuck, and John Fox to thank for its leadership and coaching. (Photograph by David Logan.)

Hurricane Ridge has turned out to be a fabulous place to ski. At a mile high, it offers a heavy snowpack and challenging terrain. Kids learn to ski well here and enjoy the challenge of varied terrain. Here, a skier jumps off a cornice of snow that is typical of the snowpack at the ridge. (Photograph by Eric Burr, courtesy of ONP.)

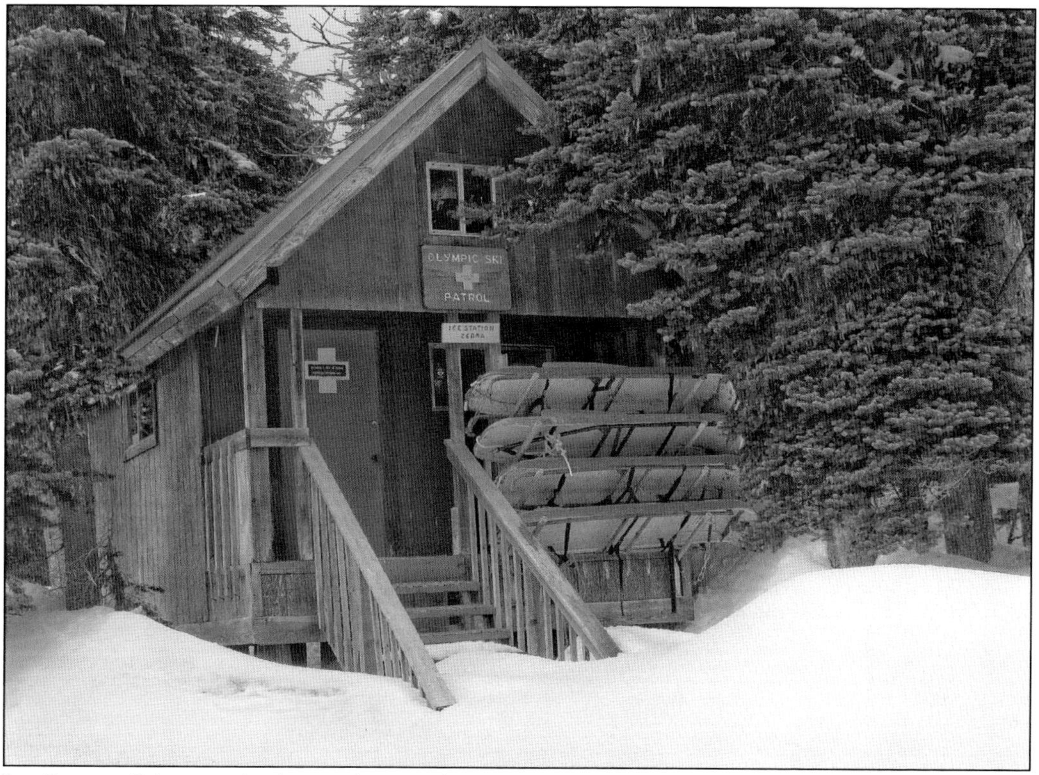

Ice Station Zebra was built as a ski-patrol cabin in the early 1980s. The Hurricane Ridge lodge was being remodeled, and the ski patrol lost its place for rescue work. The National Park Service, therefore, allowed this station to be constructed. Dan Peacock led the ski patrol's team in building the cabin, and Park Service employees were recruited to complete the work before winter set in. Many local organizations contributed materials and labor. The cabin was named after the fictional station in the Arctic-based 1960s novel and movie of the same name. (Photograph by Daniel Hudgings.)

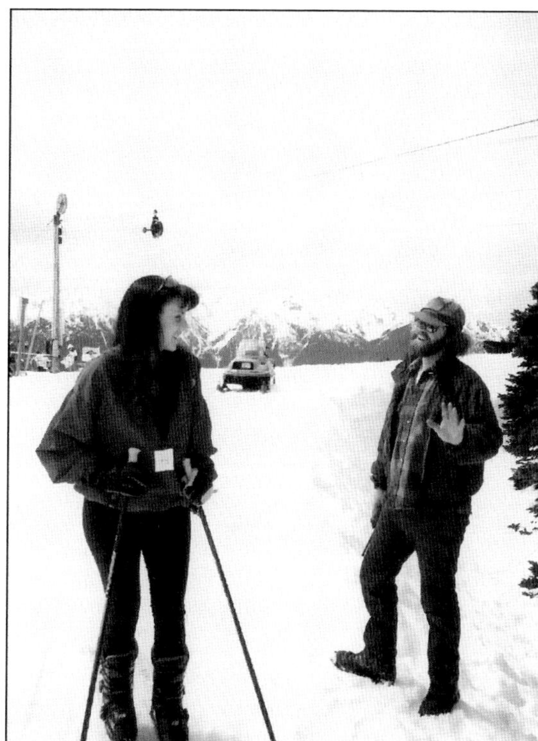

Longtime dedicated mountain worker and snowmobile operator Steve Such greets youthful skier Stephanie Currie as she approaches the intermediate tow. The bunny tow and a snowmobile used in lift operations work are in the background. (Photograph by the author.)

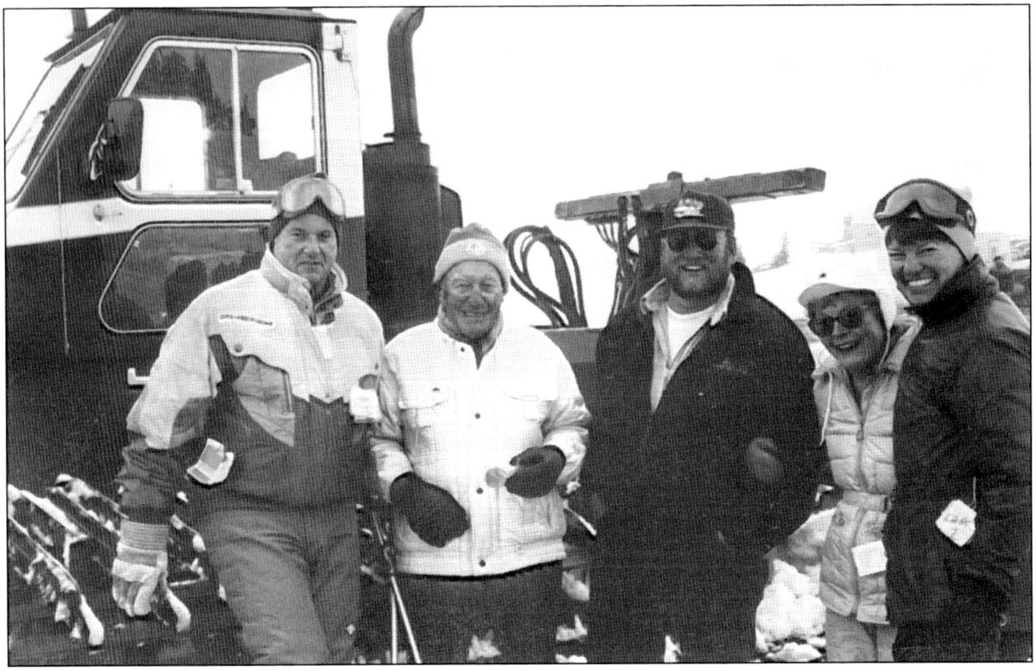

When requests for funding went out for a new snowcat, Fred and Pinkie Stolz offered their assistance. They had been active skiers at Deer Park. Standing before the LMC snowcat donated by the Stolzs (now called the "Stolzmobile") are, from left to right, Bill LaRue, Fred Stolz, Craig Hofer (mountain manager), Pinkie Stolz, and their daughter Shirley Stolz Clark. (Photograph by the author.)

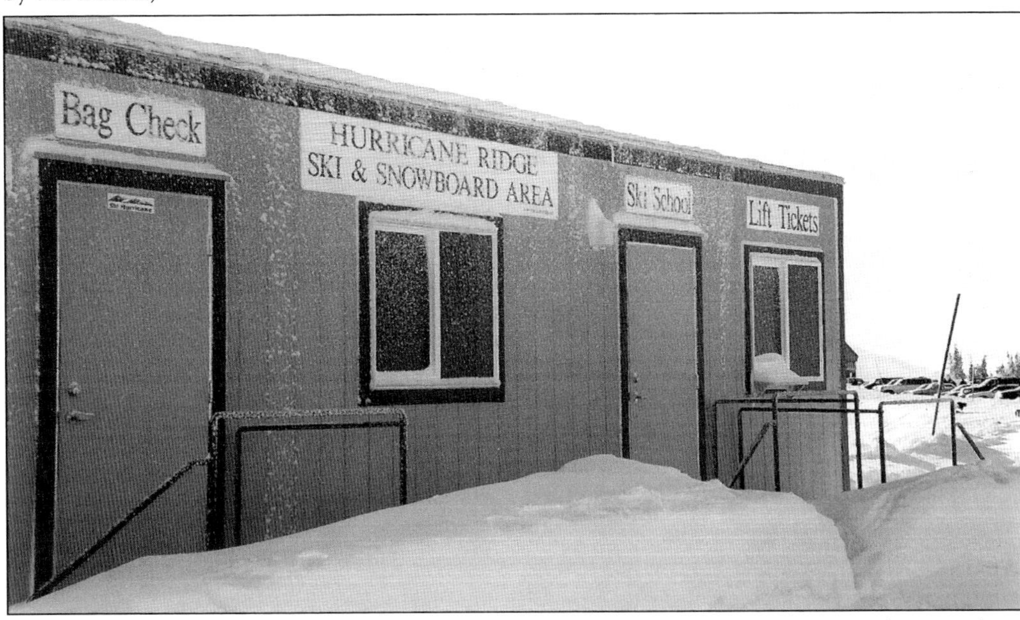

This is the current mountain operations center. Over the years, local skiing enthusiasts have maintained a viable skiing and snowboarding opportunity for the surrounding community. Visitors are now greeted by this more modern structure, which is hauled off the ridge each spring and returned in the late fall. (Photograph by the author.)

This photograph and article appear in the *Peninsula Daily News* of Christmas Day 1988. Craig Hofer became the mountain manager at Hurricane Ridge in 1975 at age 18 and continued in that role for 37 years. He was the heart and soul of the ridge during those years. His sidekick Steve Such was a big part of that success. (Photograph by Rick Ross.)

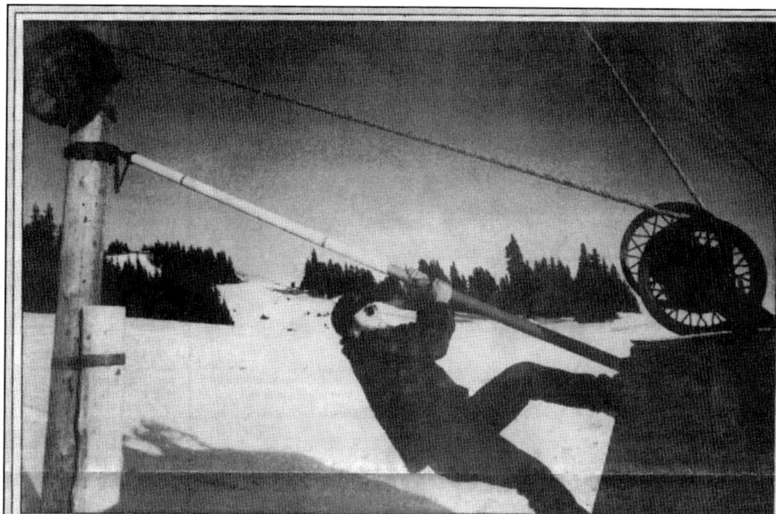

Staff photograph by Rick Ross

Craig Hofer climbs to the roof of the engine shack at the bunny hill.

A man and his MOUNTAIN

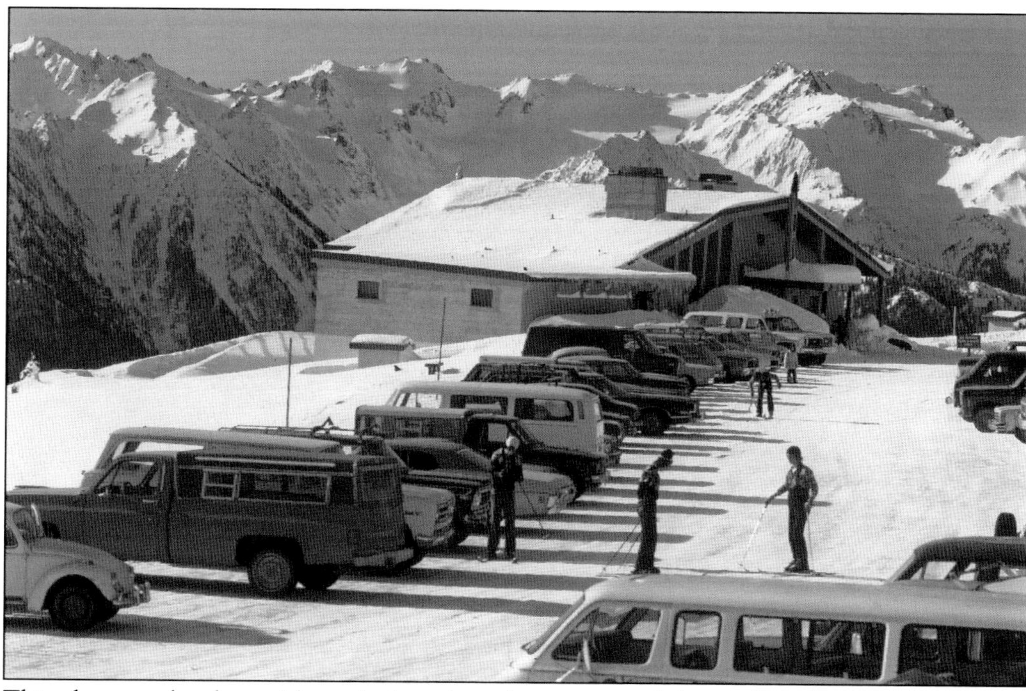

This photograph taken with a telephoto lens shows a typical day at the ridge, with sun, a busy parking lot, the lodge, and the wintery Bailey Range. The view from Hurricane Ridge is worth the price of admission. (Photograph by David Logan.)

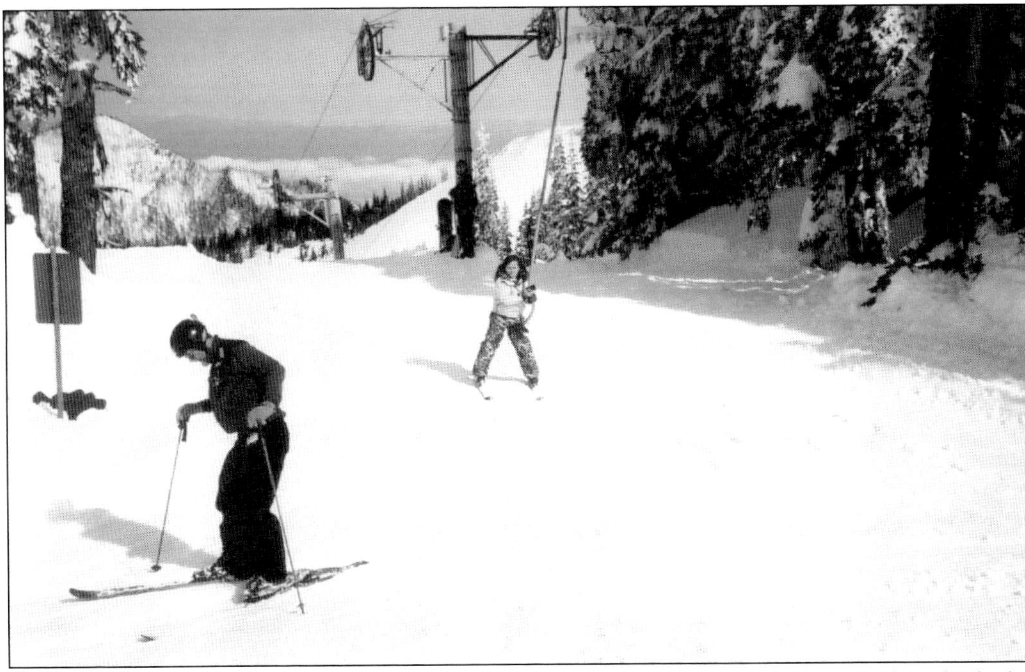

In the above photograph of a young rider reaching the exit point of the tow, notice how high the last Poma pole rises above the snow. This top landing offered a perfect platform for getting off the tow. In the winter and early spring of 1999, record snows literally buried the lifts. Below, the 25 foot Poma tower is almost buried. Some of these towers were completed buried in the heavy snow of 1998–1999. (Both, photograph by Craig Hofer.)

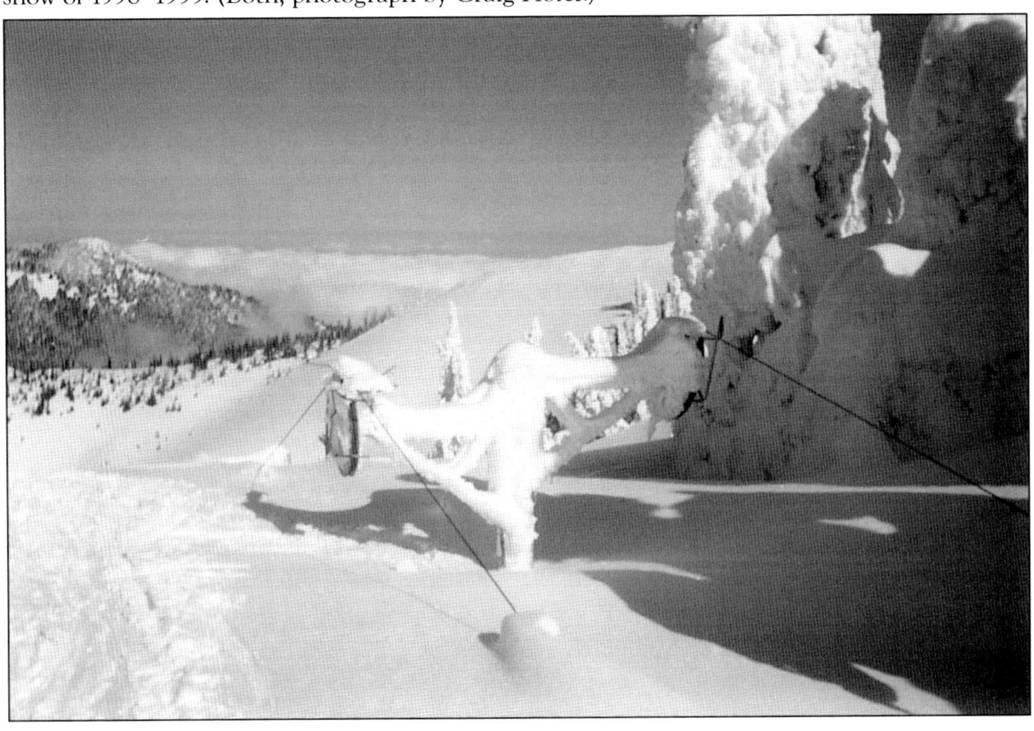

It began snowing heavily in January 1999, and by mid-January, the road to Hurricane Ridge had 40-foot drifts and large avalanches. Road crews needed the assistance of the ski-area snowcat to push snow. By March, the crews still had not reached the top. Here, local ski and mountaineering guide Jack Ganster demonstrates what they were up against. There were 40-to-60-foot drifts on the ski slopes, and 35-foot Poma towers were buried. The photograph below shows the beauty of these huge snowbanks. (Right, photograph by the author; below, photograph by Craig Hofer.)

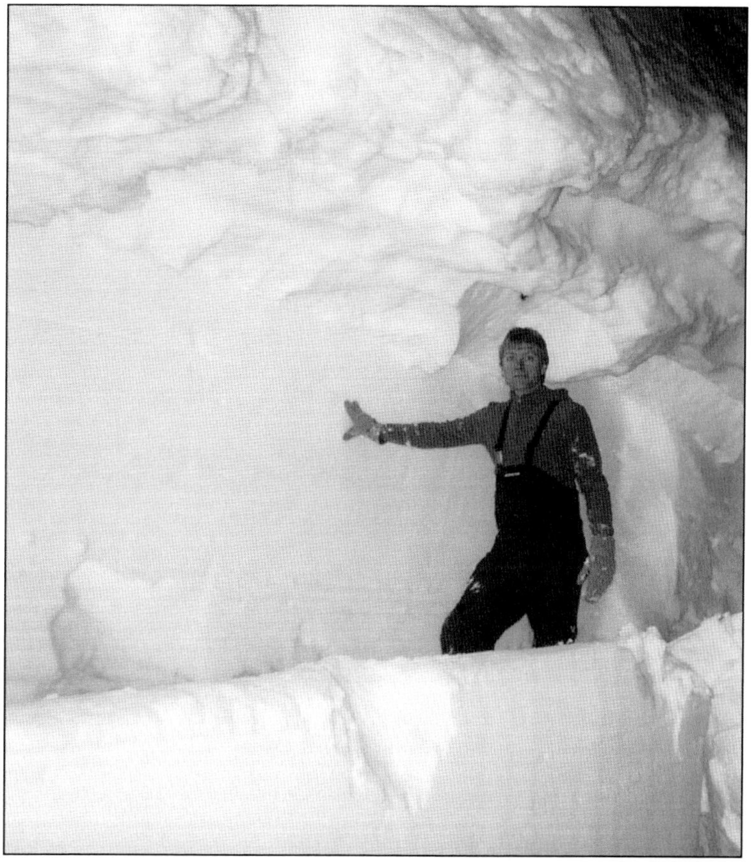

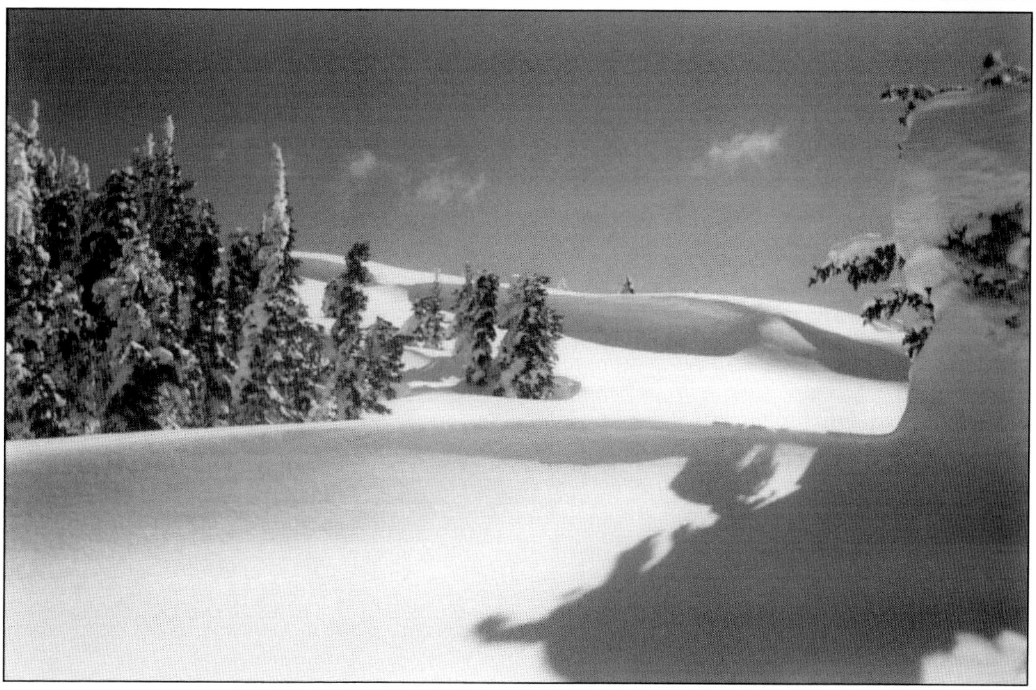

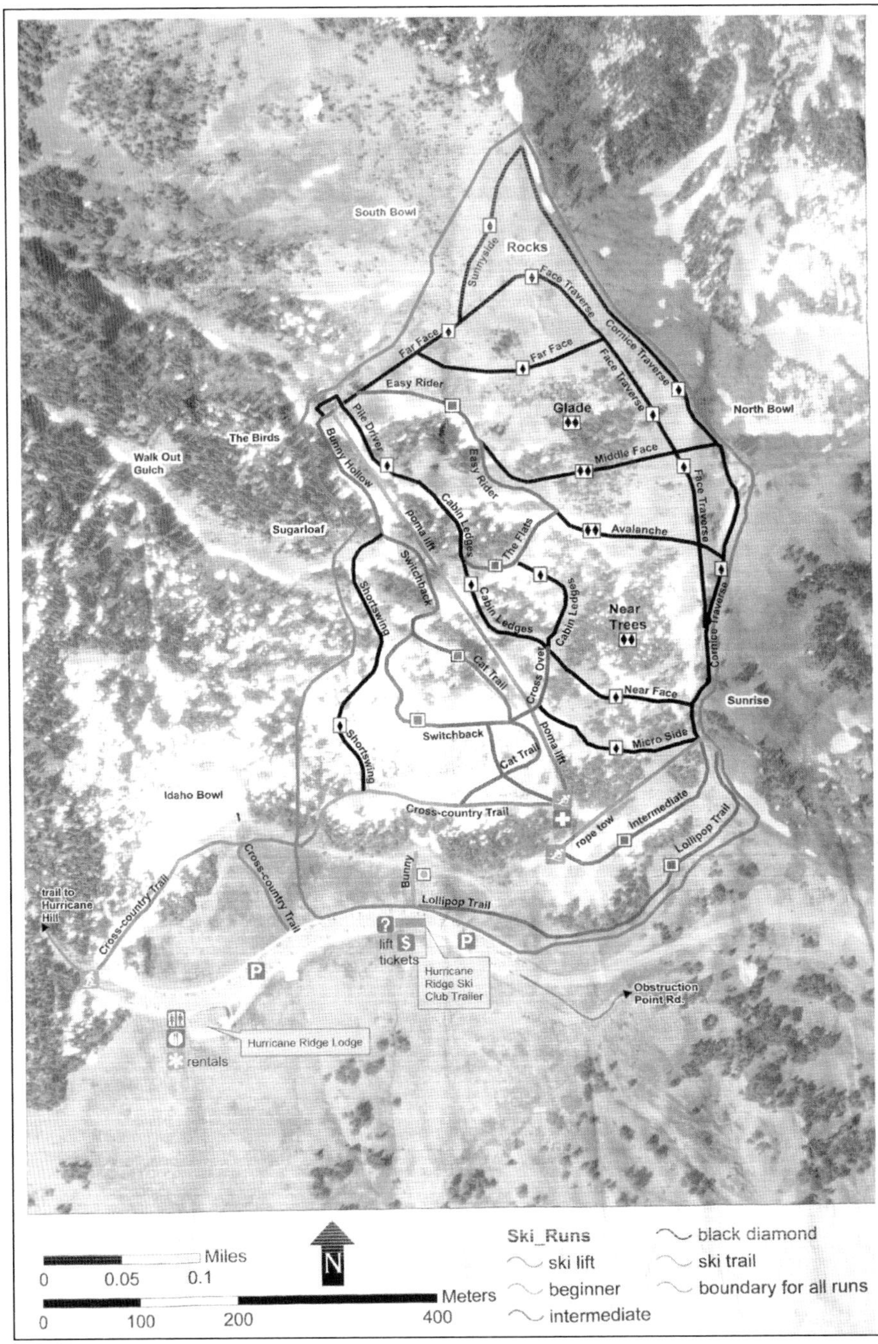

This aerial view of the Hurricane Ridge ski area was found in the Ice Station Zebra Ski Patrol hut and shows the entire ski area with labeled runs. The ski area boundaries have been established in conjunction with the national park and will not be expanded. There is more and more backcountry skiing and snowboarding outside of these boundaries that is not part of the area's jurisdiction. Note the area named Walk Out Gulch: If one makes a mistake and gets too low on this north side, the choice is (and has been) to climb back out or walk out the Little River valley. (Photograph of map by Daniel Hudgings, courtesy of Hurricane Ridge Ski Patrol.)

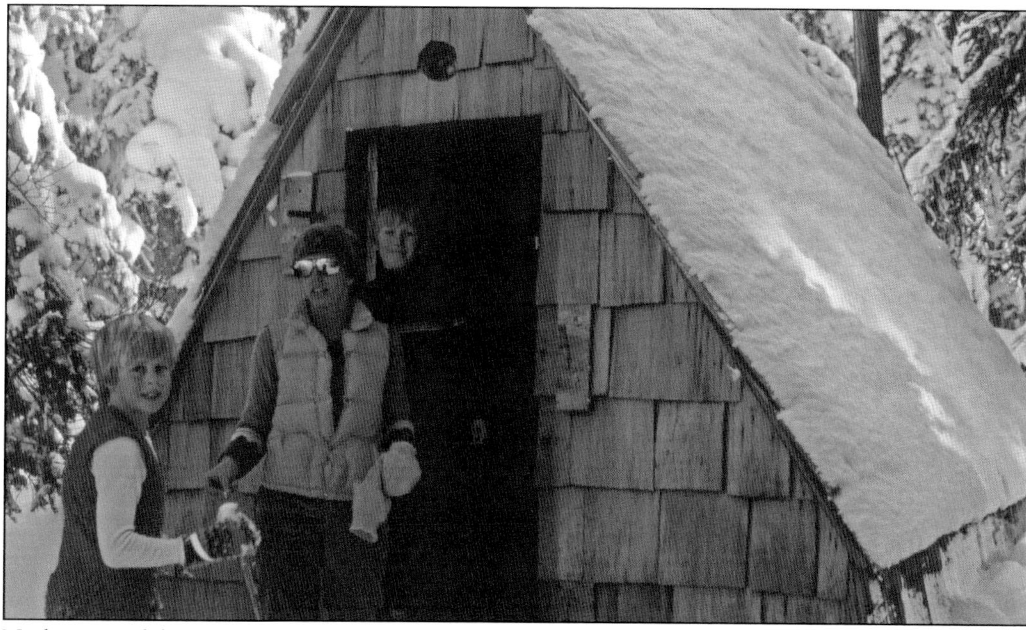

No history of skiing in the Olympics would be complete without a photograph of the Waterhole Hut, which no longer exists. This hut at the Waterhole Camp, located about four miles from Hurricane Ridge, was a cozy retreat for many years. It was constructed and placed by the "Ski Hut 7" and was said to be just big enough to hold "four good friends." Here, Joe Peterson (left) and Maura (center) and Evan Oakes enjoy the hut in the late 1970s. (Photograph by the author.)

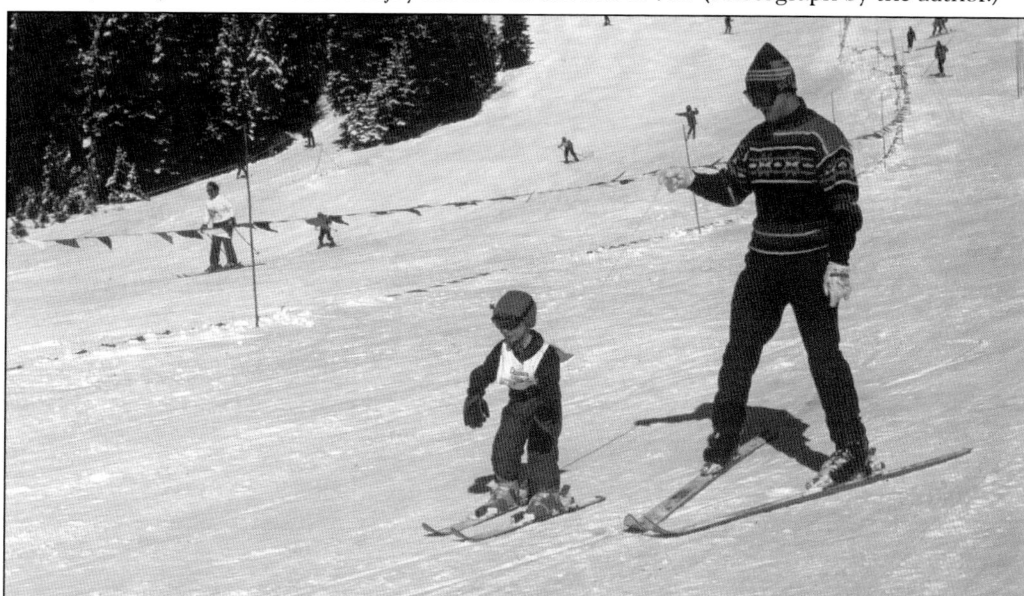

What better way to conclude this pictorial history of skiing than to see a father and a new little skier learning the sport. Warren Miller has called for a reactivation of rope tows in America. He recalls how he and others learned "on a small hill somewhere hanging onto a rope that would haul them up a hill and that would eat up the armpit of any parka or sweater that they wore." (Photograph by David Logan.)

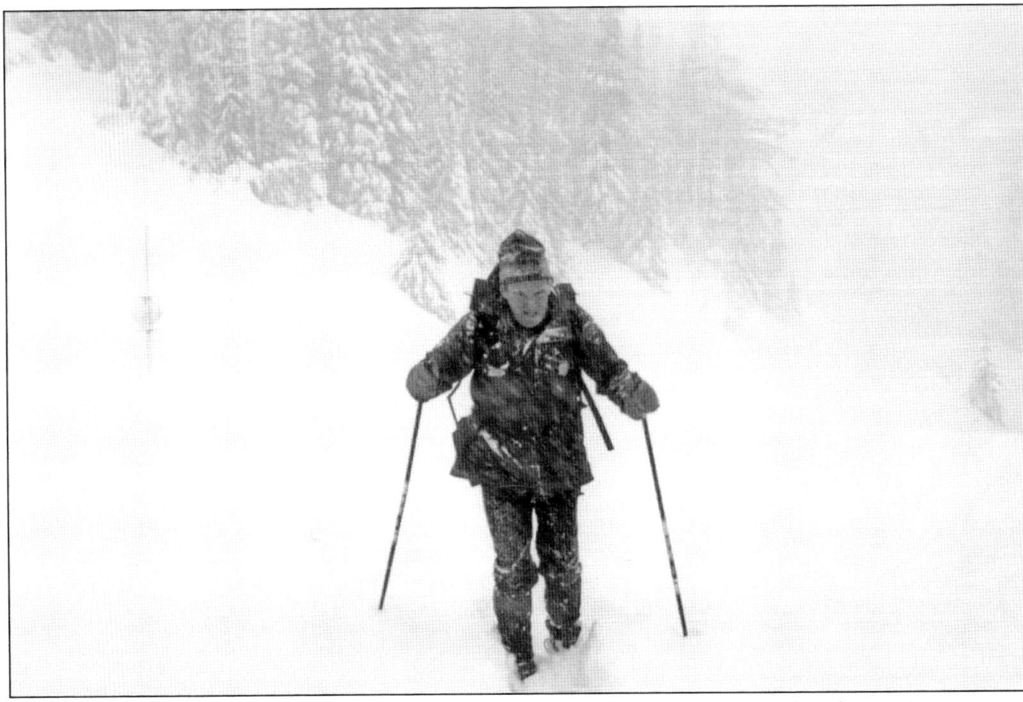

Skiing ranger Jack Hughes's career has spanned most of the Hurricane Ridge ski area's existence. Jack prided himself in skiing at least 1,000 miles each season while attending to everything from rescue work to snow and weather observations. Days like the one pictured here are common at the eponymous Hurricane Ridge. (Courtesy of ONP.)

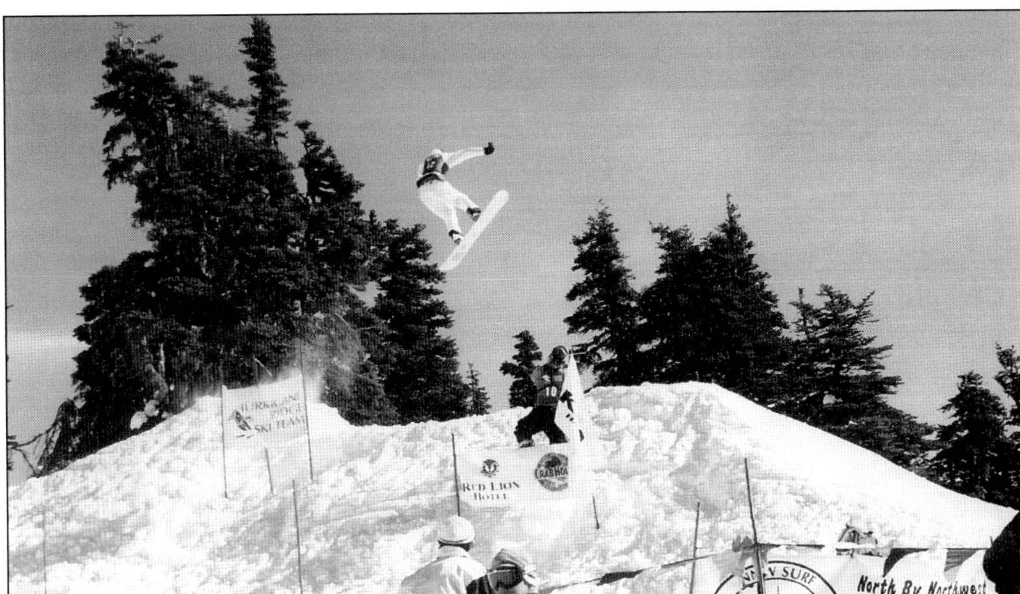

Snowboarders may be the majority now at Hurricane Ridge. They have added an element of excitement and a window to the future. Hurricane Ridge now has a terrain park, pictured here, as well as a tubing area within the permitted recreation area. (Photograph by Craig Hofer.)

BIBLIOGRAPHY

Beres, Nancy, Mitzi Chandler, and Russ Dalton. *Island of Rivers: An Anthology Celebrating 50 Years of Olympic National Park.* Seattle: Pacific Northwest National Parks and Forests Association, 1988.

Burr, Eric. *Ski Trails and Wildlife: Toward Snow Country Restoration.* Bloomington, IN: Trafford Publishing, 2008.

Danner, Wilbert R. *Geology of Olympic National Park.* Seattle: University of Washington Press, 1955.

Engelson, Keith. "Road to Hurricane Ridge." *Sturdy Folk.* Mavis Anderson, ed. Port Angeles, WA: Western Gull Publishing, 2001: 91–96.

Evans, Gail H.E., and T. Allen Comp. *Historic Resource Study, Olympic National Park, Washington.* Seattle: National Park Service Resources Division, 1983.

Fagerlund, Gunnar O. (with the assistance of Francis I. Fagerlund). *Olympic National Park, WA.* Washington, DC: Natural History Handbook Services No. 1, 1954. (Revised 1957.)

Lien, Carsten. *Olympic Battleground. The Power Politics of Timber Preservation.* San Francisco: Sierra Club Books, 1991.

Lucas, Joy. *It started in the Olympic Mountains. The History of Pacific Northwest Ski Instructors.* Seattle: Professional Ski Instructors of America – NW, 1996.

McNulty, Tim. *Olympic National Park: A Natural History Guide.* New York: Houghton Mifflin Company, 1996.

Miller, Warren. "Skiing industry may be at end of its rope tow." *Anacortes American*, November 27, 1996.

Morgenroth, Chris, with Katherine Morgenroth Flaherty, ed. *Foothills in the Olympic Mountains, An Autobiography.* Fairfield, WA: Ye Galleon Press, 1991.

Radke, Helen Neal, and Joan Ducceschi. *Olympic Leaders: The Life and Times of the Websters of Port Angeles.* Port Angeles: Western Gull, 2003.

Sellars, Richard West. *Preserving Nature in the National Parks.* New Haven: Yale University Press, 1997.

Tabor, Roland W. *Geology of Olympic National Park.* Seattle: Northwest Interpretive Association, 1987.

Webster, Esther. "Day on Hurricane Ridge brings Memories of Early Deer Park Days." *Port Angeles Evening News*, February 7, 1958.

Consistent with our mission to preserve history on a local level, this book was printed in South Carolina on American-made paper and manufactured entirely in the United States. Products carrying the accredited Forest Stewardship Council (FSC) label are printed on 100 percent FSC-certified paper.

MADE IN THE USA